# Grayling Flies

# Grayling Flies

## STEVE SKUCE

Coch-y-Bonddu Books
2016

GRAYLING FLIES
By Steve Skuce


First published by Coch-y-Bonddu Books, Machynlleth, 2016

ISBN 978 1 904784 76 0




2016 © Coch-y-Bonddu Books Ltd, Machynlleth
Text © Steve Skuce

Coch-y-Bonddu Books Ltd, Machynlleth, Powys, SY20 8DG
01654 702837
www.anglebooks.com

All rights reserved. No part of this publication may be reproduced, stored in a retrieval system, or transmitted, in any form or by any means, electronic, mechanical, photocopying, recording or otherwise, without the prior consent of the copyright holders.

*This book is dedicated to my lovely wife, brilliant children, fabulous grandchildren, and, of course, to the Lady of the Stream – long may she swim the rivers of the world.*

# Contents

| | |
|---|---|
| Preface | 11 |
| **Chapter One** | |
| Exposing the Lady | 17 |
| **Chapter Two** | |
| Fly Fishing For Grayling | 27 |
|     *Dry Fly* | *31* |
|     *Wet Fly* | *33* |
|     *Nymphing* | *36* |
|     *Tenkara* | *43* |
|     *Hints & Tips* | *45* |
| **Chapter Three** | |
| Flies and Fly Tying | 49 |
|     *What is a Grayling Fly?* | *49* |
|     *Tool Tips* | *50* |
|     *Tying Tips* | *52* |
|     *Hooks* | *53* |
|     *The Flies in this Book* | *53* |
| **Chapter Four** | |
| Dry Flies | 55 |
| **Chapter Five** | |
| Wet Flies | 109 |
| **Chapter Six** | |
| Nymphs | 121 |
| **Chapter Seven** | |
| Gray Matter | 197 |
|     *Books* | *198* |
|     *Other Media* | *204* |
|     *Further References* | *205* |

# Fly List

**Dry Flies**

| | | |
|---|---|---|
| 1 | Beacon Beige | 58 |
| 2 | Kite's Imperial | 62 |
| 3 | Greenwell's Glory | 64 |
| 4 | Duck's Dun | 67 |
| 5 | Grey Duster | 69 |
| 6 | Sherry Spinner | 71 |
| 7 | F Fly | 73 |
| 8 | Klinkhåmer Special | 75 |
| 9 | Supa Pupa | 78 |
| 10 | CM Supa Pupa | 78 |
| 11 | Milroy | 80 |
| 12 | G.R.H.E | 82 |
| 13 | Griffiths Gnat | 83 |
| 14 | Quill Shuttlecock Emerger | 85 |
| 15 | Loop Wing Emerger | 85 |
| 16 | IOBO | 89 |
| 17 | John Storey Paradun | 90 |
| 18 | CDC & Elk | 92 |
| 19 | Little Red Sedge | 94 |
| 20 | May Franglais | 96 |
| 21 | Aphid | 99 |
| 22 | Red Tag | 101 |
| 23 | Sturdy's Fancy | 102 |
| 24 | Grayling Fiddler | 103 |
| 25 | Grayling Steel Blue | 105 |

**Wet Flies**

| | | |
|---|---|---|
| 26 | Partridge & Orange | 110 |
| 27 | Waterhen Bloa | 112 |
| 28 | Greenwell's Glory Spider | 114 |
| 29 | Pink Spider | 115 |
| 30 | Black Magic | 116 |
| 31 | Copper Spider | 117 |

**Nymphs**

| | | |
|---|---|---|
| 32 | Skues Nymph No. VI | 123 |
| 33 | Skues Nymph No. X | 123 |
| 34 | BBWON | 126 |
| 35 | Killer Bug – *Original* | 128 |
| 36 | Sawyer Killer Bug – *My version* | 128 |
| 37 | Utah Killer Bug | 134 |
| 38 | Sawyer Pheasant Tail Nymph | 135 |
| 39 | Pearly PTN | 138 |
| 40 | Copperbonce | 140 |
| 41 | Black Bead CJ Ant | 141 |
| 42 | Green Genie | 143 |
| 43 | Ginger Tom | 144 |
| 44 | Juicy Tom | 148 |
| 45 | Gammy Shrimp | 150 |
| 46 | Gammy Parasite Shrimp | 152 |
| 47 | Phil White Shrimp | 154 |
| 48 | Normal Pink Shrimp | 155 |
| 49 | Fatbelly Pink Shrimp | 157 |
| 50 | UVSP Shrimp | 159 |
| 51 | Czech Nymphs | 160 |
| 52 | Hare's Ear Goldhead | 163 |
| 53 | Pedro's White Bead Nymph | 164 |
| 54 | Pedro's Pink & Grey Nymph | 166 |
| 55 | GGG (Green Grayling Grabber) | 167 |
| 56 | PPP (Pink & Purple Peril) | 168 |
| 57 | Dove Bug | 169 |
| 58 | Pink Poison | 171 |
| 59 | Grayling Special Pink | 173 |
| 60 | The Pink Thingy | 174 |
| 61 | Mr Tangerine Man | 175 |
| 62 | Hotspot Nymph II | 176 |
| 63 | Perdigón Style Flies | 179 |
| 64 | Green Caddis | 181 |
| 65 | SBE Caddis | 182 |
| 66 | Peek-a-boo Caddis | 184 |
| 67 | Chad Cad | 186 |
| 68 | Caseless Caddis | 188 |
| 69 | Der Wurm | 191 |
| 70 | Squirmy Wormy | 193 |

# Acknowledgements

FOR SOMEONE WHO is not a natural networker I seem to have been fortunate to have met so many friendly, helpful and downright nice people during my flyfishing life. So, I acknowledge, with many thanks and some significant degree of humility, all those people who have donated some of their life for the benefit of my life:

My fishing buddies over the years, including but not confined to; Mike Tebbs, Roger Cullum Kenyon, Keith and Sylvie Mason, Brian Clarke, Russell Murray, John Machin, Greg and Denise Payne, Aad van der Jagt, Wim van Montfoort, Johan Engelen and Willem Ridderbeks.

All those nice people in the Grayling Society who have worked with me to publicise and conserve this magnificent natural resource; Robin Mulholland OBE, the late Dr Ron Broughton MBE, Rod Calbrade, Rob Hartley, Alan Ayre, Bob Male, Roger Smith, Steve Rhodes, Ross Gardiner, Richard Cove, Kris Kent, Louis Noble, Hugo Martel, Ronnie Gryspeerd, Pedro Guridi, Jean-Pierre Coudoux and the late Reg Fuller, who recruited me in the first place, plus countless others in the organisation.

The writers who have influenced my fishing life; Reg Righyni, John Roberts, G E M Skues, Frank Sawyer, Oliver Kite, Arthur Ransome and Maurice Wiggin. They started me on this mad path.

Those fishing gurus whose paths have crossed with mine and who have had an impact on my thinking, fly-tying and fishing; Hans van Klinken, Charles Jardine, Malcolm Greenhalgh, Geoffrey Bucknall, Oliver Edwards, Philip White and Harry Vallack.

All those kind and generous fly-tyers who have contributed to this book and taken their time and skills to tie some of the flies they have invented or championed. They know who they are and they are all highlighted within the fly-tying pages. My special thanks goes to these guys who have all been tremendously helpful and generous with their time and talent.

Dave Martin of Go Flyfishing UK, who had the courage and confidence to let me loose on his clients, and his other guides who have made me so welcome and helped enormously with my confidence and guiding skills, especially Mick Siggery and Colin Alexander, and all the clients I have instructed or guided over the past few years.

My friends at the Fly Dresser's Guild, especially the Wiltshire Chalkstream branch, in particular Lee Hooper, Les and Trish Cooke, and Richard Vipond.

Rod Dibble who gave up his time, knowledge and materials to show me how to make my own furled leaders.

All those traders who have given me help and advice over the years, and occasional discounts! Steve Cooper at Cookshill Tackle, Pat Stevens of Fly Tek,

Phil Holding at Fly Tying Boutique, Paul Davis at Fly Tying Shop and many others who have supplied some super materials and tools.

Paul Morgan, of Coch-y-Bonddu Books, who I have known ever since we each caught a grayling (not the same one!) at exactly the same time on the River Wear in 1993 and who has taken a gamble in publishing this book. Also Pete MacKenzie, whose design skills are as galactic as the fighting ones of a Jedi Knight!

My two brilliant daughters, Karen and Nicola, who have been the treasures of my life and have now presented me with the next generation of grayling anglers.

My wife, Honor, who is indescribably precious to me and who makes it all worthwhile – who looks after my health, wealth and sanity and who makes me laugh every day – even when she is stealing my fishing tackle or flies!

And, finally, last but by no shadow of illusion the least important, that sweet little half-pound grayling who had the courtesy to grab my fly on the River Test that day and send me off on a fantastic and rewarding adventure.

Thank you all for being in my life!

# Preface

IT WAS ON a pleasant Autumn day in 1985 that I first met the Lady. She was lying there quietly minding her own business, on the lookout, as always, for any tasty morsel that the current may bring her way. I was late-season fishing for brown trout on the carrier of the River Test which runs behind the Greyhound Inn on Stockbridge High Street in Hampshire. My mind must have wandered and I had let my line drift just marginally downstream. In those days I was very keen to be seen to uphold all those bits of Victorian etiquette, like 'upstream only,' that are part of the territory when it comes to fishing chalkstreams, even though they were unfamiliar to a lad from t'North who had spent most of his previous flyfishing life lobbing spider patterns across and down.

I should add that I now consider the chalkstream rules of 'upstream only' and 'dry fly only', or 'dry fly only until 16th June' or whatever, to be bizarre: a product of the Victorian era when much was done to accentuate the gulf between the middle and upper classes and the workers. It was all very well for the landed gentry to sit by the side of rivers like the Test and Itchen patiently awaiting the first rise of the day whilst contentedly puffing on their pipes. After all, wealthy men like Halford could easily come back tomorrow if the fish were not being co-operative. But for the poor old worker on his precious day off there was no chance of coming back tomorrow. He had to catch fish today and, if given the choice, would fish the water rather than wait for the rise. And, since he had probably not been educated into the newfangled 'dray flay' approach, his natural instinct to fish downstream was just too much for the nobs to bear! Oh yes, only peasants would be so uncouth as to fish downstream, don't you know!

As I lifted off to eradicate my mistake, checking over my shoulder to make sure that no-one was watching, there was a distinct thump and a weight was suddenly on the end of the line. I played the fish for quite some time before I actually saw it. Even then I could feel that distinctive corkscrewing that is so common in the fight of a grayling. Once the fish came to the surface I was truly gobsmacked. I had read avidly about grayling in my copy of Maurice Wiggin's *Teach Yourself Fly Fishing* and lusted after catching one, but had never actually seen one. And then here I was, on Oliver Kite's 'Rolls Royce' river, and one was on the end of my line with a fly firmly in its scissors. I landed it, looked adoringly at it, marvelling at its sheer beauty, and let it swim away to grow bigger. It wasn't a big fish, maybe half a pound, but what it lacked in size it more than made up for in significance.

Even though I had bought my first fly rod in 1968 (an 8 foot Edgar Sealy Nufly split cane which I've still got, although it has long since been retired) I hadn't had that much chance to use it, having got married soon after, fathered two fabulous but time-stealing daughters, and moved around the country quite a bit as I started on my career in consumer-goods marketing. In fact I first realised that my rod was a bit outdated in the days that I worked at Farleys in Plymouth in the mid-1970s and was fishing Burrator Reservoir one evening from the bank. I was with a couple of friends, one of whom, the local doctor, had invested in one of the new 'graphite' rods. Let's just say that, after watching him cast twice the distance I was managing and, incidentally, reaching right out to where the fish were cruising, I realised that perhaps I was a bit under-gunned. It was, however, years later that I managed to save up enough for my own graphite stick.

But back to grayling, and from that single moment in that quiet backwater in Hampshire I was in love all over again, but this time with the Lady of the Stream, courtesy of a kind half-pounder and a rod, reel, line, and probably fly, lent to me for the day by that very nice man Andy Murray who worked for Hardy Brothers in their London shop. One of the highlights of my regular business trips to London was a visit to Pall Mall to see what was new in the House of Hardy.

I then started grayling fishing with a vengeance, discovered the Salisbury & District Angling Club, and spent all of my precious spare time on the waters of the Wiltshire Avon, Bourne and others, and later, on those less crowded waters of the Wylye controlled by the Wilton Fly Fishing Club. Trout came and went as well, but my sights were set firmly on the Lady between the 16th of June and the following 14th of March. My family still came first, naturally, and my career, now as head of marketing for Toshiba, based in Frimley and right next to the M3, was vital to life, but although never really a 'grayling bum' (at least not in the John Gierach sense), I fished whenever I could and in all conditions, whether pouring sweat in short sleeves, or melting ice from the rod rings with the heat of my fingers. Nothing would stop me chasing the Lady and the conduit of M3 and A303 was a swift channel to get to the river whenever I had a spare few hours.

I became an expert in detouring from the direct route to and from meetings, just to get an hour or two on a river where grayling could be found. Luckily for me the Toshiba TV and microwave oven factories were in Plymouth and, unlike my colleagues who flew from Heathrow or Gatwick, I suddenly seemed to develop an inexplicable and terrible fear of flying. My regular visits were always by car and I always went via Amesbury on the A303, where there was a particularly nice stretch of S&DAC water. The fact that they knew I was once offered a career as a navigator in the RAF didn't seem to cross the mind of my fellow managers who happily accepted, even mocked a little, my apparent fear of flying!

In those days, before the national rod licence came into being I must have had licences for nearly every water authority in the country. It became quite costly buying so many, but what is cost when you are in love?

A Hardy Smuggler travel-rod soon fell into my hands, and that gave me even more opportunity to grab moments away from work and on a river bank. In those days all other rods seemed to be two piece. Yet here I was with my rod, reel, line and flies in my briefcase!

Then, in 1989 my friend Mike Tebbs and I formed Combined Talents, a marketing consultancy partnership. I had introduced Mike to flyfishing whilst I worked at Toshiba and he was a director of a sales promotion company that worked for me. Later in life Mike moved down to the Wylye valley, as I have, to retire. He is still keen as mustard and is currently, in the year 2016, the Secretary of the Wilton Fly Fishing Club and Membership Secretary of the Grayling Society. While we had the consultancy I was always amazed at just how many business problems could be worked out by standing on a river bank waving a stick. We even thought of the grayling fishing possibilities whenever considering taking on a new client or not. The lure of the money usually held most sway, but it was nice to plan detours on our way back from meetings so we could indulge our shared passion.

In the late eighties or early nineties, I joined the Grayling Society, having seen several small grayling swimming around in a tank at the Stratfield Saye CLA Game Fair. I found a great group of like-minded lads and lasses and, for the last 21 years I have carried out some role or other on the Committee and enjoyed every minute of that time.

I was then living in Sandhurst on the Berkshire/Surrey/Hampshire border, a grayling lover in a country where the Lady was still considered little better than vermin. Yes, 20 or 30 years ago fishery owners were still netting or electro-fishing vast quantities of grayling out of the chalkstreams and, at best, trying to find someone who may like them stocked in their rivers (this, I believe, is where the stock in the River Teise in Kent came from) or, at worst, hoiking them onto the bank or into a dustbin to die. Here I must admit the rebelliousness which affected my grayling fishing during that period. One the clubs I joined (no names!) had a rule that you must kill all coarse fish, which included grayling. Well, club officials (I am still a member), I can tell you now that I broke that rule every time I caught a grayling! Isn't it amazing how fish after fish can suddenly throw the hook at the net? I am most pleased to say that this particular club, in line with many others in the south, saw the error of its ways and has, for some years now, actively encouraged catch and release of all fish, game or coarse. The club also stopped electro-fishing and removing grayling and coarse fish many years ago.

When giving talks on grayling, I often tell people that, in the 1990s and earlier, there were four distinct attitudes to the Lady in Great Britain. In the south they were considered to be vermin, having no place in a chalkstream which was the rightful home of trout, even though many of the waters were overstocked with guileless and stupid stockies. Indeed, many fishery owners stocked foreign rainbow trout into the hallowed waters of those rivers, and still do so. In Wales and the Midlands they were a well-respected fish which attracted many anglers to fish such prolific and beautiful waters as the Wye, Severn and Dee in Wales, or the streams of Shropshire and Herefordshire, and the lovely Dove, Wye and Derwent systems in Staffordshire and Derbyshire. In the north they were loved, so much so that I once had a tricky experience where a particular club would sell Mike and myself a day ticket in the trout season for trout fishing but would not entertain selling us one after the end of the trout season. We grovelled and crawled to the club's rather hoity-toity lady secretary, but, no, they wanted the grayling fishing for themselves and, in retrospect, I wonder who can blame them. I don't think I have ever fished the Nidd again since that salutary experience. I guess that's Yorkshire folk for you! Mind you in my home county of Lancashire it can be even harder to get onto a good grayling river without being a member of a club or syndicate, even though Lancastrians are renowned for their generosity! In Scotland grayling just didn't figure highly on the flyfishing agenda.

I have always been a mug for an underdog, and I guess that is part of the reason why I have been so active in trying to help the Grayling Society to achieve its primary goals of generating increased awareness of this truly wild game fish; helping actively with conservation and assisting members with advice and help for their angling.

The Society has effectively achieved most of its primary goals since its formation in 1977 and, in addition, there now exists the Grayling Research Trust which is a charity originally spun off from the Society that, now firmly established in its own right, successfully sponsors and funds original scientific research into grayling and has been particularly successful in increasing the profile of the species in scientific circles, not least in the corridors of the Environment Agency.

Anyway, this is not a book about my life with the grayling, nor a diatribe about the usefulness of the Grayling Society or Grayling Research Trust, but is an attempt to look closely at what developments there have been in grayling fishing and, more particularly, grayling flies in the years since the last book was published on these subjects quite some time ago.

If you take a look on the excellent website of Paul Morgan's Coch-y-Bonddu Books you will give up counting the number of books written about trout and trout fishing. A search for such books ends up with a list of over 5,000 titles in stock. OK, so there is much duplication in that list but even if you took only 10% of those books you are talking in excess of 500. In addition, there are also hundreds of books which cover fly-tying for trout. I know lots of those books include grayling in the title or content but they all major on trout and add grayling often as an afterthought. And how many books are there that have been specifically written about grayling fishing? Save yourself the bother of working it out because you do not need a calculator to do so. They are all in my bookcase or on my computer and there are only about twenty and one of those is purely about Arctic grayling in Alaska; one is basically a world-tour hunting grayling; another one is in Flemish, and a final one is an ebook! And, with the exception of Richard Ellis's recent ebook and the two *Favourite Flies* booklets published by the Grayling Society, I know of no book written, since perhaps John Jackson's *Practical Fly-fisher* in 1854, which looks solely at tying flies to catch grayling. I may be wrong and, no doubt, if I am there is always someone who will be keen to tell me so but the fact remains that there has been far too little interest in literary circles in the amazing, but often overlooked and misunderstood *Thymallus thymallus*.

So why should such an entertaining and beautiful fish be so poorly treated in literature in the past? Well I guess it is because it has always played second cousin to its fellow salmonid, the trout and, consequently, there has been no desire for authors to write or publishers to market books purely on grayling. To be fair I should add that recently the flyfishing magazines have done much to promote grayling, and these days there is hardly an issue of any of them that hasn't got an article, or at least a mention of this wonderful creature, particularly on fly patterns.

This book aims to add just a bit more to the literature available on the Lady and recognises the increase in interest in grayling fishing in the last 20 or 30 years. Use it as a mind-jogger to remind you of the successful techniques that can be employed to catch grayling, and tie and enjoy fishing with some of the flies it contains. Photographic representations of each fly are included along with full step-by-step tying instructions, plus a few notes about their history, successes and techniques for their use.

I have no pretentions to claim that this is a bible of grayling flies, never to be questioned or bettered. I know that more and more flies are being invented every day and that there are many in use in the UK, Europe and farther afield that I have never even heard of or seen. How many of those are truly unique of course is a moot point since many inventions are adaptations of an already successful pattern or approach. But, every once in a while a truly brand-spanking-new idea appears and adds yet another 'go to' fly to the ever-increasing armoury of patterns we all seem to carry these days.

I am also well aware that there are grayling anglers out there who are far more skilled and successful than I am or can hope to be. Good luck to those guys, especially the 'young guns,' and long may the flame of invention and ingenuity be carried by all grayling anglers as we develop better and better flies and techniques.

Last year, during a memorable weekend in Wales, fishing the Irfon with other Grayling Society members, I was asked by that well-known angling author Chris McCully what were my three favourite grayling flies. By that he meant the ones I would never be without and, if push came to shove, which I would carry as my only ones. My choice was the Ginger Tom (a nymph pattern of my own devising), the Gammy Shrimp (another of my patterns) and the Supa Pupa. Given a more reasonable selection of, say, six flies I would add a Pheasant Tail Nymph, Sawyer Killer Bug and Griffiths Gnat to that list. But I mostly fish on the chalkstreams and if asked to select an all-round set of flies I would want ten, and probably add a Pink Shrimp, Hotspot Nymph II, F-Fly and a Klinkhåmer to the list.

Ah, how easy it is to sit in front of a nice warm fire on a winter's night and dream of the mighty grayling you will catch on your slim selection of flies, and how much lighter your vest would feel. Would that we could actually restrict ourselves to just ten patterns or less. In reality, of course, we are all fly tarts and carry just about as many patterns as the seams of our vests can handle without ripping apart. At least I do, and if you are more abstemious than me then good luck to you and you have my respect!

Have fun chasing the Lady and when you catch her give her a kiss from me!

Steve Skuce
*Wylye, 2016*

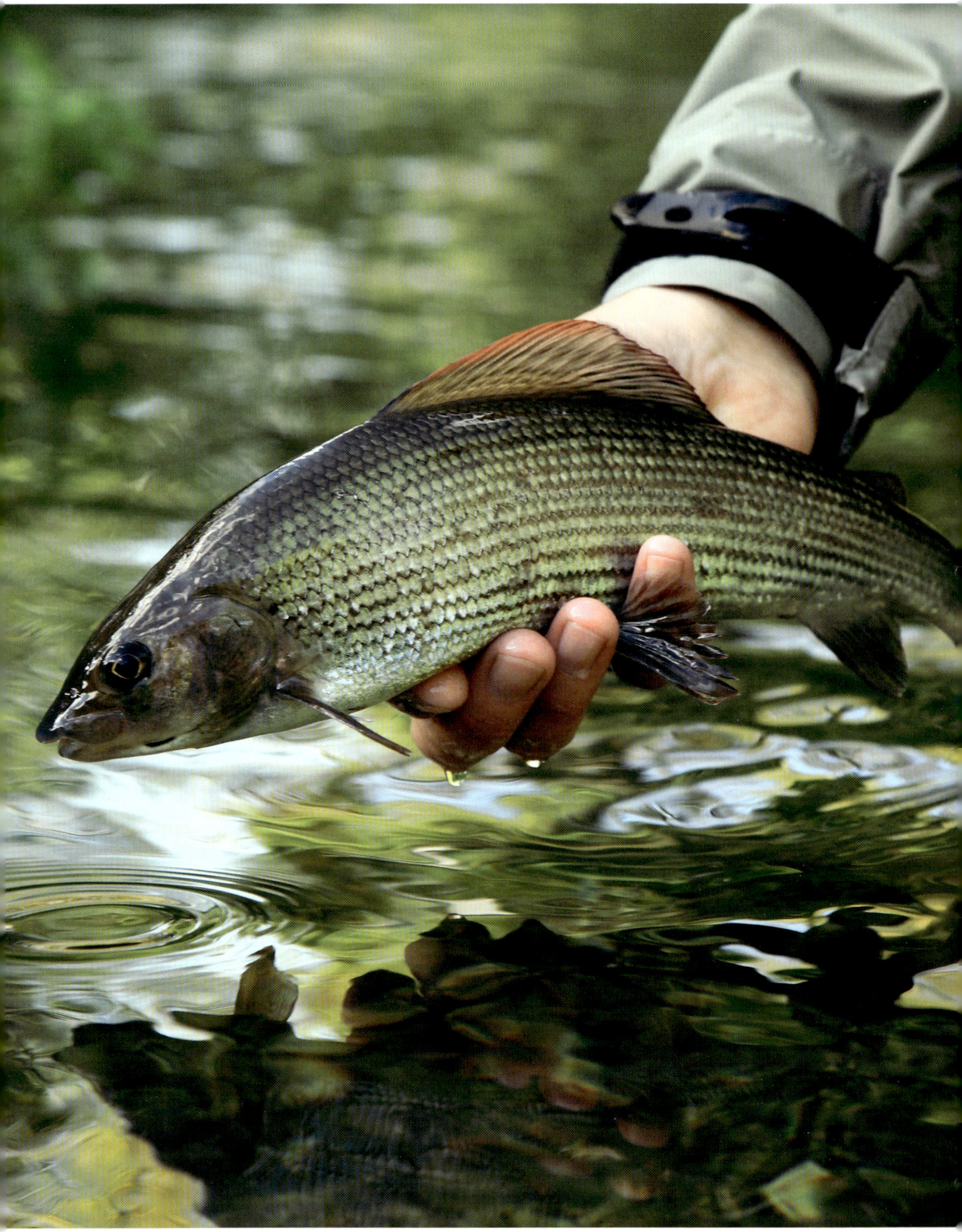

# Chapter One

# Exposing the Lady

*'Thymallus thymallus, "Lady of the Stream", so wild in your heart, and in guile so supreme!
Your scales and your fins iridescent in hue, make you and your kind such good sport to pursue.'*

Roger Smith  *An Ode to the Lady of the Stream*

I AM AN immense fan of grayling. Not surprising, you may think, as this book is all about ways to catch this beautiful fish.

When I first started flyfishing in 1968 my bible was *Teach Yourself Fly Fishing* by Maurice Wiggin. Wiggin was keen on grayling and could not understand the attitude some game-fishers had towards the fish, although he commented that coarse anglers were quite happy to catch such a 'game' fish. He did feel, however, that they were a fish to be targeted in the autumn and winter only and should not really be fished for in the summer. He believed they would not have recovered from spawning and it would not be sporting to fish for them at this time. I find his recovery argument a bit flaky since it should also, presumably, be applied to trout fishing in the early spring, but it isn't, and I suspect that he simply never really enjoyed the superb sport summer fishing for grayling can be. I have never been aware of any recovery problems when fishing for them in the summer months. Let us remember that on many rivers, especially the southern ones, the mayfly appears during the 'recovery period' of the grayling. What a wonderful, nourishing, feast for any fish. Anyway, there is no doubting his positive attitude towards the fish; "All in all, the grayling is a great fish for the fly fisherman, his stand-by in winter and ever his delight." Even so, he didn't spend too much time discussing grayling and only devoted six pages of a 200 page book to Her Ladyship.

Back to 1968 – I knew full well what a trout was since I had spent many happy hours by the little River Lledr in North Wales trying to catch them with a worm, a five-foot-long solid fibreglass rod and an Intrepid Standard reel loaded with thick heavy nylon. I had even set night-lines for them in the small reservoir in the woods on the slopes of Moel Siabod, behind the cottage where we usually spent our summer school holidays.

But the grayling? Well, this was a much more mysterious fish. Less well distributed than trout, less written about in the press (*Creel* was my usual magazine in those days), less revered and with a completely different season, this was just the fish for a left-field type like me. Looking back on life we can always see where we missed opportunities as we grew up and I can clearly see how I missed out on my first chance to catch a grayling. My first season's flyfishing was

Watercolour of a grayling, painted by Charles Jardine

on the River Wear in the city of Durham. I caught absolutely nothing in that first year, but I was to find out many years later that a relatively short trip further upstream would have put me in striking distance of reasonable grayling stocks.

Now this is not a scientific paper, just a book for grayling fly fishermen and fly-tyers, so I will be generalising to some extent. However, I think it is always nice to learn something about the history and evolution of our quarry. This book is primarily about the European grayling, *Thymallus thymallus*, but there are several other species of grayling around the world, such as the Mongolian, Hovsgol, Baikal, Amur and the well-known Arctic form. All are broadly similar in looks, and although most are considered to be distinct species and there are some differences in appearance, they can all be instantly recognised as being grayling.

The grayling is widely distributed throughout Europe, roughly between about 40 and 70 degrees north latitude. To the west their limit is Wales; there are none in Ireland which is a great pity; to the east they can be found as far as the Ural mountains; their most northerly extent is Northern Scandinavia; and in the south you can find them in northern Italy and the Balkans.

The Latin name relates to the grayling's distinctive smell which is akin to that of the wild thyme. I once stood on the banks of the Avon in Wiltshire drawing in the delightful and delicate smell of the fish and marvelling at the thyme-like odour. As I bent down to release the fish I realised that I was standing in a clump of wild thyme! Some folks tend to think it has more of a cucumber type odour and I can see, or rather smell, how they feel that. Whether it be thyme or cucumber the point is that it really does have the most

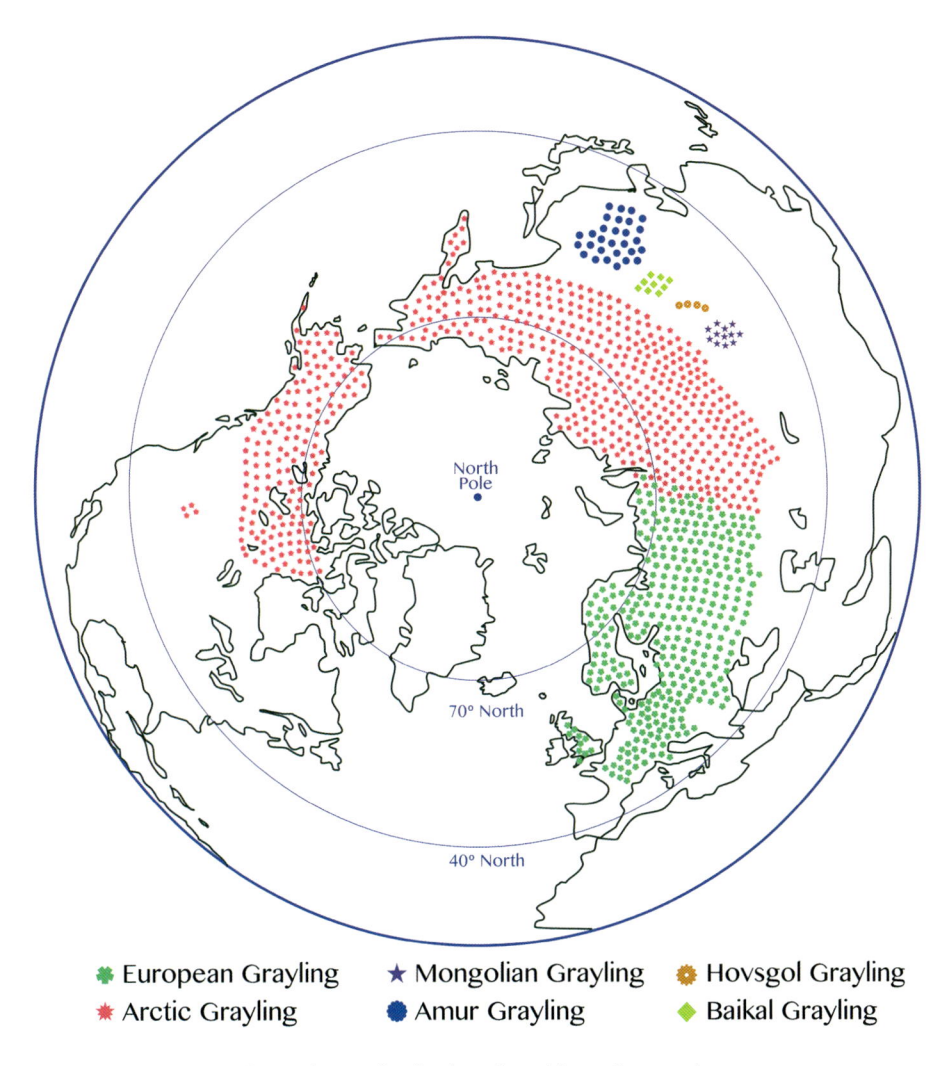

- European Grayling
- Arctic Grayling
- Mongolian Grayling
- Amur Grayling
- Hovsgol Grayling
- Baikal Grayling

Approximate distribution of world grayling species

unusual, non-fishy, odour and whenever I guide clients who have never previously caught one I insist they smell the fish and they are always amazed.

It is generally considered that the European grayling was restricted to Central Europe during the Ice Age because this area was below the southern extent of the ice. In those days, ending about 12,000 years ago, the British Isles weren't. The land that was to become Britain was a peninsula of what would become the European mainland until about 8,000 years ago, when an immense tsunami created islands somewhat along the lines of what exists today. As the ice receded flora and fauna were able to expand their distribution and colonise more northerly parts of Europe and Scandinavia and a major river, known as the North Sea River flowed northerly from what is now Central Europe and this is thought to have been the artery for the passage of several species including grayling.

Although research into grayling genetics

in the UK is still effectively work in progress, there is strong evidence that the Ouse, Trent, Hampshire/Wiltshire Avon and possibly the Severn, Welsh Wye, Ribble and Welsh Dee and their tributaries could have been colonised by grayling and possess what are now indigenous populations (Gardiner 1989; Ibbotson et al, 2001). However, it was the practice of moving fish from water to water that was common in the 19th century that has led to the pattern of distribution we know today. This process of introduction was unplanned and piecemeal so you have apparent anomalies such as the presence of grayling in the Eden and Ribble but none in the Lune although they all flow through the Pennines and discharge into the Irish Sea and are known for their brown trout, sea-trout and salmon fishing.

I can recommend looking at the work that has been carried out in recent years into grayling distribution and genetics (see the Grayling Research Trust website: www.graylingresearch.org). In particular the paper *Substantial genetic structure among stocked and native populations of the European grayling (*Thymallus thymallus, Salmonidae*) in the United Kingdom* by Nick Dawnay, Louise Dawnay, Roger N Hughes, Richard Cove and Martin I Taylor, is well worth reading. It is most enlightening to see where certain populations in well-known rivers actually originated. Did you realise, for instance, that the population in the River Annan probably originates from the Welsh Wye or Irfon, or that of the Clyde is likely to have originated in the Derbyshire Derwent, or that the Test, and possibly Itchen, seem to have received their original stocks from the Hampshire/Wiltshire Avon? No, neither did I!

These days, and quite rightly, there are controls covering the stocking of grayling just as there are of any other fish, and the distribution is unlikely to expand much further because of the provisions of the *National Trout & Grayling Strategy*, published by the Environment Agency in 2003.

Specifically Policy 21: Grayling states:

> *We will only permit stocking into rivers, streams or other unenclosed waters in catchments where the grayling is already present, except possibly:*
> - *to re-establish a previous population (even if introduced);*
> - *or for rivers recovering from long-term gross pollution where wider consideration will be given to the species stocked and the type of fisheries that might be developed*
>
> *Stocked grayling must have a suitable, generally local, provenance.*

Also there is, in early 2016, only one hatchery where grayling can be obtained, at Calverton near Nottingham, so there is little availability of fish for stocking purposes.

The grayling is an alpine fish. By that I mean it needs cool, clean, clear rivers if it is to thrive. It is less able to handle pollution than trout and has often been considered to be the 'canary' of the river, aping those sweet little birds that were once carried down coal mines to act as some form of natural gas detector.

It is now widely distributed in the UK, although has never been present in Ireland. In the south of England it is found in most, if not all, of the chalkstreams, and the Frome in Dorset is noted for its stocks of large grayling. It is from this river that, in 2009, Paul Mildren caught the current English record grayling, of just over 4lbs 4oz. There are even populations in such rivers as the Teise and the Medway in Kent. I happily caught some of them in the Teise when I was a member of a club there some years ago. It was a few years later that I discovered they had come from what are now my home waters of the Wylye. In a way I felt happy that their removal from the Wylye had not been carried out with a view to murdering the fish, as so often happened in the south, but to moving them to a location where they were welcomed. In the south-west you can catch grayling in such river systems as the Tamar and the Exe.

South Wales now has self-sustaining populations in rivers such as the Ewenny, Rhymney and Taff and there is also, I have read, a small population farther west in the Teifi. Mid-Wales is a mecca for grayling anglers, and the Wye & Usk Foundation has countless places where day tickets can be had for reasonable sums for excellent grayling fishing on the Wye system and its tributaries such as the Ithon, Irfon, Lugg, Arrow and Monnow. The Usk, however, is one of those rivers, like the Lune, which has no grayling at all. In North Wales you can fill your boots, as they say, with the Severn and Dee systems both being famous grayling fisheries and I see that the Severn Rivers Trust now has a passport scheme for fishing Severn tributaries.

Moving into the Midlands area there are grayling to be found in Shropshire, Staffordshire and Derbyshire, and the names of Dove, Wye and Derwent are synonymous with grayling fishing.

Heading North, a treasure trove of places to catch grayling can be found. From the Yorkshire chalkstream of Driffield Beck to the mighty Ribble, and up into Cumbria and the North East you can find grayling in many suitable rivers and, as pollution reduces because of the massive reductions in industrial discharges, so a natural increase in distribution seems possible.

And finally, Scotland, where some systems have grayling and some do not, even though it seems as though they have suitable water conditions. The Border rivers based on Tweed have them; the Dumfries rivers, Annan and Nith, have them; the Clyde has them; and the Tay system has them. You can even catch grayling in the centre of Edinburgh, in the Water of Leith. There are many smaller rivers with grayling stocks also, but the big north-east river systems like the Spey and Dee do not have grayling, nor do the west coast spate rivers. One feature which grayling like is a constant flow and water level, and this is not, of course, offered by a true spate river.

Reg Righyni (below), a founding father of the Grayling Society and well-known game fisherman and author, set about trying to catch a grayling from as many UK rivers, streams, beck and rivulets as he could. Over the years he amassed a huge number of separate waters where he had caught at least one grayling. Although

Fishing the Kaitum  Photo: Roger Cullum Kenyon
*I am working the central section of the river in front of me. A few steps forward it is 10 feet deep!*

the number is one of those never-to-be-proved mysteries, it was thought to have been 142 by the late Dr Ron Broughton, former President of the Grayling Society. Laid out against Reg's number my own tally looks distinctly anorexic. And I'm not saying what my total is!

In Europe and Scandinavia there are extensive populations of grayling, and in the east such countries as Poland, the Czech Republic, Slovakia and Slovenia have become bucket-list destinations for many anglers. That is not to say they are the only locations, and throughout Northern Europe and into Russia you can chase the Lady. I have visited France, Denmark and Sweden and have hopes of fishing in more European locations such as the Belgian Ardennes and some of the more eastern countries.

My visit to the Tjuonajokk Camp in Swedish Lapland some years ago with my good friends, Roger Cullum Kenyon and Brian Clarke, was a real eye-opener. The crystal clear River Kaitum and interlocking lakes were just full of large hard-fighting grayling, or *harr* in Swedish, and we caught so many that there were times when I just had to pack it in for a while and sit on the bank and have a fag – something I can't enjoy now since I gave up smoking ten years ago. The week or so we spent there changed my outlook on grayling size. A large UK grayling was a mere medium in Sweden, and we consistently caught fish well over 20 inches.

It is believed that the reason grayling grow to larger sizes in the colder more northerly climes is because of their rate of growth and length of their life. They grow more slowly but live longer and attain greater lengths and weights than those in, say, the UK because of this different growth pattern. Some Arctic grayling sampled from a lake in Alaska were found to be about 15 years old. They certainly do not live that long in the UK where they have a lifespan more like four to six years.

The relatively short lifespan of a UK fish

After fishing the Kaitum
*Brian found it hard work fighting the Swedish grayling!*

can, in part, be considered as a factor in the occasional disparity in year-class numbers in our rivers. It only takes one bad spawning year because of adverse conditions and it can have a major impact on the population densities for that individual year-class and the water's population as a whole.

Grayling spawn in the Spring which is, frankly, the cause of all the bother there has been about whether they are a true game fish or not. Some hide-bound and bigoted game fishermen, mainly in years past, just could not get their heads around the fact that it was a true member of the salmon family and should be given the same respect due to, say, a trout or sea-trout or even a salmon. Thankfully things have changed dramatically in the last 30 years or so and much of that change I think can be seen to be as a result of the efforts of the Grayling Society and Grayling Research Trust, both of which have had big impacts in educating anglers and fishery owners into a different viewpoint. Gone are the mass cullings of the south, helped enormously by the EA's National Trout and Grayling Strategy, and winter grayling fishing on a day-ticket basis is now available in many more locations and on many more rivers than was the case in the past. The Grayling Society even present their members with *The Grayling Angler's Guide*, a booklet listing over 200 day ticket waters throughout the UK. Fishery owners have got the message in Scotland too, where salmon has always been king, and there is now much excellent grayling fishing available throughout the winter.

Spawning can be a bit of a messy affair, as it can be with most creatures for that matter. Males hover around a likely female, vying for her attention, and eventually the 'chosen one' gets to fertilise the eggs. Then, however, it is highly likely the minx of a female will go off and find another 'chosen one' for another go! A typical female grayling can lay up to 5,000 eggs. These can quite easily be laid in batches with as

European Grayling spawning in Switzerland

many as six or seven different male fish being the 'fathers' of the brood!

So what do grayling eat and what can we do to match that? Well, to paraphrase an old pet food advertisement, '8 out of 10 grayling prefer gammarus!' And, where the freshwater shrimp or gammarus is readily available, this is probably true. They certainly seem to have a penchant for the shrimps, and scoop them up in droves. Is this because they really like the taste or is it that, where shrimps do exist, they are a freely available food source that requires low energy consumption to catch and is nutritious in itself? Well, it is not the purpose of this book to seek answers to questions like that. We, as anglers and fly-tyers, basically need to know what happens and not, necessarily, why it does. Too much learning means too little fishing time!

It is true that grayling take more of their food underwater than on the surface and that the proportion is, no doubt, higher than for a trout of similar size. Not only do shrimp feature on a typical grayling menu but so do all manner of other creatures, especially caddis larva and the nymphs of other flies. That, of course, is why our modern nymphing techniques work so well – while not preventing us from flicking out a dry-fly on a regular, frequent, and successful basis.

One of my favourite aspects of grayling fishing is that feeling you get soon after the strike when you just know it is a grayling and could not be anything else. I mean, of course, that determined corkscrewing movement they use in their attempts to escape. There is no other fish I have ever caught that fights quite like a grayling. Get a big one downstream and off we go on a roller coaster of a tussle as that big dorsal fin becomes a powerful drag that any wily grayling knows how to use to best effect.

I once hosted Ken Ball, who was then President of the National Federation of Anglers, to a day trotting for grayling on the Wylye. He had never been grayling fishing on a chalkstream before so he saw this as a great treat. After taking him to a good spot I left him to it since he obviously knew what he was doing, and returned a couple of hours later to see how he had got on. Well, he was a crafty old match fisherman so he had, not surprisingly, caught a lot of grayling. One thing he said to me, with a look of pure pleasure on his face, was that he just could not believe how hard they fought and how long they kept at it – even when he had them in his hand! That is how they always behave and it comes as a real surprise to many anglers when catching their first grayling.

I don't do photos of the 'Grip and Grin' type myself, but when guiding I have to accept that many clients want a photographic record of the day and of their successes. If they have caught a trout I have a simple rule which says that we keep it in the water in the net whilst I get out my camera. It's a nifty little waterproof Panasonic that I bought some time ago when I decided to stop accepting my client's proffered iPhones – you only drop them once into the river and that is the end of that! When I am ready, I get them to lift up the trout keeping it upside down and only turn it over when I am ready to press the shutter. Turned upside down a trout generally becomes quiet and relatively docile so the photographic process can be carried out quickly and with minimal stress to the fish. So, having had a couple of trout and been pleased with their photos along comes a grayling. 'Shall I just pick it up upside down and then turn it at the last minute' they say. 'Forget that' is my usual reply 'if you turn it upside down it will only get even more annoyed with you!' And that is how grayling are – they never stop fighting, which is one of the things that makes them so special as far as I am concerned.

So, when should you fish for grayling and what approach should you be looking to try at different times of the year?

In the summer, as the season commences, you could easily find grayling rising happily to mayflies. Then they will most likely be found in the shallower runs and the nice glides. You will be looking to match any hatch or any fall of terrestrials whilst always thinking of the opportunities that may exist if you fished the nymph or wet-fly, where allowed. As the season progresses the fish have a tendency to look for deeper pools and, as winter tightens its grip, they will almost certainly head for these places. Then nymphing becomes a more important technique if you are to be successful. Grayling are also, unlike trout, a shoaling fish and will gather together in quite large shoals as winter approaches. I have often tackled a sighted shoal on the Wylye and picked fish off one by one without causing too much fear amongst the rest of the shoal.

When the winter has a real grip and the waters are high and coloured then it is either time to get the fly-tying vice out and forget about fishing or turn to trotting bait. This book is about flies, of course, so we won't discuss bait fishing here except to say that it is a fun and different way to catch grayling in the winter and, with a pounder downstream of you on the end of your line the fight on a trotting rod with a centre-pin reel is quite something.

Wherever, whenever and however you go grayling fishing though you can reasonably expect to have some fun dependent on whether you are going about it correctly. Observe, observe, observe. That is key. Observe what is happening on the water, in the air and what the weather may have in store and look to fish in the most appropriate manner for the prevailing conditions. Please don't just tie on a weighted nymph and start chucking it about. And have fun. That is why we do it, isn't it?

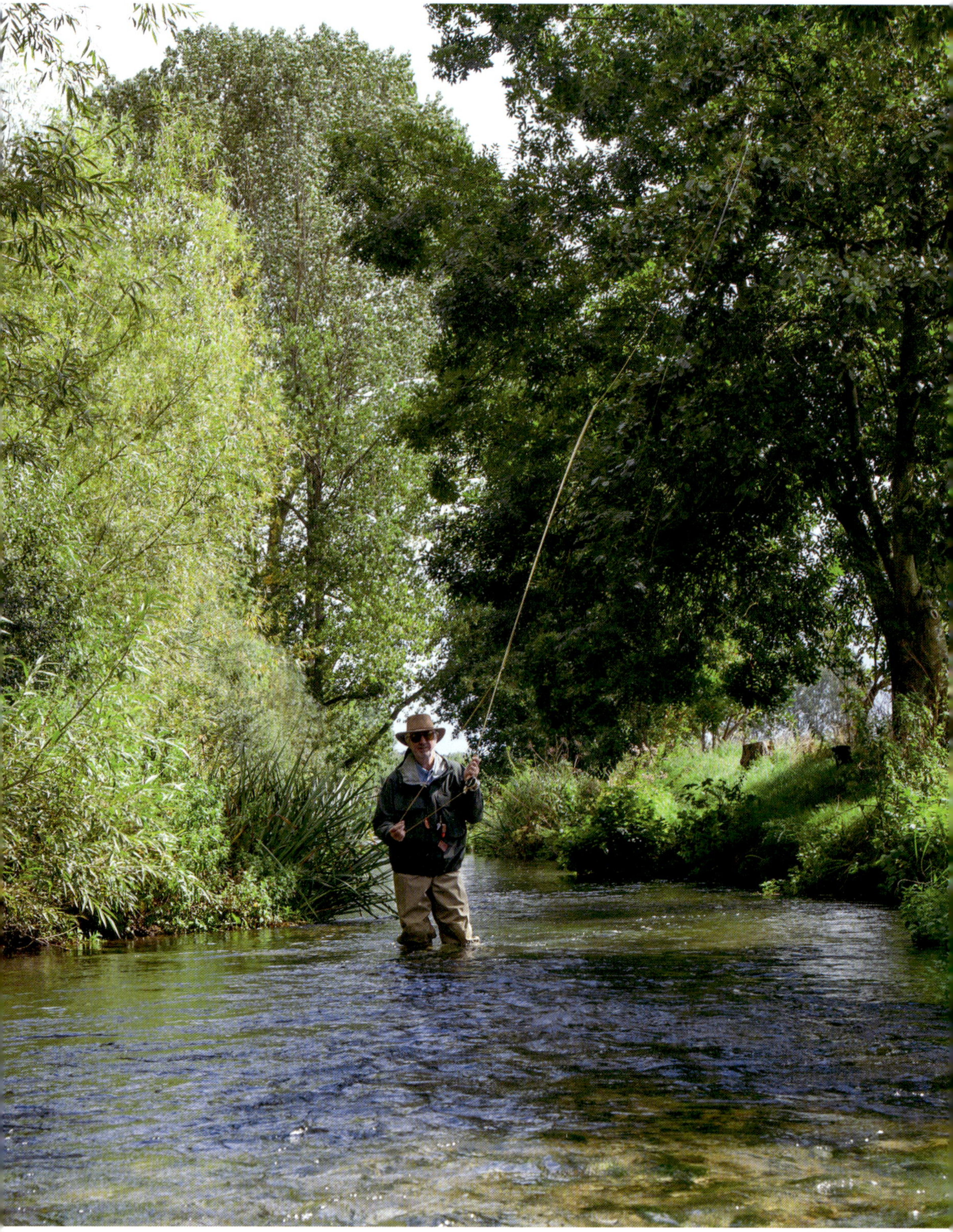

# Chapter Two

# Fly Fishing for Grayling

*'The art of capturing grayling with the fly is immeasurably the most delightful mode of angling for this lovely and gamesome fish.'*
H. A Rolt  *Grayling Fishing in South Country Chalkstreams*

THIS BOOK IS NOT, by any means, intended to be the bible of flyfishing for grayling – that job has been carried out by better and more experienced men than me. Neither is it meant to be the last word in grayling flies or fly-tying. I can tie a pretty good fly for sure but, even though I am a qualified Fly Dresser's Guild instructor and teach fly-tying at my local branch, I am basically someone who ties flies to take fishing with me not ones that are beautiful enough to show people. You aren't going to find me sitting up high on the podium at a fly fair where the expert, invited, fly-tyers carry out their demonstrations but you might see me somewhere like, for instance, the Grayling Society stand tying and talking... but mostly the latter. So, primarily, the flies in this book are ones that are relatively, in some cases exceptionally, easy to tie, and do not generally use any exotic materials nor require specialist tying techniques, skills or equipment. They are flyfisher's flies, not fly-dresser's ones.

I have tried to follow that fishing philosophy set out by the late Oliver Kite which is, essentially, to tell you what I do myself but not tell you to necessarily do it yourself.

Flyfishing has become increasingly specialist since I bought my first fly rod in 1968. In those days when carbon fibre had not been used for rod making we all wandered around with fibreglass or tank aerial, or in my case, split-cane rods. As an aside, although work had been done on fusing carbon for some years, it was only in 1963 that the true, high potential strength of carbon fibre was realised and developed at the Royal Aircraft Establishment, in Farnborough, Hampshire. The process was actually patented by the Ministry of Defence and licensed by them to companies such as Rolls Royce. Anyway, to get back to the rods of old. Our rods, and the actions built into them, were such that we expected them to be capable of all manners of flyfishing. One minute we wanted a dry-fly to be drifting down onto the water's surface like thistledown and the next we were chucking out a team of three spiders across and down.

We may have kidded ourselves that we had all-purpose rods but, in practice, they were just, essentially, a jack of all trades and master of none.

Now I am a squirrel, and over the years I have kept most of my tackle. I still have the original five-foot solid fibreglass rod I had when I was a kid but, of much more relevance, I still possess a rod which, at the time I bought it, I thought was the universal panacea for all my trout and grayling fishing. It is a Hardy Perfection Palakona nine-footer which can throw either a double taper 5 or a weight forward 6 line. If I pick it up now I wonder just how I ever fished all day with this heavy piece of kit. Not only does the rod feel heavy itself but it needs to be matched with a fairly hefty reel if it is to balance correctly and not seem excessively top heavy. But I did fish all day with it, and did so on a regular basis. I was convinced that it was a great universal tool – and it was a Hardy so it must be perfect! However, that was eventually replaced as my numero uno rod by a beautifully made Pezon & Michel 8 foot 5 inch staggered ferrule Fario Club, also rated for a 5 or 6 weight line. Lighter than the Hardy and with a much better action, it is still just too heavy for all day fishing with any degree of comfort.

Of course, as we grow older we are expected to become wiser. After many years of carbon fibre rod-waggling I have reached the conclusion that, as far as I am concerned, there is little point in making a split cane (or bamboo as our American friends more accurately describe it) single-handed fly rod that is longer than 8 foot. I know many aficionados use longer rods, and that great trout bum John Gierach famously uses one of 8 foot 6 inches, but I personally think that once you get past 8 foot there is nothing to be gained for normal river fishing other than extra weight. I still like to use my cane rods, often matched with silk lines, and have several of both. Looking at the rods as they hang in their bags down an oak column in our dining room I can easily see that my preference has settled firmly on 7 foot 6 inches as my personal ideal length, and a double taper 4 or 5 weight as the ideal line for these rods. I should point out at this juncture that I am only 5 feet 6 inches tall with, once that diet has kicked in properly, a moderate weight and strength! Obviously, taller and stronger men than me could wield bigger 'cudgels' when fishing, and for longer periods, but we each develop our own approach and preferences.

Pick up a carbon fibre rod and the world turns upside down. With increasingly clever technology in the development and use of space age materials, plus ever more sophisticated computerised taper designs and lighter weight reel seats and rings, we really have reached the stage where you can justifiably call a rod a wand – because they are now capable of magic! For instance, my Orvis Helios 9 foot 4 weight, one of my favourites and the lightest nine-footer I possess, weighs just 2.4 ounces compared to the 6.1 ounces of the Hardy! Add a reel (Danielson Original Nymph W) and line such that the centre of gravity is about at the top end of the handle – I am unhealthily obsessed with balancing rods and reels – and we are looking at 6.7 ounces compared to the 15.6 ounces of the Hardy which, of course, requires a heavier reel (Hardy Cascapedia MkIII 5/6/7) to attain the same balance point. And the action of the Helios, rated as 'Mid Flex' by Orvis, suits me perfectly whether fishing dry-fly, upstream wet-fly or normal upstream nymph fishing.

OK, so where is this heading? Towards the view that maybe we really do now have a universal rod that can be used effortlessly all day and will throw a dry-fly as perfectly as it will a weighted nymph or team of three. We are constantly being told by manufacturers, retailers and angling magazines that a 9 foot 5 weight has become the gold standard of river rods. As time progresses ideas change and the standard river rod is now probably heading towards a 9 foot 4 weight or even 3 weight for the less windy days.

But the development of lighter, more powerful and better actioned carbon fibre rods has also meant that we have also developed more specialised techniques for river flyfishing matched to more specialised rods.

Fifty years ago if you suggested making a 10 foot 3 weight rod to be used all day with two or three heavily weighted nymphs and the rod held horizontally more or less at arm's-reach whilst the flies drifted across the front of you and the fly line never touched the water people would have choked on their beer with laughter. Yet, even that specification is now being surpassed with even longer rods for 2 weight lines matched to French leaders of lengths up to 12 metres and beyond – although a highly experienced French angling acquaintance tells me they call them Spanish leaders in the south of France. Add to that the relatively recent surge of interest in the Japanese-inspired Tenkara system of long telescopic rods up to about 14 feet long or so with no reel, no rings and a leader attached to the tip by a 'lillian,' and we really have become extremely specialist and gone full circle. Why do I say full circle? Look at the famous illustration (above) from Dame Juliana Berners' *Treatyse of Fysshynge wyth an Angle*. Doesn't that smack a little bit of Tenkara with an indicator?

My dad used to regularly come out with the phrase "There's nowt new in this world, lad!" Of course, as I grew older I realised that was just a load of old bunkum that dads regularly spout just to impress their offspring into thinking they are worldly and wise and are to be held in the utmost reverence. He had, of course, conveniently forgotten manned flight, internal combustion, electricity, TV and radio, telephones, etc.

I am sure, however, that in our world of flyfishing there are lots of instances of there being 'nowt new' but many more where new ideas have been developed and successfully implemented.

I guess if I said that a curved hook was a new idea – I think I do say something like that later in the book – then no doubt someone more bookwormish than me will respond with the description or even a photograph of an example of a hook which is barbless and made from tempered metal and was used in Macedonia or Greece in 2,000 BC. Come to think of it I have seen pictures of a hook discovered in Germany which dates back 12,300 years, is made of mammoth tusk 19,000 years old and on which you could tie a Klinkhåmer Special!

There are even curved hooks found on East Timor that go back 42,000 years.

But I really doubt whether any of the ancients came up with a jig hook as we know it today and a slotted bead to make it work or had the wit to bend a standard hook by 20-30 degrees to tie a Klinkhåmer Special. Then, since demand fuels supply, up came the 'genuine' Klinkhåmer hook made by at least three different manufacturers and just about every hook maker has a jig hook range these days. (As a complete aside, whenever I go to Bakewell in Derbyshire, there seem to be several bakers who claim to be the originators of the Bakewell Pudding. Apparently, they don't call them tarts up there because a tart is someone who stands around on street corners at night, whatever that means! I always go to 'The Old Original Bakewell Pudding Shop' because that title seems to cover all the bases.)

I am not a lover of competitive flyfishing, having done it only once, reasonably successfully, as a member of the Dutch Team at Bewl Bridge one year – yes, I did become an honorary Dutchman for the day. I was disgusted with the disrespectful way in which the dead fish were treated at the weigh-in (not by the Dutch guys I hasten to add) and vowed never to be involved again.

The days of killing fish just to prove your skills are now gone, and numbers and lengths have become more important, with fish being carefully returned to the water after capture. I do recognise, however, that whenever there is something which requires both skill and luck there will be someone wanting to make it competitive, and I appreciate that competition increases the pace of development and accelerates the introduction of new and better ideas. Competitive flyfishing has spawned a host of new ideas such as the techniques of Czech Nymphing and French Leader fishing and many new fly patterns.

So, old or new, what are the ways in which we flyfish for grayling these days?

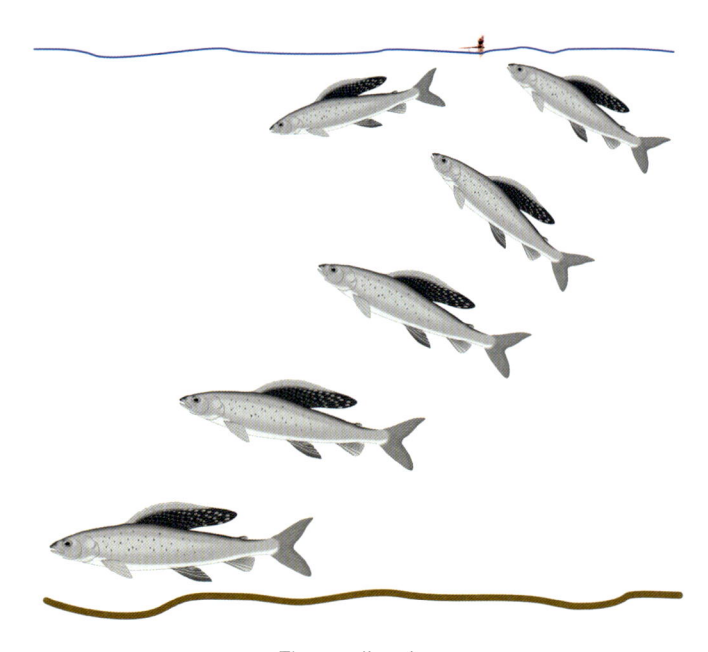

The grayling rise

# Dry-fly

Grayling eat things floating on the surface – fact. That being so, it is obvious that plonking, gently of course, a dry-fly on the surface could be a good wheeze if one wants to catch a fish.

Although not a new phenomenon by any means, it was only in the 19th century that dry-fly fishing was, in effect, codified by Frederic Halford and his colleagues on the chalkstreams of southern England. The common perception of Halford's doctrine is something that can easily polarise people and can often get them distinctly hot under the collar. There is no way I could ever be considered to be a dry-fly purist nor do I really have any problems with anglers who are (despite my wife's alarming tendencies in that direction), but there has been a lot of nonsense talked about dry-fly fishing, especially as practised on the chalkstreams.

It was fine for Halford and his cohorts to sit patiently on a bench by the river waiting for a fish to rise, then consider, by observation, exactly what fly it had taken before selecting an exact imitation from one's box and presenting it carefully to just that one fish. Process over, either successfully or by having put the fish down, one retreats to the bench, lights one's pipe, and waits until another fish does the decent thing and rises. What a load of rubbish! My socialist tendencies lead me to believe that is just a plan to keep the workers down because they can't afford to sit around waiting for things to happen – they have to be back down the pit or on the night shift tonight! OK, so this is an overly simplified proletarian viewpoint, I know, but I like it.

Seriously though, in this increasingly busy and stressful world we all have less and less time to devote to our sport, at least whilst we are still working for a living, and don't have the luxury of sitting down waiting for something to happen every time we are at the waterside. More often than not if fish aren't rising we will fish the water in places where we think there are fish, or where there have been fish before, with flies we think might bring one up anyway. Certainly that is my experience with such flies as the Supa Pupa or F-Fly or Klinkhåmer Special. If we spot a hatch of duns or fall of spinners or terrestrials then, assuming our wits are with us and not off dreaming somewhere, we will look into our box for a suitable imitation. Aha, then we can become Halfordian!

Often we don't have to fish the water because there are fish rising and they are, as often as not, smaller grayling which can turn a miserable day into a fun one. Grayling do rise well on occasion, and the little ones rise a lot.

I don't propose to say much more about dry-fly fishing for grayling because it is so similar to that for trout and, if you are not familiar with the technique then there are far better books than this to read.

There is one aspect of dry-fly fishing for grayling that should be considered though. That is when grayling 'bump the fly;' an annoying situation when a fish rises to your perfectly presented fly but misses it or, as a friend likes to put it, 'bumps' it. He takes these instances as a personal insult from the fish by the way. Why does this happen? Well, I have heard it said that it is the fish refusing at the very last moment. Yet, if that was true, then wouldn't it happen regularly with trout also? In fact, isn't it even more likely to happen with trout because they are more finicky and spook more easily than grayling?

My theory is that sometimes fish do refuse at the very last moment but, more likely, when a grayling 'bumps' a fly it is because it just got the maths wrong. When a trout is, as we say, 'on the fin' it is sitting just a short distance below the water's surface. As a fly comes towards him, trout eyesight, window and mirror view and all that stuff aside, he has plenty of time to make his mind up whether to take it or not because, when it reaches him, he only has to gently ease his way upwards and suck it down.

The grayling is invariably deeper down in the water than a trout, because more of its everyday food is down there, and so it has a lot more water to move through to reach a fly on the surface. It has to see that fly earlier and make its mind up more quickly than does the trout before setting off on its upward journey. There is a lot of geometry involved, especially when you add in the effect of varying currents. They just get the maths wrong sometimes and miss the fly. Because they only just miss it they create a bulging effect with their snouts which moves water on the surface. I don't know about you but I have occasionally seen a grayling rise and then set off almost into a backwards loop, or bunt, to get the fly. Is this because it is into aerobatics that day or is it because it got its approach wrong? Who knows, but one thing is for sure – it ain't personal!

And one final point about dry-fly fishing. Don't fall into the trap of just putting on a nymph automatically when you reach the river or even before you have got there: it is amazing just how picky grayling can be. I remember a salutary experience on the River Test one winter's day, when I had been guiding a relatively competent American angler and we had been using nymphs because there was nothing moving on the surface: we had done OK but not brilliantly. As we walked back to the car to get him to the railway station we passed a guy standing in the middle of the river playing a grayling. When I asked him how he had been getting on he replied, with a great Geordie accent, that he had been having a 'real canny time ye knar man!' In fact he had been fishing pretty exclusively with a size 20 black gnat and taking plenty of grayling on the surface. Lesson learned!

# Wet-fly

Ah, this is the real thing! Wet-fly fishing is as old as the hills. Well, not quite, but it has certainly been practised extensively, and in some places exclusively, for centuries. In the United Kingdom, these days, we tend to think of it more as a technique of the North and there are countless books about flies, flyfishing and fly fishermen written by Northerners. Yet, in reality, it has probably been practised throughout the country in years past. I learned my wet-fly fishing 'up North' and that is why the wet flies in this book are basically Yorkshire spider patterns. I have no problem with winged wet flies but I don't generally use them myself.

*Upstream Wet-fly* – "Them as knows, tha knows", as Yorkshire folk might say, realise that the proper way to fish spiders is upstream with a shortish line and a longish rod. The flies are cast upstream into likely-looking lies or, if you are lucky and have rising or visible fish in front of you, they are aimed in that direction and are then allowed to drift back with the current in as drag-free a manner as you can achieve. Takes are indicated by a tightening of the line or a sideways movement and must be hit immediately. Sound familiar? Well, if you are an upstream nymph fisherman it should do because it is pretty well the same

A typical Northern river – the Ribble at Gisburn. *Photo: Rod Calbrade*

Typical grayling weather – the Hodder at Newton. *Photo: Rod Calbrade*

technique. It isn't always easy but can be most rewarding and allows you to cover large sections of river quite quickly.

W C Stewart in his seminal book, *The Practical Angler*, advocates upstream wet-fly fishing always, so let him conclude this section;

> *The great error of flyfishing, as usually practised, and as recommended to be practised by books, is that the angler fishes down stream, whereas he should fish up.*

Downstream Wet-fly – It has been said that downstream wet-fly fishing, as traditionally carried out, is 'chuck and chance' and that it produces more fish but smaller ones than upstream fishing. I don't agree that it is chuck and chance, and I believe an experienced and skilled wet-fly fisherman can fish downstream very effectively, presenting his flies in a very natural way to the fish. I have caught lots of smaller fish when fishing downstream wets, but I have caught a lot of big ones also.

One of my delights each year is to fish spider patterns downstream on a chalkstream. Not generally a technique one would associate with the pruned, pimped and posh rivers of the south but one which is allowed by one of my clubs once the trout season is over. On the 16th of October each year I get a childish delight from tying on three spiders – Partridge & Orange, Waterhen Bloa and Black Magic probably – and launching them in the opposite direction to that which we are confined to doing when trout are in season. Daft, I know, but it is one of those snook-cocking things that I get off on. And I catch grayling!

Proper wet-fly men use a long rod, often up to 11 feet in length, matched commonly

River Tees near Widdybank Farm. *Photo: Stuart Minnikin, Yorkshire Dales Flyfishing*

with a 4 or 5 weight double-taper floating line and a leader with three flies. Many years ago rod-makers Bruce and Walker made an 11 foot 3 inch carbon fibre 'Century' rod rated for a 4/6 line. This was often used by the wet-fly men of Lancashire and Yorkshire for their downstream fishing and had the distinct advantage of being long and throwing a light line easily. Although it has been outstripped as technology has developed, it still possesses those qualities which make for a good wet-fly tool; long length, easy action and light line. It also found much use in loch-style fishing.

W C Stewart famously fished with four flies. Now, I am the Captain of the All England Untangling Team, as I tell my guiding clients when I am untangling their twentieth mess of the day, but I do not like fishing with four flies. They are just waiting to mess up your day!

Downstream wet-fly fishing is probably the most relaxing and contemplative of all my flyfishing. You cast across at about 45 degrees and apply an upstream mend as soon as the conditions demand. As your flies move downstream you are constantly mending line, hopefully without moving the flies, to ensure as drag-free a drift as possible, and keeping your rod tip high as you look for tell-tale signs of your line tightening as a fish takes one of the flies. Then, as your flies finally sweep to a position directly downstream of you there is that moment of sheer anticipation wondering if a fish has tracked them and will take at the very last moment; a frequent occurrence. The rod should always be held high to aid mending and to watch for takes.

I once fished with Harry Vallack, who is an expert in fishing the Upper Tees. Where we fished, at Widdybank Farm, about half a mile below Cow Green reservoir, the river is rocky and pretty fast flowing. Harry fished downstream wet-fly all the time with just two flies and he caught fish after fish.

This was wet-fly fishing at its best because no sooner had your line hit the water than you were thinking of lifting it off again. Harry's mantra is to always look at the line and if it tightens strike immediately. Never wait until you feel the fish, he would say, because then it is too late. How right he is, and how many of us have lost fish by waiting for the 'tug'? They say the tug is the drug but, in this case, you are just a mug if you wait for tug!

*Other Wet-fly Methods* – The traditional upstream and downstream are not the only methods of fishing wet flies.

Oliver Edwards, in his excellent DVD, *Wet Fly Fishing on Rivers*, explains and demonstrates the Square and Across method and, more interestingly, the Escalator. This method is an attempt to overcome that old problem of flies dragging across the water at strictly 'non-scale' speeds and scaring fish rather than interesting them.

Watch the DVD because it is extremely good and clearly demonstrates this great technique

# Nymphing

Nymphing is probably the most consistent and successful approach to flyfishing for grayling, and these days it is certainly the most popular and fastest growing. It is also the area where most development has taken place in terms of tackle and, probably, of flies. It is not surprising that it is so successful since the grayling takes much more of its food underwater than it does from the surface. Where freshwater shrimps are present, for instance, they can make up as much as 80% of the fish's diet, and the nymphs of upwinged and other fly species are easy pickings compared to the geometric calculations required and energy expended in travelling upwards to intercept a fly on the surface. Like wet-fly fishing we can look at nymphing in more than one way.

*'Traditional' Upstream* – This technique was pretty well the standard for many years and is, of course, that practised by Skues, Sawyer and Kite, although Skues used unweighted nymphs and Sawyer and Kite used weighted ones. In my view it is one of the most skilful methods of flyfishing and a good upstream nymph fisherman is a delight to watch.

Using a fairly standard rod – the universal 9 foot 5 weight for instance – you cast upstream beyond the fish you either know or expect to be there, and let your nymph drift back towards you. It is vital to allow the flies to act naturally on their drift because drag, as in dry-fly fishing, is your bitter enemy. Obviously, if you want to be able to hook a fish you need to retrieve line as it drifts downstream towards you. This needs to be done without moving the fly or that accursed drag will feature as a deterrent to the feeding fish. Takes are registered by either the line tightening, moving sideways, disappearing down a

The author upstream nymphing on the River Irfon. *Photo: Rod Calbrade*

'hole,' or in some cases, by a downright vicious pull! Skues, fishing the really gin clear Itchen talked about seeing the 'wink under water' as a fish opened its mouth to take the fly, although he was referring to trout with their wider mouths.

There is, however, one technique when upstream nymphing that does require you to move the fly faster than the current. This is the well-known, and extremely effective, technique, the 'Induced Take.' Originally developed by Frank Sawyer for trout, it can be a very profitable approach when grayling fishing in a situation where you can see the fish. Often a shoal of grayling will let a weighted nymph drift through them unmolested time after time. This is, of course, rather frustrating and can lead to expletives being delivered. However, several years ago Sawyer realised, when sight-fishing for individual trout with his Pheasant Tail Nymphs, that a short but sharp raising of the rod tip will cause the nymph to rise quickly in the water and this movement can be enough to trigger a positive reaction from an otherwise disinterested fish. The popularity of this technique grew rapidly and was quickly applied to grayling. In the situation where a nymph dead-drifts untouched through a sighted shoal of grayling the induced take can be quite deadly. In fact, with practice, it is possible to pick off the fish at the rear of the shoal without disturbing those nearer the front. On several occasions I have taken many fish from a shoal with this technique. It is also possible to use this technique when the fish cannot be seen, although it does require you to know where they are – time for a bit of watercraft! You can develop a kind of sixth sense when nymphing: Oliver Kite supposedly fished successfully for grayling whilst blindfolded, using his bare hook nymph, demonstrating how this

Classic upstream nymphing water on the Wylye

sense, and the induced take, can work if you are at the top of your game. Accuracy of casting and good presentation are essential when upstream nymphing, as is good line control. So often river fishing is about line control as much as anything else.

I believe it is essential to wear polarised sunglasses when flyfishing; either on clear chalkstreams or on darker rain-fed rivers. Apart from the fact that you can see more easily through the water, except when muddiness obscures any vision, you only get one set of eyes, and a hook in one of them is a catastrophe of immeasurable proportions. Very often on a chalkstream, especially as autumn approaches and the water is at its clearest, you can catch grayling just by watching both the fish and your fly as it tracks towards them underwater. Hooking a grayling by this sight method is perhaps the greatest thrill of all in river flyfishing to me, and certainly equal to, if not better than, watching a fish rise to your dry-fly.

I am (he says immodestly) very good at spotting fish in the river. It is because I have always been an observant type but also because I was once told by a guru whose name I have, unforgivably, forgotten, not to look at the water or even into the water, but to look through the water. It is not an easy difference to explain, other than to say 'ignore the water surface just look down as deep as you can through it.' Also, don't look for fish but look for bits of fish and, once found, you will see the whole thing. It works for me.

I get a lot of back-ache when upstream nymph fishing, and now fish exclusively with a back support. It is partly because of an old football injury, but mainly because of my stance. There used to be a great stillwater fisherman called Bill Sibbons, inventor of the 'When All Else Fails' stalking bug, who frequented, and probably now

'The Heron' as pictured on the cover of Clive Graham-Ranger's book

Author's typical upstream nymphing stance.
*Photo: Roger Cullum Kenyon*

haunts, the small crystal-clear stillwaters of Hampshire, especially Rockbourne, where I had the pleasure of meeting him a few times. He was an exceptional angler and on at least one occasion gave me a master class in catching rainbows. But the point is that he was known as 'The Heron' because of his stance when fishing. He didn't stand on one leg, of course, but did stoop slightly forward and looked down through the water with the keen eyes of his nickname bird, and he always wore polarised glasses.

I learned a lot from watching Bill and this is how I nymph fish with a slightly forward stoop whilst watching, as much like a heron as I can, everything that is occurring that affects my fly and line. My rod is always horizontal or even lower, ready for an instant strike and giving me as big an arc as possible to ensure that the strike is successful.

I know others may advocate keeping your rod tip high but, when using this technique, I think the opposite is better with grayling. This is because you can then hit the fish quickly with a swift and short flick of the rod tip which, bearing in mind how fast they are at taking and rejecting a fly, is stacking the odds onto your side somewhat.

Grayling certainly can, and frequently do, hit and reject flies instantly. When I am guiding and my client is fishing upstream nymph on a chalkstream, especially for grayling, I always tell them to strike at absolutely everything. If the line tightens or goes sideways, or the Klinkhåmer or indicator goes under or even flutters slightly, strike immediately for it is much better to hook Hampshire (or Wiltshire) than to miss a fish!

I have seen grayling mouth the fly many times, and am always amazed at the speed at which they can take in and reject a fly without anything registering at the business end of the system. I once lay on the riverbank alongside a small shoal of grayling, when the water was crystal clear, and watched a friend upstream nymphing relying purely on seeing his leader tighten, move sideways, or just disappear down the hole where it enters the water, as Sawyer would say. I counted the number of takes I saw as grayling took in the nymph and then spat it out and it was at least twice those which my friend detected by watching his leader.

Bite detection, therefore, is critical when upstream nymphing and particularly so on the rain-fed rivers where currents are less predictable and water clarity seldom as good as on a chalkstream. When I was younger it came easy to me. I have excellent eyesight, although age is causing it to deteriorate now, and I could easily see my leader in virtually any light conditions. So, detecting the movement of a leader with a lightly greased butt was no problem. As I get older I increasingly need to resort to some form of assistance in detecting bites. The New Zealand style or Klink & Dink method (also known as Duo or Hopper & Dropper) is, of course, a great technique where it is allowed. The upside is that it can be sensitive enough to readily show bites, dependent on the relationship in size between the nymph and Klinkhåmer Special or other buoyant dry-fly, and you also have two chances because you are fishing both a dry-fly and nymph.

The downside to this method is that your fishing depth is fixed. This can be a great disadvantage when grayling fishing because you so often have to get right down to the river bed especially as winter tightens its grip. With depths varying along the river it can sometimes be a pain fishing Klink & Dink. A brilliant alternative is the New Zealand Strike Indicator Tool whereby you hook your leader with a specially designed needle and slide a piece of tubing off the needle shaft down onto the leader itself. Now you have a loop of leader into which you put some wool – New Zealand, of course. Once you tighten up the indicator by sliding the tubing back over one end of the wool you have something which doesn't possess a hook, obviously, but has the massive advantage of being instantly movable up or down the leader thus making depth changes a breeze. Pop a bit of floatant on the wool and you are in business with it floating all day. You only need a very small piece of wool so it will go under very quickly if a fish takes the nymph.

I have spent a lot of time in my grayling fishing life using the traditional upstream method and I am very fond of it as a relaxing way to fish and a very profitable one. It gives you backache though!

*Czech Style Nymphing* – Ironically, it is said that Czech Nymphing was started in Poland by the Polish team in a 1984 flyfishing competition between them, East Germany and Czechoslovakia! This was five years before the Poles and Czechs threw out the communists and became a democracy and six years before the East Germans did the same. I have seen it written that the equipment the Polish team had available was hardly state of the art. Thus the Poles resorted to fishing their heavy caddis-type nymphs on whatever nylon they had and fishing them on short lines deep down

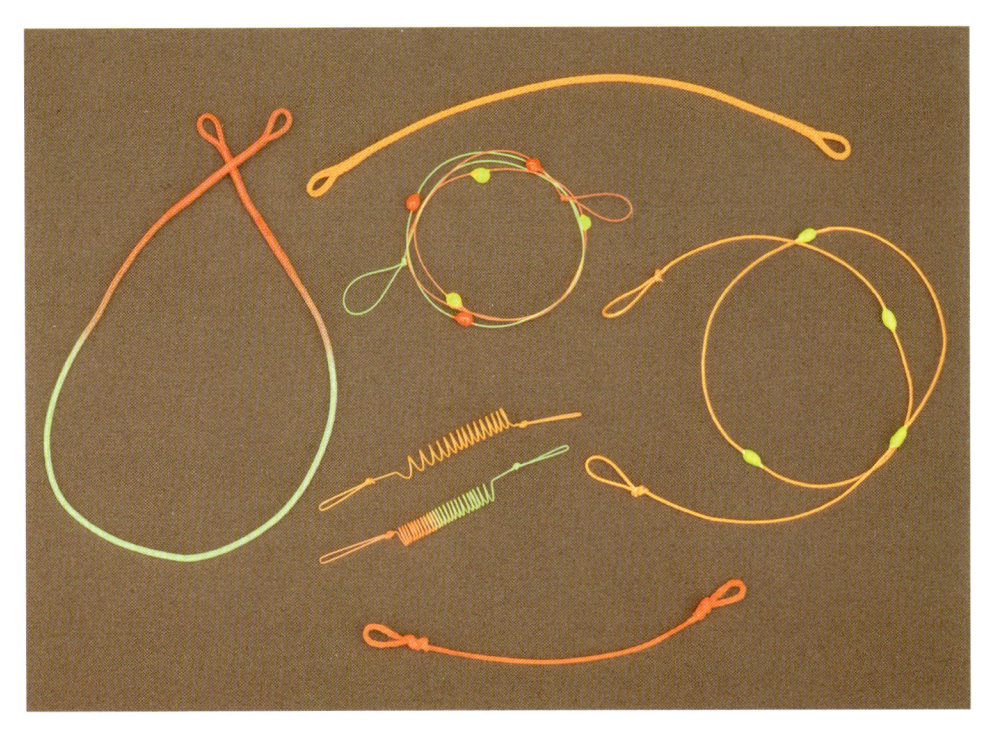

Popular types of indicator

and tracking the flies as they drifted downstream. Was this the birth of Czech Nymphing? Well, nearly. In practice the Czechs, not slow to pick up a good tip or two, went home and developed a slightly more refined version with nymphs of their own designs, known to us unsurprisingly as Czech Nymphs and to them as Bobeš or Bobesh, and, hey presto, we then really did have the birth of Czech Nymphing as we know it today.

Over the years there has been a lot of mysticism about the technique although it does seem fairly basic to me. Take a long rod that takes a light line, put a heavy reel on it to balance it in the hand not at the top end of the handle – it helps when you are holding the thing at arm's length for a day. Tie a shortish leader to your fly line with a dropper or two and tie on two or three slim but heavy flies and you are ready to go. Most folks build an indicator into their set up and thus spiral ones or braided ones are readily available all in bright fluorescent colours to enable them to be seen easily in any conditions.

Casting is a fairly basic affair and, with this method you don't want your fly line to touch the water, ideally, but just fish with the leader itself. After your short cast upstream you track the flies downstream holding your rod horizontally and following the drift of the flies with your rod tip. Once they have passed your position you should always lift with what is, in effect, a strike and re-cast. This sharp lift often produces fish although they can take at any time throughout the drift.

The key is to get your flies down to the river bed and, with the right equipment, you can literally feel them bouncing along the bottom.

The method has spawned a host of nymph patterns and, of course, the jig hooked ones are ideal for this method because they swim upside down and are less likely to snag during the drift.

Czech Nymphing has led to the development of longer and lighter rods and I was even talking with someone recently who uses a 10 foot 6 inch 2 weight for his nymphing. This seems a little extreme to me because you have to consider that we generally release grayling and I wonder if one of the modern 2 weight rods can subdue a fish as quickly as one with a higher line rating. However, I am quite happy using my own 10 foot 3 weight when fishing this way and find it can bring a fish to hand quickly enough so I can release it without it having been tired too much.

Stealth and watercraft become paramount when Czech Nymphing because you are fishing in quite close proximity to yourself and need to be conscious of the water depth and flow characteristics if your nymphs are going to fish properly and with the best opportunity of tricking a fish. Used well the technique can be quite devastating and, in the winter months, when grayling have shoaled it can account for several fish without having to move position as you pick them out from the shoal one by one. There is no doubt that this is a very effective method for catching grayling although, as I get older, I find it strains the old arm muscles a bit. Still, no pain, no gain, I guess!

*French Nymphing (or Spanish Nymphing if you are French!)* – Now from short leaders to unbelievably, incredibly, enormously, extraordinarily long ones! Like most of the recent developments it has its history linked to international competition fishing. Around the turn of the century the French and Belgians were using this type of approach in internationals. It soon caught on and is now becoming increasingly publicised and popularised.

It requires a longish light line, say up to 11 foot and 3 weight, rod which can be softer than the Czech Nymph equivalent and a leader which can be up to 12 metres long. The leaders can be quite complex in their make up and I have seen them with reverse tapers and built in indicators plus the use of camouflaged nylon. The idea is to cast a long line to minimise fish disturbance and raise the rod tip as the flies drift towards you. Like all river nymph techniques it requires the flies to fish drag-free moving only as the current allows and not pulling as you would on a stillwater.

Casting with this set up is a skilful affair and requires some degree of practise to master. I was once fortunate enough to guide a one time member of the French national flyfishing team who, not surprisingly, was a real expert at this type of fishing. I guided him for four days in total during which time I put him onto the fish and he showed me how to use the technique with devastating effect. Incidentally, he hailed from the Pyrenees and does most of his fishing in Spain and he insisted that the leaders should be called Spanish leaders!

Having said that, it is a technique that I don't really like. I was brought up as a traditionalist in my flyfishing and although I can and do fish Czech Nymph style regularly I don't often pull out the French, or even the Spanish, leader. It just isn't my bag as they say, even though there is one in my bag. But it is a real pleasure to watch someone using it who really does know what they are doing. And there is no doubt it catches a lot of fish. But, I never started fishing to catch lots of fish just to catch some fish and have a good time whilst doing so. When I worked in a high pressure job I went to the river to relax and wash away the troubles of my day not to pressurise myself into catching lots of large fish. And I guess that philosophy has stuck with me, not that I don't enjoy catching lots of large fish – I just don't set out with that as my goal.

Oh, and if you have never tried French Leader fishing then try a four-fly wet-fly approach first. If you can fish four wet flies without a tangle then you might just get away with a French Leader.

# Tenkara

I worked for Toshiba for some years, back in the 1980s, but, even on trips to Tokyo, Fuji and Kyoto, I never got to hear about Tenkara. It hit the headlines a few years later with a bit of a bang, fuelled to some extent by an American, Daniel W Galhardo, and his firm Tenkara USA, having previously been the subject of a magazine article by the late Peter Lapsley. Like a lot of other folks I bought one of the rods and tried out this, apparently, wonderful piece of kit. As the American advertising guru Jerry Della Femina, 'The Madman of Madison Avenue', once said it

A typical Tenkara set up

was 'From those wonderful folks who gave you Pearl Harbor!' Needless to say that line wasn't, actually, used in advertising – just as part of the title of his best-selling book.

Anyway I have used my Tenkara kit, although not that often, just as I don't fish with a French Leader too often, but it can be fun. In fact, I caught probably my biggest English grayling whilst Tenkara fishing. I was with a friend, Steve Harrison, at Wherwell on the River Test on the 14th of March one year, the last day of the season, of course. He was keen to try out Tenkara so we set up my rod and wandered upstream from the lodge. There is a footbridge about a hundred yards upstream, and a ford above it which housed a large shoal of grayling that year. I tied on a Gammy Shrimp and, just as I was about to cast upstream, along came the local farmer who wandered over the bridge telling us we had no chance of catching any of those fish because they had seen everything. Secretly, I agreed with him because they had been fly-bashed for months. Anyway, first cast a fish took the nymph. I turned to Steve and said, rather smugly, something like 'Of course, you have to have faith in the strength of your leader and the flex of the rod.' Just then the fish, which was now below us and under the bridge, rolled and we looked at each other and both blurted out, loudly, some choice and distinctly Anglo-Saxon expressions. It was big and my tippet was only about 2 ½lbs. breaking strain. Eventually the fish was landed and, just pushing 20 inches, made my day and my season. So I packed up for the year and passed the rod to Steve who caught several fish before he decided that his season was over also. Not a bad introduction to the technique then.

Now, Honor gets fed up with me whenever there is cricket on TV because I always start saying, in my best David (Bumble) Lloyd accent, 'I don't like cricket, I love it!' And that is just how Tenkara seems to get some folks. They go overboard with it all carrying dinky little curved, misshapen, landing nets made from bamboo and fishing with reverse hackled 'sakasa kebari' flies, sometimes with silk eyes instead of proper metal ones, and carried in glass bottles! They can get carried away with it all and end up like one of the English lads who used to work with me at Toshiba who became more Japanese than, well, the Japanese!

Seriously though, before folks start stalking me and planning to throw me into the river, or forcing me to buy a tantō knife and commit *hara-kiri*, for my blasphemy then let me say that I believe Tenkara is yet another technique which has prompted the development of rods and flies and equipment new to the West even though it may have been used for years in the East! But I still think Dame Juliana would have been quite familiar with the technique and, since the rods are telescopic I often go fishing with one tucked down the back of my fly vest just in case I fancy a go with it.

I see they are now selling Tenkara rods of 7 and 8 feet in length which seems a bit bizarre to me. I can't help wondering if they should call these short ones Fivekara instead!

# Hints and Tips

*Don't cast too far in front of a fish* – I know we get terrified of scaring fish but we also want to have the best chance of catching them. The experience I have of guiding competent anglers and teaching beginners is that many folk cast too far ahead of a rising or sighted fish. What you gain in stealth you can so easily lose in drag. The farther ahead of a fish you cast the more chance of drag before the fly reaches it. I have seen anglers casting huge distances to reach a fish when a gentle and stealthy move farther upstream will enable them to cast shorter and have a better chance of a drag-free drift. Never use a long cast if you can use a short one.

*Don't try and cast too far* – Apart from the reasons shown above, just how can you easily hook a rising fish at 25 yards? And how can you present a fly delicately enough at that distance? The answer to both of these questions is – not easily at all! The development of faster rods and distance lines seems to have prompted a desire to cast as far as possible. I can't see how double hauling has much place on a river. On lakes, then sure you do need to do it often to get out to the fish, but on a river you can usually just move nearer. Presentation is so important in river fishing that we should be more conscious of that than we are of the distance we cast, or even the flies we have on the business end.

*Don't just turn up and start casting to the far bank like so many anglers seem to want to do* – If you were on that bank you would cast to this one wouldn't you? So why not cast to this one first anyway? That way you can search the nearest water then work your way across the river.

*Don't cast at the water, cast above it* – If you want your flies to land like thistledown then you have to aim high. A fly aimed at the water surface will have more chance of smacking down and not floating properly or, even worse, scaring fish. Even nymphs cast above the water can have a chance of entering it at a steeper angle and thus sinking faster.

*Don't tie on a fly before you get to the water* – It is tempting to just tie on a nymph or Klinkhåmer or Supa Pupa etc. whilst tackling up. Why not get to the water first and see what's happening? Then you can tie on the fly that seems best in the prevailing conditions.

*Push the hook out with your rod tip* – Sounds scary? Well it isn't. I was fishing in the mayfly season on the Wiltshire Avon at Amesbury some years ago. I had hooked a nice trout and was trying to net it rather unsuccessfully because of the high bank I had to reach down. Someone came along and asked me if it was a barbless hook, which it was. So he then suggested I push the hook out with the rod tip. That sounded a bit scary to me because of the possibility of breaking the rod. Anyway I did what he said and, hey presto, the hook came out sweetly and easily. I turned to look at the guy and it was Geoffrey Bucknall, the well-known angler, author and tackle dealer. Since then I have pushed thousands of hooks out with my rod tip and never, no never, damaged a rod. You have to be careful, of course, and check that the hook is in a suitable place to try the technique and the hook has to be barbless. If the fish has swallowed the hook then, obviously, the idea is a no-no, but if it is sitting in the scissors or top lip and seems to be moderately hooked then the idea will work. Move the rod towards the fish keeping the line tight with the fish still under water and, usually, once the tip ring has touched the bend of the fly one quick push and out the hook comes. Fish generally sit there for a few moments with a quizzical look on their faces and then casually drift away.

If the fly does not come out after a couple of goes then land the fish as normal since the hook may be too firmly lodged in the jaw and will require too great an effort to push out which will not be fair on the fish. The technique works best if you are on the bank. When wading it is not as easy because of the lower angle of the rod versus the fish. In these circumstances I keep the fish in the water and use a pair of forceps to whip out the hook.

*Missing the first fish of the day* – If you are fishing together with a friend then do the chatting bit before you start fishing. On countless occasions I have been with friends and we are so busy chin-wagging that one or other of us misses his first fish because he isn't concentrating on what he is doing!

*Tippet material* – I know we all have our favourite tippet material but if you were thinking of changing or haven't settled on one yet then here is my personal choice – STROFT – which stands for STrong and sOFT and is made in Germany by a company called WAKU GmBH. I was first introduced to this by Hans van Klinken some twenty years ago and I have used it ever since. The GTM version is the one I use. This is a co-polymer and has a remarkable breaking strain for its diameter, knots easily, and is neither too supple nor too stiff for leaders and tippets. For example, the 1.4 Kg (3 lbs 1.3 ounces) BS line is just 0.10 mm in diameter. The only other co-polymer that I can see anywhere near this is Frog Hair which is a little weaker for the same diameter and more than twice the cost of Stroft. The other 'standard' nylons are all thicker, some considerably, for the same breaking strain. Stroft isn't always easy to find in the UK but can be obtained directly from WAKU through their ASPO shop at www.aspo-gmbh/de/shop/ where there is a large range of products with several more nylons plus fluorocarbons and braids as well as a tippet dispenser system and pre-formed tapered leaders.

*Photographs* – Hang on a minute while I struggle up on top of this soapbox. I'm not very tall and it is hard work climbing up so I can evangelise! My pet hate is 'Grip and Grin' type photos! On the rare occasions that I have been pictured holding a fish it has always been because of the insistence of the photographer and not out of personal choice. I am not proud of those lapses and have vowed never to let it happen again. I feel strongly on this issue.

The reason I don't like them is because I consider them to be self-gratification and something which does the fish no good at all. If you want a photo of your fish then do it while the fish is in the water or as you are releasing it , not whilst you are holding it up so you can demonstrate how clever you are to have caught it in the first place! And please don't pull its dorsal fin up to show it off because it probably does the fish no good at all!

I fish for pleasure as most of us do, not competition, and I have a strong respect for the quarry so I won't mess with a fish for the sake of a feel-good factor and a pleasing snap. Neither do I need to know how much each fish weighs, or even how much the big ones do, or how long they are. I think I have only actually measured fish once or twice and that has been with them lying in the water. Not recording my achievement doesn't dim my enjoyment one jot – our lasting memories are in our minds not on mobile phones, computer drives or pieces of paper. If it is your bag to have photos then OK that's your choice but it certainly isn't mine. Remember that grayling are precious and do not take too well to long periods out of water or heavy handling. And, please, if you are going to lift them up to admire them make sure your hands are wet.

Keith Mason playing a large chalkstream grayling

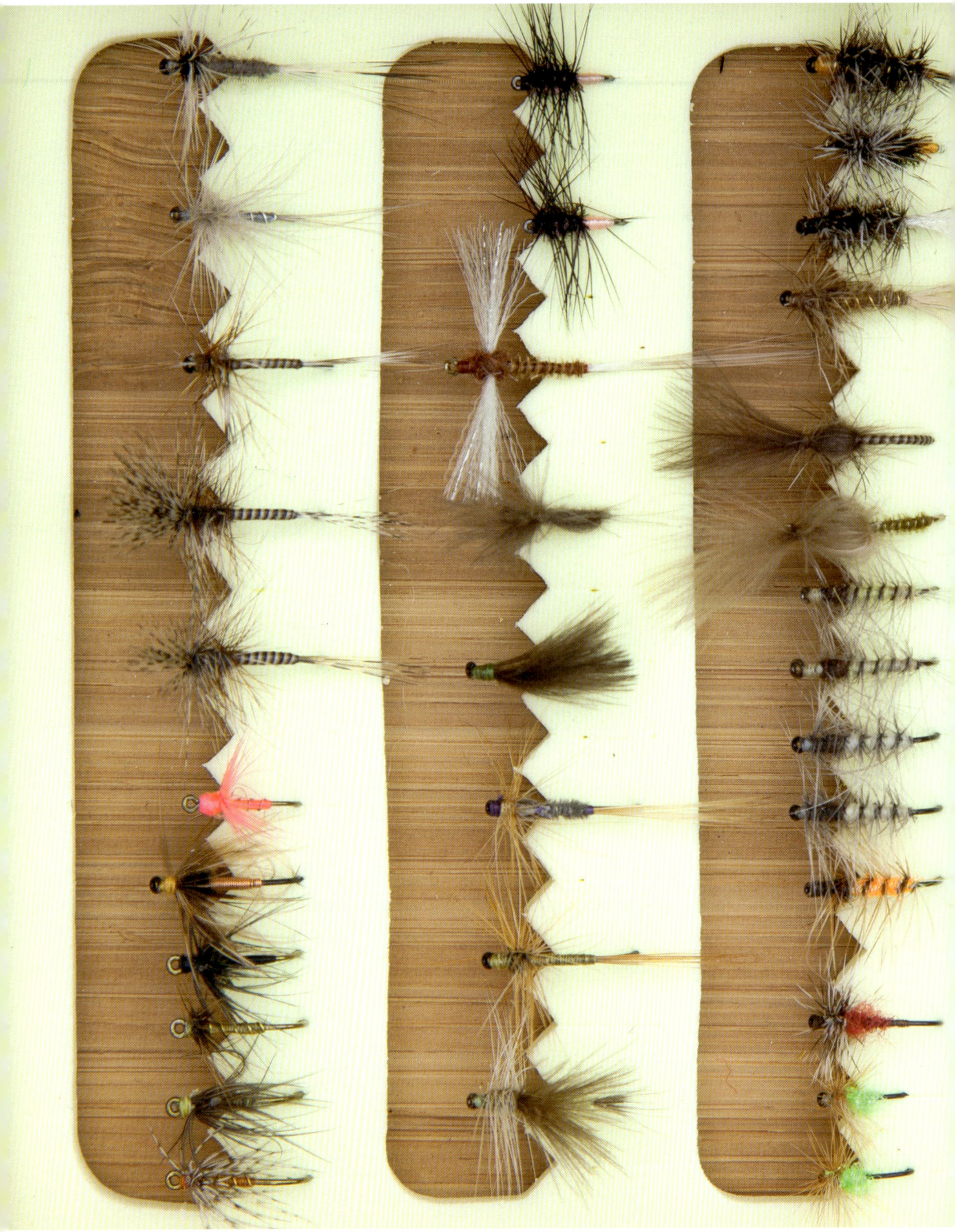

# Chapter Three

# Flies and Fly Tying

*'The bright scaled umber as it passes by, flits as a shadow o'er the gazer's eye'*
Ausonius, Roman Poet c. 310-395 AD

TROUT AND GRAYLING live in an environment where there is a defined food supply. Unlike humans, who may go to, say, Tesco for most of their shopping but always prefer to visit Waitrose for some items, fish will not waste energy going to the other side of town, as it were, when there is food right in front of them. To them food is more fuel than anything and, although they do have particular favourites, I guess, they will, generally, eat most things that come their way. How else can we explain some of the strange things found in fish autopsies – cigarette butts, stones, sticks, etc. OK, so I am generalising a bit, but the point is that flies designed for a specific species will often be taken by other species.

## What is a Grayling Fly?

When I give talks on grayling to angling clubs I am often asked this question. My answer is that there is no such thing as a grayling fly, just flies that catch grayling. Now, that may seem to be just a bit of weasel wording at first glance, but let me explain.

Take, for example, Frank Sawyer's Killer Bug. Frank designed this specifically for taking grayling out of the Avon in Wiltshire. And we know, from autopsies and fishing experience, that chalkstream grayling seem to be particularly fond of freshwater shrimps. But is that fondness because of the ready availability of shrimps or because they particularly like the taste, texture or size of them? Or is it that the shrimps are just easy to catch, rather abundant and the ratio of energy expended to energy gained is a good one for the fish? There are many questions about fish and fishing that we will never be able to satisfactorily answer, so we must use judgement and experience plus some educated guessing.

Frank's Killer Bug also catches lots of other fish. He famously caught a salmon on it when fishing the Hampshire Avon, and I have taken brown and rainbow trout, grayling and chub on the same fly. All, I think, because it is in the water, near the fish, behaving naturally and looking like food. I think it is no more clever than that. As they say, if it looks like a duck, walks like a duck and talks like a duck then it is probably a duck!

Fish eat when they want or need to eat,

and dependent on how hungry they are they will eat most things. Have you ever been shopping in a supermarket when you were starving hungry? I have, lots of times, and it is lethal because you want to buy everything in sight, even those things you aren't particularly fond of. And so I think it is with fish. If they are hungry they will eat anything going but will be very fussy if they are full despite there being an abundance of food.

There is not one single fly in this book that does not, and has not, accounted for trout as well as grayling; even the most gaudy creations that have been specifically designed for grayling. Yes, even the Fatbelly Pink Shrimp has been eaten regularly by trout. This is why I long ago gave up having separate boxes for trout and grayling flies. Everything is in one box and is used for all species.

## Tool Tips

These are just a few ideas about tying tools which you may find useful.

*Vices* – Does your vice rotate easily? It is a very useful idea, not just for tying tube flies, but so you can easily see the fly you are tying from all angles and make any adjustments to the dubbing, ribbing, hackling etc., as you go. Also, it is very handy to have a set of midge jaws because they can be very important if you are tying flies smaller than about size 16 – which you often need to do for grayling.

*Bobbin Holders* – Don't buy cheap bobbin holders because they can easily fray your silk if they don't have lined or ceramic tubes. There are some excellent models available so don't think of this as an area where you could save money because a broken thread halfway through tying a fly is a real pain in the whatsit! I invested in a Norvise Automatic Fly Tying Bobbin Holder a couple of years ago and now I wouldn't be without it. As the advertising blurb says 'It is a true marvel that will automatically rewind itself, making thread management simple, quick and efficient. This bobbin automatically retracts instantly to the correct tying position, yet remains suspended from the hook where released.' It has a clockwork clutch mechanism in the centre of it which winds up as you use the tool and enables you to let the holder hang at any distance you want below the hook without all that manual rewinding of the bobbin if you have let too much silk come off the spool. If that doesn't make any sense then I encourage you to look on the Norvise website for a proper explanation and demonstration.

*Scissors* – Buy the best scissors you can afford. Friends who use my kitchen knives often remark upon how sharp they are. My standard response is that if they aren't sharp they aren't knives! Similarly if the scissors you buy can't keep an edge they aren't scissors. And don't use your best scissors to cut wire – just get a cheap pair for your wire cutting.

*Applying Varnish* – Lots of the flies in this book are best used in small sizes and need correspondingly small heads. For varnishing I use an acupuncture needle to apply the gloop (if not using the varnished silk idea below). It works brilliantly. You can get them on-line for about 10 or 11 pence each although you usually have to buy a hundred!

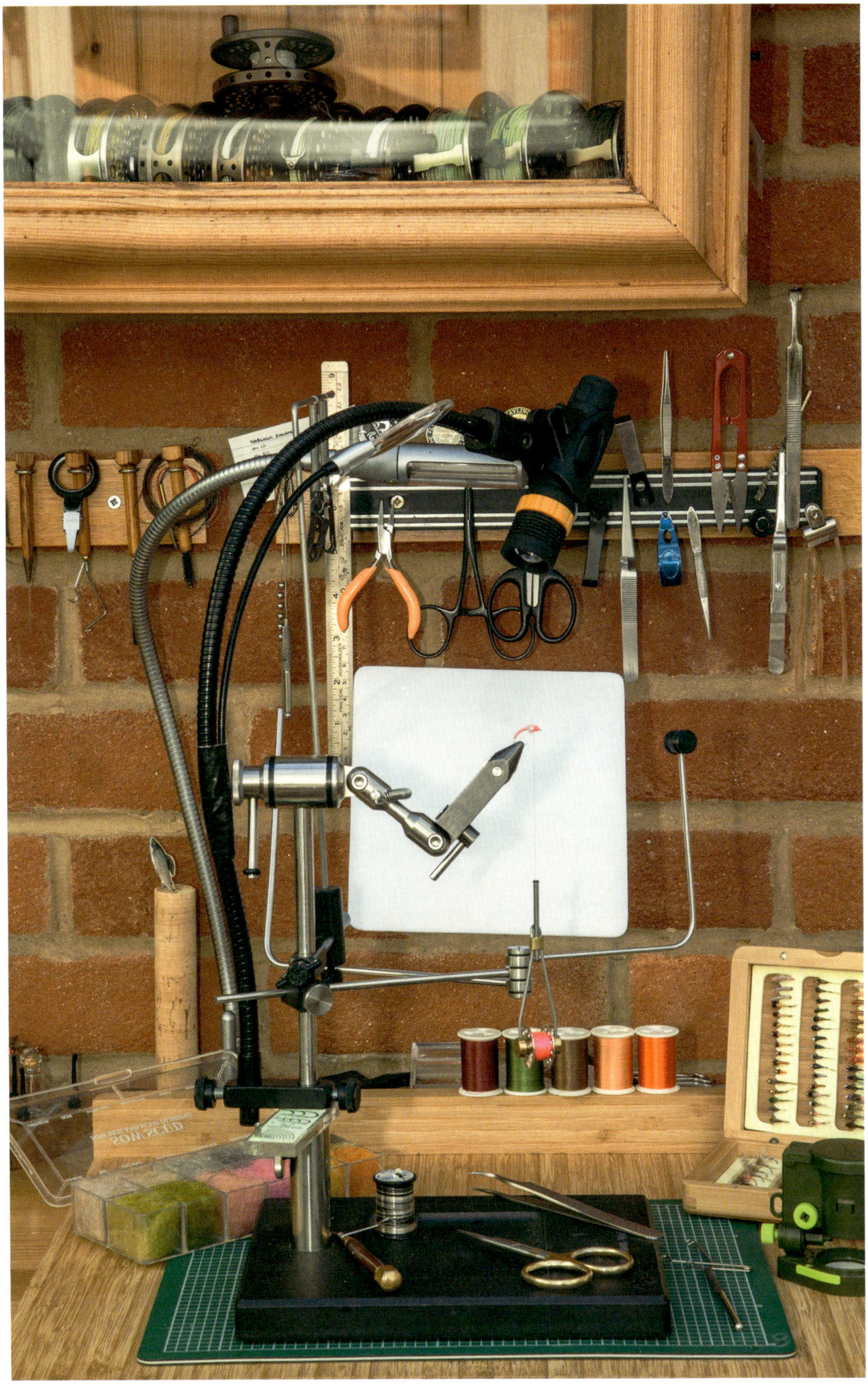

*Dubbing Teaser* – Rather than buying yourself a specialist tool to tease out dubbing, just 'borrow' one or two of the wooden stirrers from a coffee shop and glue a bit of Velcro onto the end. It works brilliantly.

## Tying Tips

*Debarbing hooks* – Always debarb your hooks before you tie the fly. It is frustrating to spend ages tying a superb fly only to nip off the hook point accidentally when trying to flatten the barb.

*Running thread down hook* – When running your silk down the hook shank in the famous 'touching turns' hold the tag end upwards at an angle of about 45 degrees then each turn of thread will effectively slide down that tag and butt up nicely on the previous one.

*Always tie in first that which you will use last* – An old standard statement which helps produce a neat fly. So, if ribbing a fly, you will generally tie in the rib before the body material or palmered hackle for instance. I always tie in the tail fibres before this though since they need to sit right on top of the hook shank.

*Splitting dry-fly tails* – Lots of dry flies require tails that are split so they splay out as do those, for example, on olive duns and spinner patterns. There are several ways to accomplish this and different tyers may recommend passing the silk through the middle of the fibres and tying a figure of eight or fixing a tiny ball of dubbing underneath or even tying individual fibres on each side of the hook. In my experience all of these methods can be difficult. A far easier method, to me anyway, is to split them with a piece of silk. Cut off about 1 inch of the tying silk and tie it in on the shank ensuring it is on top and that most of its length is beyond the bend. After tying in your tail fibres simply pull the piece of silk back towards the eye splitting the fibres down the middle. Tie it down and you have split tails. Simple!

*Hackle dry flies backwards* – I often find that after hackling a dry-fly there are hackle fibres which just insist on getting trapped in the whip finish and ruining the front end of the fly. You can easily end up with a blocked hook eye or a messy look because you have cut away or cauterised stray fibres. One way to overcome this is to hackle backwards. Tie the hackle in quite close to the eye with just enough space in front for a neat head. Take your silk back about 3 or 4 turns and then wind your hackle back to meet it. Wind the hackle away from you. Tie off and then take the silk forward through the hackle to the eye. Make sure you jiggle it all the way to avoid trapping any fibres. At the eye form a small head and finish off as normal. Then cut away the waste hackle at the back. There are two advantages to this approach. Firstly it looks much neater and secondly it fastens the hackle much more securely because the silk has been wound forwards in the opposite direction to the hackle and thus traps the quill firmly.

*Varnish the silk not the head* – If you have problems putting varnish on and always get it in the eye of the hook, try running some varnish onto the last few inches of thread before you do your whip finish. Then your head will be whipped and varnished in one hit.

*Do two whip finishes* – I always, except perhaps for a really small fly, do two whip finishes. That way if one gives way, which can happen, you don't lose the fly because you have a back-up whip finish!

## Hooks

For me a hook is a functional item and I select them on the basis of design, strength and value. There are certain manufacturers who I would not use again because of quality control issues, but if you choose a good quality brand then you will have no problems. After all you just need it to be the right shape, size and weight with a suitable bend for its purpose and be very sharp and stay that way for a reasonable period of time. I use hooks made by Partridge, Grip, Tiemco, Kamasan, Varivas, Fulling Mill, Veniard, Dohiku, Daiichi, Maruto, Hanak, Hayabusa, and both Fly Only and Fly Tying Boutique's own brands, and am happy with them all. Where no specific hook type or brand is mentioned in the tying instructions then that is because I am not fussy about it for that particular fly. Where I, or my contributors, feel that a specific hook is required then it will be mentioned by name, type and size.

## The Flies in this Book

The flies in this book have been carefully selected by me and should be capable of being used successfully for grayling wherever they are found. Not all will work well in every situation, but between them all, I believe the bases are covered. When I say 'carefully selected' that means over a period of 30 years! Some, such as the Greenwell's Glory, Partridge & Orange, Red Tag and others have been in my box for all that period whilst others have appeared in it more recently.

Malcolm Greenhalgh; author, angler, raconteur and all round good guy, with whom I have had the immense pleasure of fishing on the Wylye, has a rule of thumb that a fly hasn't arrived unless it has caught 50 fish. I'm not that precise myself but I can soon tell if a fly is a 'keeper' or a 'duffer' and these are all in the former category.

There are flies in here which have been used for over 100 years; flies which have been invented between the end of World War II and the millennium, lots of them; and flies which are strictly 21st century. But they all have two things in common – they catch grayling and they have merited inclusion in my fly box. I hope you feel that some of them can grace your box too.

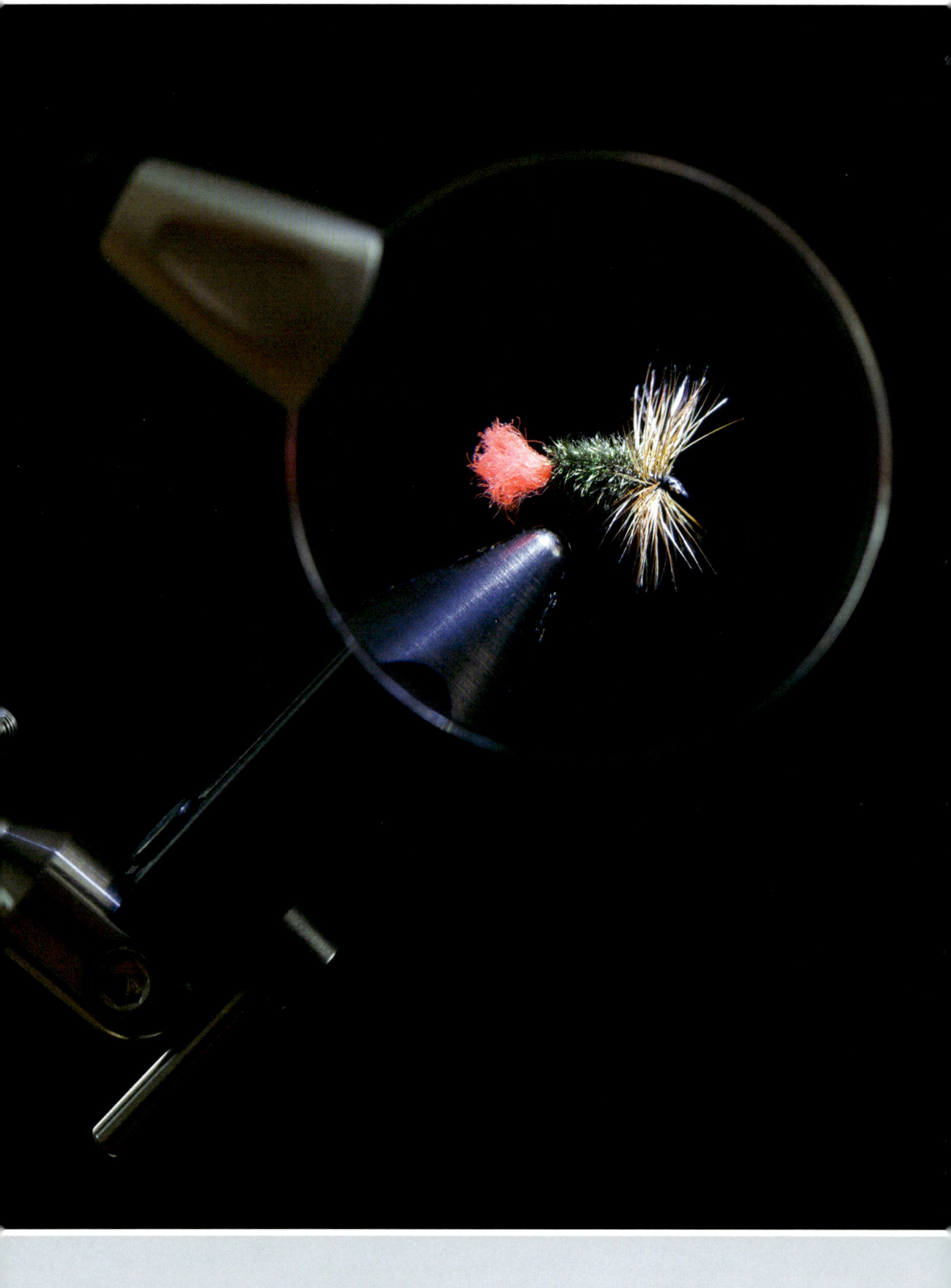

# Chapter Four

# Dry Flies

I LIKE DRY-FLY fishing. I suppose it is the visual aspect: I see that movement, whatever form it takes, and watch as my fly disappears under water, hopefully followed by a successful strike. I'll never, however, have the courage to do what I think Lefty Kreh once suggested and remove the hook point from my fly. His idea was that the buzz came from the take not the fight so why bother having a hook at all. Let the fish rise; strike or set as Lefty would say; feel the fish before he lets go and then he is gone feeling foolish but unharmed and you have the satisfaction of having fooled him. Brave stuff and certainly it is the thrill of knowing that something you have crafted has fooled a fish into thinking it is real that is paramount in all successful dry-fly fishing. But, although it is a nice philosophical thought that all that matters is the take, I think I will always still want to feel a fish fighting on the end of my line and have the pleasure of landing it, or the agony of its loss.

I can't see me ever becoming a dry-fly purist. In fact, I can't even understand why an angler would want to possess such a character defect! I remember, many years ago the great Bernard Venables hosted a TV series entitled *Anglers' Corner* and in one episode he held a discussion with a gentleman called Dick Bartholomew who was a dry-fly purist. I don't really wish to be unfair but the DFP did look a bit like Captain Mainwaring might on his day off, bedecked in sports coat, waistcoat and tie and wearing those round spectacles we associate with the war years. Of course, this was the 1960s so I shouldn't really take the mickey out of his dress code. It was his attitude that needs some comment. Basically Dick, a chalkstream man all his life, derided wet-fly fishing as being little more than 'chuck and chance' whilst dry-fly required a more thoughtful and skilful approach. Fighting talk indeed, and Bernard did not let him get away with it. I personally think that kind of attitude should be kept where it belongs in the box labelled 'Tunnel Vision.' However, as they say 'whatever floats your boat' or in this instance 'your fly'!

I will never understand dry-fly only rules on rivers though. That is just too crazy a concept for words. And even worse is a situation such as exists on a certain stretch of a well-known Derbyshire river where, apparently, you can't even use a fly such

Alex Martin Parachute Flies

as a Klinkhåmer Special. Why not? Do they think that normal dry flies sit proudly above the water surface? Of course they don't because there is always some part of the fly, in addition to the hook bend and point, that is under water. It may be the tail or the body or the hackle or all three but it sits underwater just as clearly as a Klinkhåmer Special. Dry flies sit neatly on top of the water if we drop them gently into a tank for testing purposes but after casting one it will hit the water in such a way that some part of it will almost certainly break the surface tension no matter how gently it lands. And why do some clubs on the chalkstreams have a dry-fly only rule until the 16th of June or so, or even the 1st of August, which is the rule at one fishery I have visited? It is all beyond me.

Over the years fashions have changed in dry-fly design. Centuries-old illustrations show flies which are winged and look like they would have fished on the surface, probably until they eventually sank. Well, this was before Gink! It was, however, in the 19th century that the upright split-winged phenomenon originated, although there are questions as to who first conceived the idea.

Vintage split wing dries

Certainly, when I first started fly-tying in the 1980s we still tied split-winged dry flies such as the original dry-fly version of the Greenwell's Glory. But fashions change and the wingless hackled fly is most common now along with parachute-hackled versions of most dry flies. But even the parachute hackle is not new and I have flies in my modest collection which were sold, and even patented, by the Glasgow tackle shop of Alex Martin many years ago. I have even seen it written that they invented the concept back in the 1920s. What is cute is that each one has a tiny label pinned to the point showing the patent number and the maker's name.

Among several hackle-only flies in this section, the Beacon Beige is wingless and relies just on the hackle to fool the fish, as does the Grey Duster. However, there are always new kids on the block, so there is also a Beacon Beige tied with the inclusion of a Coq de Leon wing, and a Grey Duster tied paraloop-style.

# 1  Beacon Beige

People of a certain age – mine for instance – will remember the great TV programmes made by Oliver Kite. In one of these he is fishing at Two Lakes in Hampshire alongside Peter Deane. Captain Deane is seated in his wheelchair on the bank of one of the lakes and demonstrates he is no slouch at catching rainbow trout. It is quite some time before he accepts that it may be time to go indoors to warm up and dry out. He is, by this point, entirely covered with snow but still fishing and puffing on his pipe!

During the Second World War he was posted to India with the 1st Battalion the Somerset Light Infantry. Whilst on leave, probably bird watching, he contracted polio and returned to the UK in 1943 via a spell of hospitalisation in South Africa. He was now, and would remain, wheelchair-bound. Having never been interested in flyfishing, despite now living near to the River Culm, in 1948, following a 'wake up' call from a friend, he decided to become a fly-tyer and tied his first patterns in March that year. Eventually he built a fly-tying business which ran for 40 years and, at its height, employed 12 lady fly-tyers, all taught by him.

The Beacon Beige is his most famous fly and he stated in his excellent book *Peter Deane's Fly Tying* that he probably tied more Beacon Beige than all his other dry flies put together. The pattern was essentially an improvement of a fly called simply the Beige, given to him by Fred Tout who was a well-known tackle dealer in Dulverton and father of one of Peter's army colleagues. Peter developed the fly and it entered the realms of legend one day on the River Test

Peter Deane

in 1952 when he used one to catch his limit in not much more than half an hour on a day when it was felt that nothing would be caught!

Whilst it is thought of first and foremost as a chalkstream fly I have had great success with it everywhere I have fished when there are olives about. In its large sizes it can be used happily to represent Large Dark Olives and in the smaller sizes will be a good match for any other varieties of olives or other similar upwinged flies. It has definitely become one of those 'go to' flies for me whenever olives are hatching.

There are two things to be conscious of when tying the fly. The first is the body. The single stripped peacock eye feather quill should be as well marked as possible. Strip the quill using finger and thumb or an eraser. It is also possible to use bleach but I would not recommend this since it is rather skin-unfriendly and can result in quills that are too brittle. I have used this method in the past and it does strip a

## Beacon Beige Original Version
*Fly tied by the author*

**Materials:**

- **Hook:** A suitable dry-fly hook sizes 14 to 18.
- **Silk:** Mid-brown.

  *Peter preferred yellow but I like mid-brown.*
- **Tail:** 5 or 6 grizzle hackle fibres.

  *The fly also looks good and works well with tails of Gallo de León.*
- **Body:** A single, natural-coloured, stripped peacock eye feather quill, as well marked as possible.
- **Hackle:** One red game and one grizzle cock hackle, both longer in the flue than you would normally use for the relevant hook size.

  *Peter generally tied the fly with hackles slightly longer than might be considered normal as he felt it floated better that way.*

**Tying Instructions:**

1. Tie on silk and run it down to bend.
2. Tie in hackle fibres or Gallo de León fibres as a tail.
3. At bend of hook tie in stripped peacock quill by its thin end.
4. Run silk to a point just back from the eye.
5. Wind stripped peacock quill towards eye in touching turns, tie off and remove waste. Be careful because sometimes the quill can be fragile. Also, for strength, it can be advisable to varnish the quill after it is wound on. The fly looks best if you can wind the quill with the dark edge forwards. Peter Deane recommended using the quills from the left-hand side of the eye feather to ensure the dark edge was uppermost.
6. Tie in red game hackle then grizzle hackle.
7. Wind on two turns of grizzle hackle, tie off and remove waste.
8. Wind on three turns of red game hackle: one behind the grizzle, one in the middle of the grizzle and the final one in front of the grizzle, tie off and remove waste.
9. Form a neat head, whip finish and varnish.

## Beacon Beige Lee's Variant
*Fly tied by Lee Hooper*

**Materials:**

- **Hook:** Good quality dry-fly hook such as Dohiku 301 or Hanak 130BL, sizes 14 to 18.

**Silk:** Brown (UTC 70 denier).
**Tail:** Gallo de León, light pardo.
**Abdomen:** Stripped well-marked natural peacock quill.
**Thorax:** Mole fur dubbing.
**Hackle:** Grizzle and red game cock.
**Wing:** Gallo de León, light pardo.

**Tying Instructions:**

1. Wash hands, make a cuppa, sit down, put hook in vice, tie on silk.
   *It takes a bit of time to tie this one!*
2. Cut off some light pardo Gallo de León fibres (size 16 about ¾ of a medium sized feather) and stack these fibres. Ideally you will need a really small stacker or an empty .22 cartridge case.
3. Tie in these feathers as a wing (fibre tips forward) just back from the eye of the hook. Only put silk wraps in the thoracic region and trim off the cut ends.
4. Run silk down the shank in touching turns and tie in a small bunch of light pardo Gallo de León for the tail.
5. Strip a well-marked natural peacock quill (*I prefer to strip my own quills with an eraser*) and tie in by the tip, ensuring that when the quill is wound the dark side of the quill is toward the rear. (*The opposite way to Peter Deane.*) Wind the quill up the thorax, tie off and trim waste. Give the quill a VERY LIGHT lick of thin glue or varnish and leave it to dry. This makes the fly a lot more durable.
6. Tie the hackles in by the butts at the rear of the thorax so when they are wound the grizzle is foremost and dub the thorax with mole fur up to the wing.
7. Wind the hackles together so that the grizzle is foremost up through the thorax (3-4 turns) and then, still holding the hackles, push the base of the wing (Gallo de León) back with your thumb-nail so it fans out. Pull back the wing and make one turn in front of it. Tie off, trim waste and build up a neat head, pushing the wing back.
8. Ensure the wing is upright. It sometimes pays to pull the wing back and apply a spot of super glue right in the base of the wing. Trim out the hackles directly below the hook shank so it creates a fly that sits flush in the surface film.

*Well, there you are, not the easiest of flies to tie but extremely good looking as you can see in the photograph.*

**Fishing Method:** The Beacon Beige is an excellent dry-fly whenever any olives are hatching. Choose an appropriate size and you can feel confident in its use wherever you fish.

**A word about Coq de Leon/Gallo de León:** These highly attractive and useful feathers come from roosters first bred in the León area in north west Spain in the early 17th century. We use spade feathers from mature cock birds which are renowned for their stiffness, glossiness and translucency, and make ideal tails for a variety of flies. My stock came from a small supplier in the Pyrenees some years ago who now appears to have closed down. However, they have become fashionable so there are several suppliers now and the feathers can be obtained easily from fly-tying shops in the UK.

If you have had a good day at the bookies or a tax rebate then treat yourself to *The Pardon de Meana and the Feather of Gallo de León*, a book written and published by Luis Meana

Baeza in a limited edition of 500 copies. His book tells you all you need to know about these feathers, and includes highly detailed step-by-step instructions on tying a host of exceptional flies with some super dry-fly patterns. I watched Luis tying flies incorporating Gallo de León at the British Fly Fair International in 2016 and his flies are amazing.

whole feather pretty-well instantly but you have to dip the feather into and out of the bleach extremely quickly.

Although it seems a simple material it is not always easy to find a quill which is as well-marked as is ideally needed. If possible, and it is not always easy to establish the source of a material, buy quills or feathers sourced from birds in hotter climes. The feathers of British-bred birds are less exposed to high levels of sun and this results in less well-marked quills. Whenever possible buy quills or feathers at a shop or show where you can examine them. Ready stripped quills have recently become freely available and some are excellent, with superb marking, and are available in a variety of colours to enable you to experiment.

Secondly, be wary about how many turns of hackle you take. Since there are two different hackles to wind you need to be a bit frugal with your turns. Often less is best when hackling. Although you want the fly to stand up on the water, it also needs to look reasonably natural and a great big thick hackle does not fulfil the latter need. In reality it will almost always sit partially on and partially in the water because that is what dry flies do.

My good friend Lee Hooper ties his own special version of the Beacon Beige which uses Gallo de León feathers in a more extensive manner and this is his description of the fly and tying instructions:

*I've always been a fan of the Beacon Beige but prefer flies that float flat in the surface film. I am also a great believer in the wings of a dun being the first thing the fish sees as the fly drifts into its view (ghost wings), so I really like my dun patterns to have a good wing. This fly was inspired by my friend Luis Meana and his Gallo de León winged flies. It's a bit of an extravagant wing but the sparkle does seem to add some attraction and is very easy to see, even if fished at range. This fly can be tied with an ordinary cock hackle fibre wing but it won't look anywhere near as good.*

Well there you go, Lee's colours are firmly fastened to the mast! In my experience both patterns work really well though there is a certain magic about the look of Lee's version.

# 2 Kite's Imperial

If you set out to design a fly to represent olives would you choose grey, gold, honey and purple as the key colours? No, neither would I, but Oliver Kite did and he created a legendary dry-fly.

Oliver was a soldier, author, TV personality and angler supreme, who regrettably died on the banks of the River Test, at the relatively young age of 48, in 1968, which was co-incidentally the year I first started flyfishing. If my memory serves me right, the first issue of *Creel* I bought contained his obituary.

His home river was the Avon in Wiltshire, where he was a member of what was then known as the Officer's Fishing Association, living in Netheravon across the road from Frank Sawyer, the well-known keeper of the Association waters, and also a supreme fly inventor and angler.

The Imperial, so called because of its use of 'royal' purple and gold was designed to represent the Large Dark Olive during one of Kite's regular spring trips to the Teifi at Tregaron in March 1962. It uses heron herl, which is now pretty well impossible to obtain legally. Since herons became protected under the Wildlife and Countryside Act 1981 it has become illegal to kill or attempt to kill one. So, unless you happen upon a roadkill you are unlikely to find any heron herl these days. There are substitutes available from good suppliers of fly-tying materials and, basically a mid-grey herl such as goose also works. I seem to fall on my feet from time to time as opposed to more usually falling on my face. Thus it was that one day, travelling between meetings many years ago, I was passing Knebworth in Hertfordshire and called into Olivers – no, not Kite, but Olivers of Knebworth, who were once well-known for cane rods as well as having a great shop – just as they were closing down their fishing section to concentrate on equestrian stuff. They had loads of fly-tying materials and, spotting packs of beautiful heron I made a cheeky bid for the lot and walked away with a lifetime's supply.

Incidentally, Ted Oliver used to make the most wonderful split-cane coarse and fly rods, all beautifully finished and with excellent cane. I had a fly-rod of theirs once, which I guess I must have bought that same day, hence the good deal on the heron probably, and it was a work of art although it turned out to be just a wee bit too soft-actioned for my needs. The lesson learned that day was to never buy a fly-rod unless you had tried it, or an identical model, with a suitable line, at least on grass and preferably on water!

Anyway, a key element of the Imperial is the prominent thorax and this is a feature on which Kite was very keen. He even referred to it as the Netheravon style in his book, A Fisherman's Diary. This should not be confused with his, or more correctly, Frank Sawyer's use of the induced take when fishing nymphs upstream. Kite also seemed to call this the Netheravon style.

The fly can be tied in two different ways to represent either the early or late-season olives by simply changing the tails from a greyish brown in spring to a honey dun later in the year. The honey dun hackle is another hard-to-find material. In fact, I have only ever seen one cape which I could honestly say was a true honey dun, with a definite blue dun list and rich honey-

## Kite's Imperial
*Fly tied by the author*

**Materials:**

**Hook:** A suitable dry-fly hook, size 14 to 18.

**Silk:** Purple.

*The original probably used Pearsall's gossamer shade 8 which, in early 2016, is still available from fly-tying suppliers. It may be a little too thick for the smaller sizes however.*

**Tail:** Several fibres of greyish brown (spring) or honey dun (rest of year) cock hackles.

**Rib:** Fine gold wire.

**Body:** Heron herl or substitute. Use two to four herls dependent on hook size.

**Hackle:** Good quality, stiff, honey dun or light ginger cock hackle.

**Tying Instructions:**

1. Run the silk down to the bend in neat touching turns.
2. Tie in the tail fibres.
3. Tie in the rib material.
4. Tie in the heron herls.
5. Wind the silk back towards the eye in neat touching turns.
6. Carefully, because they are not the strongest material, wind the heron herls towards the eye and trap them just behind the eye leaving enough room for the hackle and head. This is very important or you will have difficulty in forming a head and tying off when completing the fly.
7. Rib in the opposite direction to that you have wound the herl and tie off just behind the eye again and remove the waste.
8. Take the tying silk back a short distance to where you want to create the back of the thorax.
9. Double the herl back to form a thorax and take a turn with the silk to trap the herl then take an open turn of the silk back towards the eye.
10. Re-double the herl and tie off at the eye and remove the waste.
11. Tie in the hackle in front of the thorax.
12. Wind hackle for about three or four turns, tie off and remove waste.
13. Form a small head, whip finish and varnish.

**Fishing Method:** Oliver's olive. Nuff said!

coloured outer on the full length of each hackle. The cape belonged to the instructor at my fly-tying class in the mid-eighties when I was learning and he was lucky to get out of the place alive because we all lusted after his cape. If you do not possess a honey dun cape then you are unlikely to find one. In this case use a light ginger hackle. I have a barred ginger saddle cape and the hackles from this work very well on an Imperial.

Several of Oliver Kite's TV programmes can be seen on YouTube, including the one entitled *Season Opening on the Teifi* where he starts his season on what he describes as a 'wicked day' in March at Pont Llanio on the River Teifi. All this being elegantly filmed, despite the outrageous weather, by his cameraman, Ted Channell. And as you will see, despite the weather he catches trout on the Imperial.

Having, in my younger days, copied Ollie and started my season at Pont Llanio, also on a wicked day, along with my great fishing friend Mike Tebbs, I can relate directly to this footage although our 'generous libation' poured into the river to appease the water gods was a bit more palatable than his seems to have been, and less went into the river and more into ourselves, to ward off the worst of the weather.

Imperial by name and also by effectiveness, Oliver concocted a right good 'un here.

# 3   Greenwell's Glory

Many a clergyman has been associated with flyfishing. Perhaps they have a lot of time on their hands, or is it that they are just better at communing with nature, or the man upstairs? Certainly they have been responsible for some great flies. Take, for example, Rev Edward Powell and his Baby Sun Fly, Orange Otter, Paragon and Doctor flies, all renowned on the Dee and Severn and other rivers of the Welsh Marches, and still regularly and successfully used today.

But, of all the flies in all the world, there is one that is forever known to be linked to a clergyman even by those who are only vaguely interested in the origins of flies. That fly is, of course, the Greenwell's Glory.

Canon Greenwell was a native of County Durham and Canon of the great Norman cathedral in the city of Durham itself from 1854 to 1918.

As an aside, I was an undergraduate at Hatfield College, University of Durham, in the mid-1960s and my room was just a double-haul from the bell tower of the cathedral. Well, I can tell you that it may be a magnificent sight to behold, but the bells drove me quite insane!

Medium Olive Dun
*Photo: Dr. Cyril Bennett MBE*

# Greenwell's Glory
*Fly tied by the author*

**Materials:**

**Hook:** A suitable dry-fly hook, size 12 to 18.

**Silk:** Yellow well-waxed with brown cobbler's wax to create a light olive hue.

**Tail:** Several fibres of furnace or Greenwell's cock hackle.

**Rib:** Fine gold wire.

**Body:** Tying silk.

**Hackle:** Good quality, stiff, furnace or Greenwell's cock hackle.

**Tying Instructions:**

1. Run the well-waxed silk down to the bend in neat touching turns.
2. Tie in the tail fibres.
3. Tie in the rib material.
4. Wind the silk back towards the eye in neat touching turns again.
5. Rib in the opposite direction to that you have wound the silk and tie off at the eye and remove the waste.
6. Tie in the hackle, sized to suit the hook size.
7. Wind the hackle for about three or four turns, tie off and remove the waste.
8. Form a small head, whip finish and varnish.

**Fishing Method:** A truly great olive pattern. You can tie it on with every chance of success whenever they are on the water.

Anyway, having learned his craft on the little River Browney, near his birthplace of Lanchester, Canon Greenwell fished regularly on Tweed and one day in 1854, having been relatively unsuccessful at Sprouston, asked a local and well-known Scottish fly-tyer, James Wright, to match a natural fly which he, the Canon, had seen trout taking readily. That fly was probably an olive and from this enquiry came the Greenwell's Glory. Almost certainly a wet-fly originally, and still a very successful one, it excels also in its dry form.

Like other olive imitations it can be used, unless you are excessively purist, to represent several different species. Hence tied on hooks from 12 down to 18 it is an extremely worthwhile addition to any grayling angler's dry-fly box. The size 12 is there ready for a hatch of really Large Dark Olives whilst the 18 can work well on those annoying little olives that sometimes appear to frustrate your efforts to rise a fish.

Originally the dry-fly version was tied with upright split wings of two slips of fibre from the inside of a blackbird's wing. Tie it this way if you wish with upright back-to-back split wings so set that the natural curve of the fibres is outwards at the tip with the 'pointy' end, i.e. the part which was originally nearest to the feather's tip, towards the eye. However, there is an increasingly modern thought that traditional winging is not strictly necessary. Hence the fly here uses just a hackle and no wing. It is quicker and simpler to tie and works just as well as the winged version. I like 'quicker and simpler' because, although I have taught the beginners and intermediates at my local Fly Dresser's Guild branch for a few years, I am not a totally committed fly-tyer per se, and only tie them to fish with. No award winning works of the fly-tyer's art are likely to come from my vice!

Alternative and successful approaches could be to tie in an upright wing of grey polypropylene yarn or Tiemco Aero Wing or even CdC. All will work and are considerably easier than tying the traditional split wing, although it must be said that an upright split wing is quite remarkably attractive.

The original fly used yellow silk well waxed with cobbler's wax. Now, old cobbler's wax is dark brown and adds this hue to the silk thus changing the colour. In my personal experience, the new type of wax that cobblers seem to use looks brown but, when applied to the silk, makes no colour change whatsoever and is, therefore, not much use. What is needed is for the brown wax to cause the yellow silk to change to a light olive colour and this is fairly critical if you want to replicate the original body. If you can't get the right wax, and after a long period of unavailability I see that some fly shops have begun stocking brown cobbler's wax again, then you can try tying the fly with a light olive silk instead. I have, and it does work.

Exactly what hackle is used has been an area of controversy over the years. Canon Greenwell is said to have gone into print saying it was a coch-y-bonddu, whilst others have said it was a furnace. Essentially what you want is a stiff hackle with a dark, even black list or centre, and a ginger to red outer. If offered Greenwell hackles then keep in mind this colouring when deciding if they are worth buying.

My advice when buying any cape, saddle or pack of hackles is, whenever possible, look at them, feel them and splay them in your hand before you buy. This is where flyfishing or fly-tying shows are a great opportunity to stock up since there are usually a super selection of capes, saddles and packs of individual hackles on several different stands and most, sensible, retailers will let you take them out of the packs to look at them more closely. Buying a new high quality genetic cape or saddle is, after all, a fairly major purchase these days.

I haven't bought any hackles, unseen, by mail order for many years although I did start my collection back in the early 1990's when the UK£/US$ exchange rate was heavily in our favour and myself and a friend stocked up on a variety of Metz Grade 1 capes from Dan Bailey's in Livingston, Montana. We simply split each cape carefully down the middle of the back with a scalpel and had plenty of hackles each for our fly-tying for years to come.

# 4  Duck's Dun – *Charles Jardine*

Now, if Charles Jardine doesn't know a good fly then who does? He himself needs no introduction and neither, I think, does his Duck's Dun olive pattern. I have used this fly a lot and it performs extremely well in all its sizes. Knowing it has at times lost something in translation between various writers and exponents I asked him for the real story and instructions. This way we all get the chance to tie it properly:

*The whole truth and nothing but the truth – Charles Jardine:*

*The Duck's Dun was utterly and unequivocally an accident. The story began with my first trip to the Austrian Traun with the late Partridge boss, Alan Bramley, many years ago. It was cathartic: not only did I get to fish with, and befriend one of our flyfishing giants – John Goddard – but meet someone who became and remains one of the most influential river fishers I have ever come across – Roman Moser. Roman's fly design is legendary, but fishing with him for that period just jolted me into another flyfishing dimension. That trip was the first time I had ever seen gold beads used on hooks – I am not sure anyone had in the UK. I had never seen deer hair dubbed, understood that caddis patterns could "actually" work, and to top it all, be introduced to a rather dowdy, odd, wispy material – and in those days almost unheard of in the UK – CDC. Some trip.*

*I was gripped and intrigued: then catapulted into a frenzy of creativity at the vice when I returned to my beloved chalkstreams. But I did not understand, or indeed, know then, the intrinsic nature of CdC – floatability. I was intrigued by the structure, shape and colour, but simply saw the grey feather as just something, well, that was perfect for the aspect I was seeking; namely representing the wings of a freshly emerged, upwinged dun.*

*The tail was also pure Moser. Simply using the soft 'webby' semi spade hackle from a jungle cock neck – a bit grizzly, a bit cree-ish, a bit buggy – was perfect. I fiddled with the design a little, but not much and of course over time a few adjustments have been made. Rather than clipping the underside of the hackle, I now incinerate it with a cauterizing tool. But beyond that, very little has changed.*

*And the really weird thing is, it was always designed to take paste/gel floatant. The wings go into a wonderful 'insects' configuration when the unction is applied.*

*The pattern's longevity and success? Well to give you an idea, I was fishing recently on the pristine upper River Lambourn – wild fish darting like missiles at any hint of danger. The fly choice of my companions, and unsolicited I hasten to add, to represent the clusters of Medium and Large Dark Olives scuttling across the surface in the spring chill; the Duck's Dun. Even my son Alex, grudgingly admits that 'it's OK!'*

Accident? Oh yeah! It sounds like a bit more thought went into it than that. But however Charles came to create it, there was a touch of fairy dust in the mix that has given it near magical properties. Thanks Charles.

## Duck's Dun
*Fly tied by Charles Jardine*

### Materials:

**Hook:** Standard dry-fly hook, e.g. Tiemco 103BL, size 14 to 20.

**Silk:** Yellow, orange or claret micro such as Veevus 14/0.

**Tail:** Jungle cock spade feather fibres – about 4. This is important for softness. I believe this softness and near collapsibility of the structure leads to far fewer rejections – especially with grayling.

**Body:** Well, anything really, as long as it corresponds to the underside of the fly you are imitating – the bit the fish inspects! I favour dyed muskrat or beaver underfur.

**Wing:** CdC – full, short and curved.

**Hackle:** Dun or grizzle cock hackle with a barbule-length just shy of the hook gape. Avoid dark colours.

### Tying Instructions:

1. Take the silk down to the bend and tie in the jungle cock spade feather fibres as a tail.
2. Dub silk with the chosen body dubbing. To form the abdomen – and this is important – do try and make a small gradual taper covering two thirds of the hook shank up to the thorax area.
3. Tie in the hackle at the point where the thorax will eventually be formed.
4. Place your CdC feathers, convex to convex, with the tips aligned so they make a gradual sweep outwards.
5. Using the pinch-and-loop method, tie in the feathers immediately at the end of the tapered abdomen.
6. Dub the thorax. As far as this pattern is concerned the thorax is multifarious. It covers all the work that you have done tying in the wings and hackle, covering the butts and so on and providing the perfect bed on which to wind the hackle. You actually use this point, where the dubbed body taper finishes and your hackle has been tied, as a support to raise and support the paired wings. It sounds complicated but, in essence, it is easy once you have got into the swing of things. A vital aspect of the wing is to slope it slightly back along the body as a natural olive dun's would.
7. Wind the hackle in tight open turns. When winding the hackle make at least one, if not two, turns immediately at the thorax to support the wing, which should be inclining back along the body. If you have done this procedure correctly you will both bring the wing into the right aspect and flare the two feathers.
8. Form a neat head, tie off, whip finish and varnish.

9. Now, carefully – with an ophthalmic cauterizing pen/stylus – melt the hackle fibres below the hook to get wonderful 'bobbly' ends to them that emphasise the footprint and puddle light at the surface. Alternatively you can, carefully, cut a 'V' configuration into the underside of the hackle (as one would a spinner or thorax dun) to offer a semi-parachute aspect.

**Fishing Method:** It's a superb olive dry-fly so fish it that way when olives are about.

# 5  Grey Duster

None other than A Courtney Williams, author of the bible of fly-tying, *A Dictionary of Trout Flies*, considered the Grey Duster to be perhaps the best dry-fly he knew for trout and grayling, even stating "it is the only fly which has nearly tempted me to become a 'one pattern' angler"! Praise indeed for this modest, somewhat drab-looking, dry-fly. Once thought more valuable on rivers where small *perlidae* are present – willow fly, needle fly, etc. – and not on chalkstreams, it nevertheless works well 'darn Sarf' in my experience and that of others. It can be particularly useful when any pale olives are about, especially pale watery duns.

Originally it was tail-less, but I like tails on my dry flies so my version has them.

My good friend Bob Lomax, who hails from Jacksdale, Nottinghamshire, is a magnificent fly-tyer and has fallen in love with the paraloop method of hackling which he executes with consummate skill. His variant, using a light-blue dun hackle and pale grey mink, is a truly excellent fly and so I give the dressing for this also.

The Grey Duster has a reputation for bringing up fish when there is no noticeable hatch, which is a pretty useful attribute in these days of increased pressure on our fly life.

## Grey Duster – *Original Tying*
*Fly tied by the author*

**Materials:**

**Hook:**   Dry-fly hook, size 14 or 16.
**Silk:**   Grey.
**Tail:**   Fibres from a badger cock hackle or Gallo de León.
**Body:**   Light rabbit fur mixed with blue underfur.
**Hackle:** Sharp badger cock hackle with a strong black list and cream fibres.

**Tying Instructions:**

1. Run the silk down to the bend in neat touching turns.
2. Tie in the tail fibres.
3. Dub the silk with the rabbit fur and wind back up towards the eye stopping short to leave room for the hackle.
4. Tie in a good quality stiff badger cock hackle, sized to suit the hook size.
5. Wind hackle for about three or four turns, tie off and remove the waste.
6. Form a small head, whip finish and varnish.

## Grey Duster – *Bob Lomax Variant with Paraloop Hackle*

*Fly tied by Bob Lomax*

**Materials:**

**Hook:** Grip 11011 hook, size 16.
**Silk:** Veevus Grey 14/0.
**Tail:** Fibres from a light blue dun hackle – no more than 6.
**Rib:** Fine silver wire.
**Abdomen:** Mink fur dyed grey.
**Thorax:** Mink fur dyed grey.
**Hackle:** Sharp light blue dun cock hackle.

**Tying Instructions:**

1. Ensure you have a gallows tool or alternative attached to your vice. This is essential to hold 2 loops of silk around which you will tie the hackle.
2. Run the silk down to the bend in neat touching turns.
3. Tie in the tail fibres.
4. Tie in the rib.
5. Dub the silk with the mink fur and wind back up towards eye stopping short to leave room for the hackling procedure and thorax.
6. Rib the body, winding in the opposite direction to the silk. Remove the waste.
7. Take 2 loops over the gallows tool.

   *Note: Most gallows tools have only 1 spring. If yours is like this then take 1 loop over the spring and 1 over the tool arm itself. Some have 2 springs, as in the Griffin version, although one is longer than the other. However, with some tin snips and small pliers it is very easy to reduce the length of the longer spring to that of the smaller one. Then you can take each loop of silk over a spring of equal length and tension. The reason there are 2 loops is because experience has shown Bob that if only 1 loop is employed there is a tendency for the hackle to twist to one side. The presence of a second silk loop balances everything out nicely and the hackle winds vertically.*

8. Tie in the hackle so it lies alongside the hook shank where you have created the loops.
9. Wind the hackle up the silk loops for about four or five turns and then back down again.
10. Tie off the hackle with a few turns of silk around the base of the silk loop post

and trim the waste. The hackles can be stroked back towards the bend, doubling them, if required. This allows the hackles to form a more 'V' shape when pulled over towards the hook eye.

11. Dub the silk and form a small thorax in front of the hackle leaving enough room to fold over the hackle and tie off behind the eye.

12. Leaving the silk at the eye now fold the hackle over towards the front of the hook and tie down. Tie off and remove the waste.

13. Form a small head, whip finish and varnish.

**Fishing Method:** Fish as normal as a dry-fly, especially when there are olives about.

# 6   Sherry Spinner

Don't you just hate it when the powers that be change things just when you have got used to them? I can't visualise a litre but I know what a pint looks like; grams are a mystery to me but ounces aren't; and I always have to do a mental calculation (double it, take off 10% and add 32), when the weather forecast is on TV, to change Celsius temperatures to Fahrenheit to which I can relate! I wouldn't really mind if it got down to -40 degrees because then I won't have to do any calculations because it is the same temperature in both systems. It might be a bit chilly though.

Anyway, after years of calling the Blue Winged Olive *Ephemerella ignita* along come some taxonomists and they change it to *Seratella ignita*! Why? What about those poor folks in years to come who pick up old books and end up wondering what an *Ephemerella ignita* is, or was!

Well, whatever you call it, the Blue Winged Olive remains one of our most common and most valuable upwinged flies for the fly fisherman. Its nymphs come into the moss-clinger category, living their lives under stones or in moss, algae or weeds. It is when they rise to hatch that they become most vulnerable to fish and the BBWON fly described in the Nymphs chapter covers this situation.

The duns are unmistakeable as they float downstream showing their large and dusky blue wings. On closer inspection it can be seen that the BWO has three tails rather than the two found on most other upwinged flies. But it is the adult, imago form we are interested in here. Known universally by fly fishermen as the Sherry Spinner, it is a most useful fly as it returns to the river to lay its eggs. It is a favourite of both trout and grayling and it is the cause of the evening rise on many occasions in the summer months.

I remember guiding a client on the River Test one evening in late June. We had done OK on small nymphs, Griffith Gnats and Supa Pupas, but the takes suddenly fell off despite the trout and grayling still rising. I looked up and there was a veritable swarm of Sherry Spinners. I changed fly as fast as my shaking fingers would allow and, first cast, my client had a fish. From then on the magic of a full-blown evening rise happened matched to huge grins on both our faces.

There have been many fly patterns created to imitate the Sherry Spinner including those by Skues, Woolley, Lunn and Peter Lapsley. Various materials have been used for tails, bodies and wings but all have combined to create the look of a dying BWO spinner trapped in the surface film. My own pattern uses more modern materials and works very well in a spinner fall. Always carry at least one spinner pattern in your box because when you need it you really need it!

## Sherry Spinner
*Fly tied by the author*

### Materials:

Hook:     A suitable dry-fly hook, size 14 or 16.
Silk:     Orange.
Tail:     Microfibets, grey or light olive, or paint brush fibres.
Rib:      Extra fine gold wire. If using turkey biot this can be dispensed with.
Abdomen:  Rust-coloured turkey biot or Flyrite Extra Fine Poly Dubbing #5, rust or equivalent.
Thorax:   Flyrite Extra Fine Poly Dubbing #5 rust mixed 50:50 with #28 dark reddish brown.
Wing:     DNA Holo Fusion white or Tiemco Aero Wing white.

*I prefer Holo Fusion because it is stiffer and won't fold back when casting. It also contains some fine pearlescent fibres which help imitate the glistening wings of a spinner.*

### Tying Instructions:

1. Run the silk down to the bend in neat touching turns.
2. Tie in the tail fibres. You can run a turn of thread under the tail fibres to lift and separate them a little or, even, run turns between them for separation, but I am not sure it is essential, just as having exactly 3 fibres isn't because grayling can't count beyond 2! An alternative approach to separating the fibres could be to dub an extremely small ball of bright pale green, extra fine, dubbing just under the tail fibres where they meet the hook. This will lift them and give the impression of the egg ball of a female.
3. Tie in the rib material if using.
4. Tie in the turkey biot and wind in neat touching turns to about a third back from the eye at which point you tie off and remove the waste. Alternatively dub the silk with the abdomen material and wind up to the same point. Make sure you dub this tightly because you don't want it to be straggly. Sherry Spinners have reasonably smooth abdomens.

5. If using then rib in the opposite direction to that you have wound the silk and tie off at the silk and remove the waste.
6. Tie in a small amount of the wing material. Don't pick too much because we just want to create a transparent wing which is sufficiently structural to hold the whole fly in the surface film and give the impression of the gossamer-like wings of the natural. However, have the wing a little too long at this point so it is easy to handle. It can be cut to size (width) later.
7. Having tied in the wing, manipulate it by running figure-of-eight turns over and under it until it is at a right angle to the hook shank, and is sticking out as a real wing would on a trapped and dying fly.
8. Dub the mixed thorax dubbing onto the silk and wind a thorax behind, over, in front and under the wing where it is attached to the hook shank using a figure-of-eight technique.
9. Take the silk to the eye, tie off, remove the waste and form a small head, whip finish and varnish.
10. Finally, pull the wings upwards and trim to a width you feel is right, then let them sit down horizontally again.

**Fishing Method:** Whenever you sense a fall of Sherry Spinners tie one of these on as fast as you can!

# 7   F-Fly – *Marjan Fratnik*

The F-Fly, named after the initial of the inventor's surname, Marjan Fratnik, is another of those system flies which can be used to represent many different types of naturals. By varying the size, body material and colour and the size and colour of the CdC wing you can have a complete box of dry flies, covering all eventualities, all based on just this one pattern.

The key thing to remember is to use the very best CdC you can obtain. Much cheap CdC is of dubious quality and provenance and its floatability and resilience can be questionable. Whatever CdC you use it should be remembered that it is relatively fragile and should be handled gently. Also remember that CdC will get wet quite quickly in use and will need regular drying. Amadou is an excellent product for this purpose. Considering this is a fungus that was used for many years by dentists to dry out cavities and it grows on tree trunks before being treated in some process that seems close to alchemy, I wonder how anyone ever discovered its magical properties. Man is amazingly creative at times! I just can't imagine a dentist walking through the woods thinking he needed a drying compound and deciding to break off a bit of horseshoe fungus to try! Of course, many anglers just tie lots of F-Flies and replace them when they start to get too wet rather than go through the laborious and time consuming rigmarole of drying the CdC, and considering they are so easy and quick to tie, that's not a bad idea.

CdC is not a material to which you should apply floatant, although there is at least one product on the market that claims to be useful for application to this material. Also, of course, the white fumed silicon powders that are marketed under several brand names work well in drying any fly. I am not a keen user of any white powders though! I still prefer to apply nothing and let the natural oils in the feather do the job of keeping the fly on the surface and just tie on another one when it gets too wet to float even after having the magic amadou treatment.

The original fly just used tying silk as a body and this works very well producing a slim fly. I generally apply a small amount of dubbing since I think it can help flotation properties yet can still be dubbed finely to leave a body which is quite slim anyway. I have never used a rib for this fly because it just adds weight and has never seemed necessary.

Its beauty is that it sits well-down in the surface film whilst the CdC wing gives it great life above the surface. It must be a very tempting target for a hungry grayling and will always have a place in my box.

My favourite body colours are Superfine cream or light olive dubbing, or yellow silk with a whisper of mole dubbing, à la Waterhen Bloa.

## F-Fly
*Fly tied by the author*

### Materials:

**Note:** This being a 'system fly' means you should consider what you are trying to represent and match that using different body and CdC colours and a suitable hook size.

**Hook:** Any suitable dry-fly hook, size 12 - 26.

**Silk:** Vary to suit body colours and vary thickness of silk to suit hook size.

**Body:** Fine dubbing, e.g. Superfine, in a pale colour – cream, grey, olive, etc. – sparsely dubbed.

**Wing:** CdC plumes, number to suit size of fly. Usual guidance is three to four for a #12-14, two for a #16-18. For #20 and smaller just use some barbs stripped from a plume. Vary the colour of the CdC to suit the fly colouration you wish to achieve. There are some excellent coloured CdC plumes available these days.

### Tying Instructions:

1. Run the silk down to the bend in neat touching turns.

2. Lightly dub the silk with the body material and wind back towards the eye stopping just short of it.

3. Take the CdC plumes and stack one on top of each other. It helps if the feathers are each of similar size, shape and curvature.

4. Trap the CdC on top of the hook with a pinch and loop technique between the body and hook eye.
5. Gently pull the CdC plumes forward to thicken the wing and to set the correct wing length, which as a rule should be level with or just beyond the back of the hook, whilst keeping some tension on the silk.
6. When happy with the wing thickness and length, tie down the CdC firmly and trim off the tips.
7. Lift up the wing and take a turn or two of thread tight in the angle between the upper part of the shank and the lower part of the wing. This lifts the stems, and fibres clear of the shank.
8. If you have not been able to set the length of your wing as indicated above then you can trim it to size. My recommendation if trimming CdC is to pluck it with your finger nails rather than cut it as this produces a finer, more appealing, and less sharp end.
9. Whip finish and varnish. The head may end up quite large but that is fine on this fly.

**Fishing Method:** Use confidently whenever there are upwinged flies on the surface. Even when there is no surface activity an F-Fly can bring a fish up.

# 8 Klinkhåmer Special – *Hans van Klinken*

This is one fly, and one fly-tyer, who needs no introduction, especially to any grayling angler throughout the world. Hans is a former career soldier in the Dutch Army, now retired and enjoying his fishing even more, and I had the great pleasure of getting to know him and his lovely wife Ina some years ago when I was a regular visitor to the Dutch and Danish Fly Fairs on behalf of the Grayling Society along with my great friend Roger Cullum Kenyon. Hans is the secretary of the Grayling Society in Holland and has succeeded in making it the second largest national area of the Society after the UK. Roger and I would man the Society stand, ably assisted by Hans when he was not involved on the invited fly-tyers podium, and other members of the Dutch area. Afterwards, at the Danish shows, we would decamp to Braedrup in the north of the country and have a few days fly-tying and fishing together. Great days and ones to remember forever.

Hans created the Klinkhåmer Special as a result of his fishing experiences in Norway and it underwent a lot of development in its early years. Most anglers know its history and uses so let's just see what Hans tells us are the important elements in a successful Klinkhåmer Special:

*Visibility*
*Your ability to see this pattern on the water is vital. Tie the wing so that it can be easily spotted in fast, turbulent waters.*

*Durability*
*User Spiderweb thread to tie in and secure the parachute. This is very important for steps 12, 13 and 14 as it does not damage the wound hackle fibres.*

*Build a Strong Base*
A strong base for the hackle is essential and very important for the fly's durability. You gain additional practice using the Spiderweb when you build a stronger base.

*Hooking Power*
For more proven hooking power use wide gape hooks. If the original hook is not available find the hooks with the widest gapes.

*Quality Hackles*
Use top quality hackles and make as many turns as required until the fibres start to change direction. I find at least five full turns will be required as the entire fly will be supported solely by the fibres of the parachute hackle. Sparsely tied parachute hackles may do well on calm waters, but they will easily sink in the strong rapids of a wild turbulent river.

*Dark for Success*
My experience has taught me that a fly tied with a darker coloured thorax will catch more fish than a similar fly without the darker thorax.

*Thin is In*
Body colours may be varied and according to the tyer's preference. I find bodies made of Fly-Rite light tan, dark tan or rusty olive have been my most effective. Tie the body very thin and well tapered. Start as close to the barb as possible. The thinner the body the more successful the pattern.

*Use Floatant Wisely*
Do not apply floatant to the body. Apply floatant only to the wing and/or hackle.

*Varnish for Strength*
Use a varnish applicator to properly secure the hackle, thorax and wing.

Some wise words there from Hans, and ones we should all take to heart when tying our Klinks!

The Klinkhåmer Special is a top fly from a top guy and one that has changed the way we fish forever.

## Klinkhåmer Special
*Flies tied by Hans van Klinken*

### Materials
**Hook:** Daiichi 1160 or Daiichi 1167 Klinkhåmer hook, size 8-20.
**Thread:** Uni-thread, 8/0, grey or tan for abdomen and thorax. Spiderweb to tie off the hackle.
**Body:** Fly-Rite Poly 2 dubbing any colour of preference or Wapsi Superfine waterproof dry-fly dubbing for smaller patterns.
**Wing:** One to four strands of white poly yarn depending on the size and turbulence of the water you are intending to fish.
**Thorax:** Three strands of peacock herl.
**Hackle:** Blue dun, dark dun, light dun, chestnut – all in good combination with the body colour.

*This is THE way to tie a Klinkhåmer Special courtesy of Hans – accept no substitute!*

### Tying Instructions
**1.** Place the hook in the vice and wrap the

entire shank with the tying thread. This avoids the difficulty of a slipping wing when the fly is finished.

2. Cut off a strand of poly yarn and taper the tip with your scissors before tying in to ensure the underbody is as slim as possible.

3. Secure the yarn onto the top of the hook shank with the thread just forward of the middle of the hook shank leaving a long section pointing forward to eventually form the wing.

4. Wrap your thread down to the bend trapping down the poly yarn and then bring back again. Try to make a nice slim well-tapered underbody. Be very critical at this stage! The better the underbody the more beautiful and effective the completed fly.

5. Tie in the hackle so it lies in the same direction as the yarn.

6. Form an upright wing by winding up the poly yarn and hackle. This must be done accurately to avoid potential hackle problems in the remaining tying steps.

7. Take the thread back to where you finished tying down the body at the bend. Apply a small amount of dubbing to the thread. Use enough dubbing just to cover the underbody. Dub a very slim and well tapered body, starting as close to the barb as possible. The thinner the body the more successful the pattern.

8. Wind it along the shank and stop just behind the wing and cut off surplus or use the last piece of dubbing as an underbody for the thorax. In that situation it is not really necessary to cut off the surplus. I recommend trying both techniques because for some people it is much easier to produce a better-looking thorax when you have made an underbody.

9. Tie in three peacock herl fibres. Tie the herl in by their tips. This will help to create a much nicer thorax. I secure the strands well behind the wing. This ensures that the thorax will not come off. Tie off the thread at the eye.

10. Wind the herls, starting with two or three turns behind the wing and then form a

thorax by winding the remaining herl in front of the wing.

11. Make a few extra turns of thread, whip finish and cut off the waste.
12. Turn the hook in the vice so that the eye is pointing downwards and the wing is now horizontal. Grasping the tuft of poly yarn, wind several turns of Spiderweb around the base of the poly yarn to create a rigid wing base on which to wind the hackle.
13. Starting at the top of your wing base wind on successive turns of hackle, taking each turn below the next and thus closer to the hook shank. Small flies will require about five turns of hackle and bigger flies at least seven or eight. Remember the fly has to float mainly on the parachute. A lot of people wind their hackle working up the wing. This makes the hackle less durable and it may come off. When you work from the top downwards you ensure a compact, well-compressed and durable hackle.
14. Pull the hackle tip in the opposite direction to the wing and secure it with a few turns of Spiderweb. Secure well around the base of the wing between the wound hackle and body. Finish off using a whip finish tool going between the wound hackle and the body.
15. Trim away the waste hackle tip and any hackle fibres that are pointing down. Take your varnish applicator and apply some lacquer on the windings just under the parachute.
16. Trim the wing as required.

**Fishing Method:** It's a Klinkhåmer Special! You know what to do with it!

# 9 & 10   Supa Pupa & CM Supa Pupa

The Supa Pupa is one of those system flies like, for example, the F-Fly or Klinkhåmer Special. Tied in a variety of different colours it can be used to represent many different natural flies whether they are in a state of hatching, dying, or just struggling in the surface film after being blown or having fallen onto the water. It is a great fly.

I was introduced to it by Hans van Klinken in the late 1990s. After the Danish Fly Fair we went to a campground at Braedrup with some other English and Dutch guys, to have a few days fishing on such rivers as the Gudenå and Kongeå and a bit of fly-tying – and drinking! I still have Hans' handwritten instructions for the original pattern which is shown in the tying instructions below. The secret of the fly is that it sits right down in the surface film. That is why cutting off the hackle below the fly body is critical to its success. Failure to cut off the hackle will result in yet another palmered fly that will ride high on the surface and defeat the objective. However, although the fly is meant to sit down in the surface film it will still need greasing slightly or it will eventually become a wet-fly!

The Supa Pupa is a system fly which can be tied in a variety of colours and sizes. Being a system fly means that you should, therefore, consider what you are trying to represent and match that using different body, thorax and hackle colours. The original, as demonstrated to me in Denmark, has a cream body, dark brown thorax and blue dun hackle. This works very well in the UK. However, I have also had great success with one with a light olive abdomen, dark thorax and an olive grizzle hackle.

My friend Steve Rhodes, who lives near, and guides on, the rivers of the Yorkshire Dales, champions a variant which was originated by a mutual friend, Christian Mohr of Germany, and a former Area Secretary for the Grayling Society in that country. Christian's version has an orange Ice Dub body and is one of those flies that can bring up a fish when there is nothing hatching or visible on the surface. He originally dressed it for the rainbows of the Weisse Traun in Bavaria but found that it was a big hit with the local trout early in the season around the time when the large stoneflies sporting orange abdomens were about. At that time he dressed almost all of his flies with a bit of hot orange material, but only the super pupa stood the test of time.

When you see a big grayling rise to this fly it makes you wonder what the logic of fly design really is! Steve has gone on record stating that if he only had just one fly to do all his grayling fishing with it would be this one. Praise indeed!

Tyings for both the original and Christian's excellent pattern are shown below.

## Original Supa Pupa
*Flies tied by the author*

**Materials:**

**Hook:** A suitable dry-fly hook, size 14 to 20.

*I normally use Tiemco 103BL sizes 15 to 21.*

**Silk:** Vary to suit body and thorax colours.

**Abdomen:** Fine dubbing e.g. Superfine in a pale cream colour – two thirds body length.

**Thorax:** Same material in a dark brown – one third body length.

**Hackle:** Blue dun cock hackle not too long in the flue.

*A saddle hackle is best if you can get one. Whiting are excellent – they are an even width and very long, so several flies can be tied with one hackle.*

**Variants:**

**Abdomen:** Similar fine dubbing but using other colours such as light olive, grey, etc.

**Thorax:** Same in a darker colour – brown, dark olive, black.

**Hackle:** Blue dun, grizzle, ginger, red game, etc., cock hackle.

## Christian Mohr's CM Supa Pupa

**Materials:**

**Hook:** Tiemco 103BL, size 17 to 21.

**Silk:** Danville Spiderweb coloured to suit thorax dubbing.

**Rib:** Very fine copper or gold wire – optional.

**Abdomen:** Orange Ice Dub – or similar such as Hends Spectra – two thirds body length.

**Thorax:** Any fine dark brown dubbing – one third body length.

**Hackle:** Dun or ginger cock hackle.

**Tying Instructions:** Either version

1. Run silk down to the bend in neat touching turns and tie in rib if using.
2. Tie in the hackle by its tip.
3. Dub the silk with the abdomen material and wind back towards the eye increasing thickness slightly as you go. Stop about two thirds of the way up the hook shank.
4. Dub the silk with the thorax material and wind to just behind eye.
5. Wind the hackle towards the eye with the fibres pointing forward.
6. Stop just behind the eye and tie off and trim.
7. If using a wire rib then now is the time to do the ribbing in the opposite direction to which you wound the hackle. Wiggle it as you go to avoid trapping hackle fibres.
8. Tie off at the eye and remove the waste.
9. Form a small head, whip finish and varnish.
10. With scissors cut off the hackles at the top and bottom of the fly.

**Fishing Method:** You can fish this fly, in any of its guises, confidently anywhere in the world. It will bring fish up even if there is no other surface activity.

# 11 Milroy – *Lee Hooper*

My friend Lee Hooper introduced me to the next fly and I am very glad that he did. It is one his grandfather used to tie and fish with on the River Wylye in Wiltshire and it has stood the test of time extremely well. The Milroy is one of those patterns we use to cover any of the 'black stuff' that appears from time to time on the river

# Milroy

*Fly tied by Lee Hooper*

**Materials:**

**Hook:** Dohiku or Hanak dry-fly, size 18 to 22 barbless.
**Silk:** Fine black.
**Tag:** Pinky peach Antron yarn or poly yarn.
**Body:** Bronze peacock herl (one strand).
**Hackle:** Black cock. Oversized for hook (feather barb length = hook length).

**Tying Instructions:**

1. Run the silk down the hook shank in neat touching turns and catch in about 10 strands of peachy yarn just before the bend.
2. Wind a peachy butt round the bend and back up to the tying-in point, tie off and trim waste.
3. Catch in a black cock hackle and one strand of bronze peacock herl. I like to tie the hackle in with the shiny side facing the hook shank, this gives the hackles a slight forward orientation.
4. Wind a small peacock body up to the eye, tie off and remove the waste.
5. Palmer the hackle up through the peacock herl (five or six turns) up to the eye, tie off, trim the waste, make a neat little head and whip finish.
6. Very carefully trim out the hackles directly above and below the shank to create a flat fly.

**Fishing Method:** Watch the water and watch for your fly. Like a Supa Pupa it will sit right down. My own maxim for fishing flies like this is to always ensure you think you know where your fly is and strike at absolutely everything!

and it performs its duties admirably in this respect.

As Lee tells us:

*Whilst looking through my late grandfather's fly box, I noticed an unusual fly amongst all the usual black gnats, sherry spinners, etc. I was inspired by this unusual fly (up-eye dry #16, peachy tag, herl body, traditional black hackle). It was not a million miles away from a grayling witch. So I thought I would have a tweak and get it back out on the River Wylye again for fish feeding on the small black flies but with a slight bit of pinkish grayling attraction. A simple pattern that sits flush in the surface film. The fly is nigh on impossible to see, being dark with no wing, you just have to watch for any rise. I find I sometimes need reassurance that the fly is still floating when using small flies I can't see, so it is tied on a light hook with oversized hackles. Could imitate gnat, smut, midge, beetle or terrestrials. I also tie a more sombre natural version where I replace the peach tag with stripped peacock quill.*

It's a belter! And the fly's name? It was the christian name of Lee's Grandad.

## 12 GRHE

The Gold Ribbed Hare's Ear, or G R H E, is one dry-fly pattern you can use pretty well all year round and is particularly effective when there are medium olives about. It is also a fly you can tie on with complete confidence on virtually any type of river where you might find grayling. Its origins are lost in the mists of time but it is believed that it was being tied in Redditch as early as 1832. Even Halford and his disciples were impressed, and in Victorian times it seemed to sprout wings and a hackle – no doubt to satisfy the precision requirements of the Halfordian mantra.

It has evolved since then and become simplified again. Gone are the wings and hackle and it now uses picked out guard hairs to represent the general disturbance in the legs and wings area of a hatching or newly hatched fly, and has probably come full circle to be closer to the original tying.

The fly can be fished dry with a judicious application of floatant, or allowed to sit in the surface film more in the manner of an emerger. In those situations where it is washed underwater and acts like an unweighted nymph it can also pick up fish.

All in all a very versatile fly and one of the top 'dryish' flies that you can tie and use in complete confidence that it will attract fish.

### GRHE
*Fly tied by the author*

**Materials:**

**Hook:** Dry-fly, size 14 to 18.

**Silk:** Yellow or tan.

**Tails:** Several guard hairs from a hare's ear.

**Rib:** Flat gold tinsel originally. However I don't like tinsel so I use gold wire.

**Body:** Dark hair picked off (not cut off) the hare's ear by thumb and finger nails.

**Hackle:** Guard hairs picked out with a dubbing needle.

**Tying Instructions:**
1. Run the silk down to the bend in neat touching turns.
2. Tie in the tail hairs.
3. Tie in the rib material.
4. Dub the silk with the dark hair back towards the eye and don't bother too much about how rough it is because you want it to look 'hairy'.
5. Rib in the opposite direction to that you have wound the silk and tie off at the eye and remove the waste.
6. Run the silk back to the point at which to start a thorax.
7. Dub the silk with the guard hairs and wind a 'hairy' thorax.
8. Pick out the guard hairs with a dubbing needle or by giving them a gentle brush with a piece of Velcro stuck to a wooden stirrer from a coffee shop – a lot cheaper than buying a dubbing teaser!
9. Form a small head, whip finish and varnish.

**Fishing Method:** A truly great year-round pattern which is especially good in a hatch of olives. Sitting in the surface film with all the disturbance going on caused by the hairy parts it can be most attractive to any hungry grayling.

## 13  Griffith's Gnat – *George Griffith*

The surface of rivers is frequently littered with 'small black stuff,' and at times this is the only colour that a grayling wants. I guess we have all experienced the phenomenon known as smutting, where the little blighters seem to be eating with great relish something we just can't see. There have been several attempts to devise flies to crack the smutting situation but they have all had limited success. I remember in earlier years how I expended lots of effort in devising different smut and simulium patterns and testing them on unsuspecting grayling. Some worked, most didn't. In addition there are regular falls of small black stuff, which we often just classify as gnats, on rivers virtually every day of the year, and we need to be ready to capitalise on such an event.

This fly does just that and with some aplomb! Created in the USA by George Griffith, who was incidentally one of the founders of the Trout Unlimited movement over there, it is actually intended to be a fly to use to represent midges, which it does admirably, but it is also a great all-rounder that can be used to mimic many different mini-beasties just by changing the size or adding little touches such as a small tail of fine mylar, pearl tinsel, holographic tinsel or crystal flash, etc.

It is one of those flies which I never tie on before getting to the river – let's face it you shouldn't ever tie any fly on before you have carried out a period of observing what is occurring down at the riverside – but often do once I have seen that there is nothing, apparently, hatching. This is because, when there is no other activity, a small black fly can usually produce something. It is like the old adage, true on small upland reservoirs like Fernworthy on Dartmoor in Devon, that you can use any colour fly you like as long as it is black! I call these small black things the Henry Ford Flies.

It is a simple fly to tie and can be used in sizes right down to what we used to call in the advertising and marketing game, when writing packaging copy, 'fly shit bold' or, in other words, really really small! In fact the limit in terms of smallness is governed by what hooks you can buy and what small hackles you have. For example Tiemco 518 midge hooks go down to size 32 and Varivas 2300 to size 30. Small stuff and not easy to find a suitable hackle. But fish do take flies as small as this. Dave Southall regularly catches grayling on tiny flies.

I have loads of these flies in my box – just a recognition of the effectiveness of it.

## Griffith's Gnat
*Fly tied by the author*

**Materials:**

**Hook:** Any dry-fly hook in sizes from 16 downwards.

**Silk:** Black and make it as fine as the hook requires. For the really small sizes you could use something like Danville Spiderweb, and colour it black before use with a marker pen.

**Tail:** If you want a tailed variant then use a little fine mylar, pearly tinsel, holographic tinsel or Crystal Flash, etc.

**Body:** Peacock herl – just one.

**Hackle:** Grizzle, tied palmer style.

**Tying Instructions:**

1. Take the silk down to the bend in neat touching turns.
2. If you want a tail then tie it in now. If not then go to step 3.
3. Tie in the grizzle hackle. If using a hackle from a cape tie it in at the hackle point. If using one from a saddle, which are usually even width from butt to tip, tie it in at the butt. Usually the hackle will 'angle' either forwards or backwards when you are winding it. Try to make it angle forward.
4. Tie in the peacock herl by the tip.
5. Take the silk back towards the eye and stop just fractionally behind it so there is room to tie everything off and form a small head.
6. Wind the peacock herl forward in touching turns. Tie off and remove the waste. Be careful because it can easily break if you

are heavy handed – and don't sneeze whilst doing it!
7. Palmer the hackle forward in nice open turns trying to ensure that it angles forward if at all.
8. Tie off, remove the waste and form a small head then whip finish and varnish.

**Fishing Method:** Watch the water. If fish are smutting, put one on; if they are taking something small and black, put one on; if there are lots of small black flies in the air, put one on; if nothing is happening, put one on! There is nothing to stop you giving the fly a haircut above and below the shank, as with a Supa Pupa, and fishing the fly in the surface film.

# 14 & 15   Emergers

I suppose, when you think about it, that the most vulnerable times in the life of an upwinged fly (or mayfly if you are reading this in North America) is when they are just hatching, or after they return as spinners to lay their eggs. In both situations the flies are virtually stationary and completely under the control of the current and the surface tension. It is not surprising, therefore, that fish target both these situations for such easy pickings. So let's look at hatching flies.

The nymph has moved up through the water column to the surface film and the sub-imago or dun has broken through the nymphal exoskeleton as it crawls out leaving an empty shuck behind. During this process it is quite helpless, stuck between water and air and all a fish needs to do is sip it down.

Of course anglers have known this for years but it is only fairly recently that we have codified it and started tying what we call 'emergers'. The name is pretty self-explanatory and general and covers many types of pattern. A Klinkhåmer Special is, of course, an emerger since it was originally tied to represent a hatching sedge and a significant element of the fly hangs down below the surface supported by the parachute hackle in the surface film. Any dun pattern can be tied in a parachute fashion on a slightly curved hook to create the same effect.

A modern approach to emerger patterns involves the use of Cul de Canard feathers which can be used in a variety of different ways. Perhaps the most common are as a Shuttlecock style of fly, drawing on the stillwater flyfishermen's approach to fishing with emerging buzzer patterns, or as a loop wing version of a broadly similar fly. These are the two variations I favour and which work well for me on the river.

Body materials can vary although I prefer to use stripped peacock quill and goose or turkey biot. I don't tend to use goose biot on larger flies because they are generally smaller than turkey and are too small for my ham-fisted approach, although they are a bit tougher.

The two patterns that follow use quill and biot.

## Quill Shuttlecock Emerger
*Fly tied by the author*

**Materials:**

- **Hook:** A fine wire grub hook, size 14 or 16. It must be lightweight.
- **Silk:** Brown and use a fine one such as Benecchi 12/0, Sheer 14/0 or Veevus 14/0.
- **Body:** Stripped peacock quill, either natural or dyed. Olive or yellow work well but I think natural is generally best.
- **Thorax:** Hare's ear fur or squirrel with plenty of guard hairs.
- **Hackle:** One CdC feather is usually enough but you may like two on a size 14.

**Tying Instructions:**

1. Take the silk down around the bend in neat touching turns.
2. Tie in the stripped peacock quill trying to keep the darker edge towards the bend if you can. Be careful because they can be a bit brittle. Wetting them may help or applying a little varnish to the silk just before you wind the quill can also be a big help.
3. Take the silk back to just behind the eye.
4. Wind the quill in neat touching turns to where the silk is hanging then tie off and remove the waste.
5. Take a CdC feather and tie it in just behind the eye using the pinch and loop method with the tip of the feather facing towards the back of the hook – very important! First just position it with a couple of loose wraps before pulling it towards the eye to force the fibres to compress together and give more body to the end which will form the thorax cover and wing. Position the feather such that, after pulling it towards the eye there will be sufficient feather to fold back towards the eye over the thorax yet still allow for a wing to protrude beyond the eye of about 10 mm on a size 14 and, say, 8 mm on a 16. It sounds complex, I know, but it is easy once you start on the process. Once you are happy that you have positioned the feather correctly tie it down tightly with a few wraps going back to a point where you will dub a thorax.
6. Dub on a thorax of hare's ear fur or squirrel, ensuring there are lots of guard hairs in the dubbing. Pinch the hair to remove it from the ear or skin, don't cut it.
7. Ensure the silk is now just behind the eye after dubbing the thorax.
8. Pull the CdC feather tightly back over the thorax towards the eye and, while still holding it firmly put a couple of turns of silk over it just behind the eye. You will have to do this backhanded because your right hand (if right handed) will be pulling

the feather forward. If you are happy that all looks good then add some tighter turns.

9. Now move the silk in front of the tied off CdC and put a few turns in front of it behind the eye before doing a whip finish and cutting off the waste. If you varnish the head then do so carefully to avoid varnishing the CdC. I use an acupuncture needle for varnishing the heads of small flies.

10. You could now varnish the exposed quill if you want to give it some strength against the ravages of fishing.

## Loop Wing Emerger
*Fly tied by the author*

### Materials:

**Hook:** A fine wire grub or emerger hook, size 14 or 16. I like emerger hooks for this fly, often sold as being suitable for stoneflies or caddis. They are usually less curved but a little longer than a grub hook which helps with the loop wing. Good examples are Partridge K12ST, Tiemco 2488 and Grip 14582.

**Silk:** Brown, and use a fine one such as Benecchi 12/0, Sheer 14/0 or Veevus 14/0.

**Tail:** Cock pheasant centre tail feather fibres – about four to six – tied short – optional.

**Body:** A single turkey or goose biot either natural or dyed. Olive, brown or mahogany work well.

**Thorax:** Hare's ear fur or squirrel, with plenty of guard hairs.

**Hackle:** CdC feather, two for a size 14 and possibly just one for a 16.

### Tying Instructions:

1. Take the silk down around the bend in neat touching turns.

2. Tie in the pheasant fibres, if using, to form a short tail about a quarter the length of the hook.

3. Tie in the goose or turkey by its tip. Be careful because it can be a bit brittle. Wetting it may help. Try to tie it in so the raised notch is to the back when you wind the biot up the hook. It is quite obvious what this is and it will stand proud of the body to give a superbly segmented look.

4. Take the silk back to just behind the eye.

5. Wind the biot in neat touching turns, or even overlapping slightly if you have managed to keep the notch to the back, to where the silk is hanging then tie off and remove the waste.

6. Take the CdC feather and tie it in just behind the eye using the pinch and loop method with the tip of the feather facing towards the back of the hook – very important! If using two feathers then

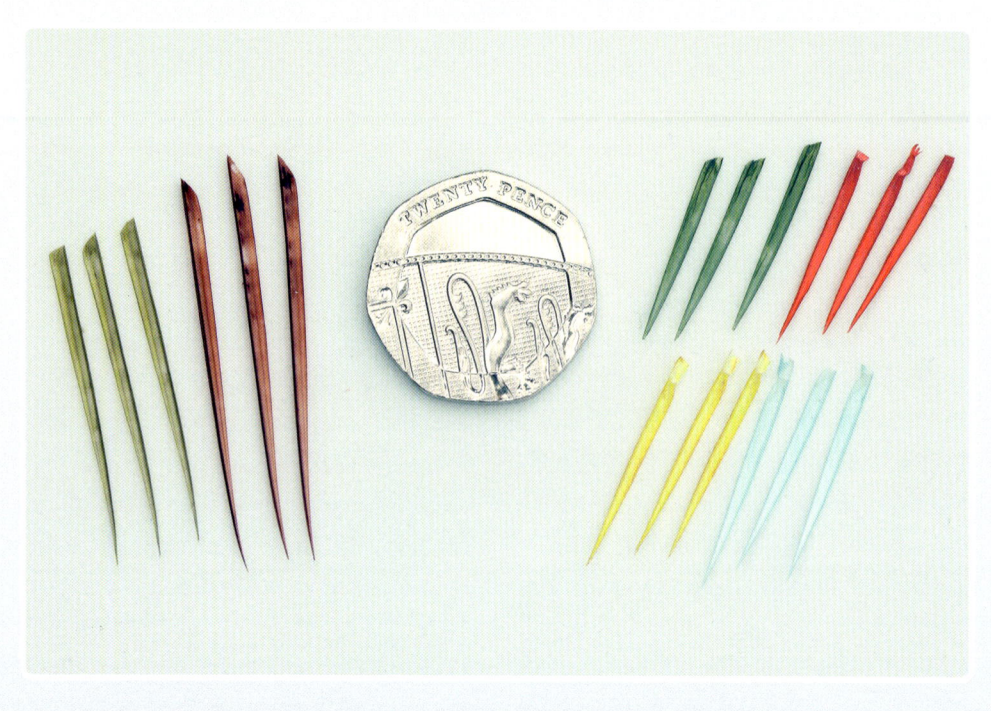

Comparative sizes - turkey biot on left and goose on right

lay them onto each other so that the tips are lined up before tying them both in together. Stroke the fibres towards the tip to get them to squeeze together a little before applying the loose turns. First position the CdC with a couple of loose wraps before pulling it towards the eye a little to force the fibres to compress together further and give more body to the end which will form the wing. Position the feather such that after pulling it towards the eye there will be sufficient feather to fold back into a loose loop wing towards the eye over the thorax yet still allow for a little of the feather to protrude beyond the eye for about 10 mm on a size 14 and less on a 16. Leave the feather in position such that about one hook length of it is protruding from the back of the hook. This a rule of thumb guide to getting the length correct to fold over into the loop wing easily. Once you are happy that you have positioned the feather correctly tie it down tightly with a few wraps going back to a point where you will dub a thorax.

7. Dub on a thorax of hare's ear fur or squirrel ensuring there are lots of guard hairs in the dubbing. Pinch the hair to remove it from the ear or skin, don't cut it.

8. Ensure the silk is now just behind the eye.

9. Pull up the CdC feather back over the thorax towards the eye forming a loose loop. Don't pull tight to the thorax or you are tying a Shuttlecock variant! Now, whilst still holding it firmly put a couple of turns of silk over it just behind the eye. You will have to do this backhanded because your right hand (if right handed) will be pulling the feather forward. If you

are happy that all looks good then add some tighter turns.

10. Now move the silk in front of the tied off CdC and put a few turns in front of it and behind the eye before doing a whip finish and cutting off the waste. If you varnish the head then do so carefully to avoid varnishing the CdC. I use an acupuncture needle for varnishing the heads of small flies.

11. Usually several of the CdC fibres spring out from the back of the loop which all helps with the general feeling of disturbance in the surface film.

**Fishing Method:** Fish these whenever there is a hatch starting and fish seem to be rising with gentle sips, rather than full-bodied rises to flighty duns.

# 16  IOBO – *David Southall*

Dave Southall is a well-known and highly successful angler, who writes regularly for *Fly Fishing & Fly Tying* magazine and contributes copious high quality material to the Grayling Society's journal, *Grayling*. He has fished all over the world for many different species but the grayling is his favourite. He is a great promoter of the IOBO fly and I asked him to tell us about it in his own words:

> IOBO stands for 'It Oughta Be Outlawed' (it's that good!). Devised in 1996 by Jack Tucker of Pennsylvania it is, in my opinion, one of the world's best ever dry flies.
>
> I was introduced to it in 2003 by a friend, Brian Pinning, who had seen it on Hans Weilenmann's website. I immediately saw its potential in small sizes for those grayling that are preoccupied with tiny midges or aphids, and it has accounted for lots of very picky grayling (and trout) all over the world. In sizes 26 to 12 it resembles a host of surface insects, midges, aphids, olives, fluttering stoneflies and sedges, plus various terrestrials.
>
> In April 2015 I was delighted to receive an email from Jack himself thanking me for crediting him with devising this when I wrote about this brilliant fly in Fly Fishing & Fly Tying magazine and saying that he would in future use my 'better' method of tying it.

I was introduced to this fly by Dave's writings and I have never regretted tying some. It is one of those great all-purpose dries which can represent all manner of naturals.

It also, of course, uses a minimum of materials and is very easy to tie although care needs to be taken, as always in fly-tying, in getting the proportions right.

## IOBO
*Fly tied by David Southall*

**Materials:**

**Hook:** Light wire dry-fly hook, size 12 to 26 – yes 26!

**Silk:** Tan, camel or yellow 8/0.

**Body & Wing:** Two natural grey CdC plumes (one or two, depending on plume size, for very small flies).

**Tying Instructions:**

1. Wind well-waxed thread from the eye to the bend of the hook.
2. Line up two matching CdC feathers with their fronts touching so that the tips flare slightly. Orientate them vertically over the hook and tie in with two slack turns of thread. Pull the butts gently until their tips extend one and a half to two times the shank length behind the hook bend. Then lock in place with two tight turns of thread.
3. Rib over the CdC butts in open turns to just short of the hook eye and cut off the excess. (If you want a fat body, wind the thread up to just short of the eye; rope the CdC butts and wind them to just short of the eye and tie in).
4. Pull the CdC tips forwards over the body (I like to leave a few fibres trailing as a tail/shuck) and tie in just behind the eye with 4 tight turns of thread.
5. Post up the wing to an angle of 45 degrees with thread turns in front and whip finish.

**Fishing Method:** Use it whenever there is 'small stuff' on the water.

# 17  John Storey Paradun – *Steve Rhodes*

I have a lot of time for Steve Rhodes. He is a very hardworking, Orvis endorsed, flyfishing guide and instructor operating in the Yorkshire Dales, and is co-owner of the guiding organisation Go Flyfishing UK. He has fished the Wharfe and other Dales rivers all his life and is a particular expert on the mysteries of Malham Tarn. He has been a member of the Grayling Society since time immemorial and was for some years the Chairman. Now he looks after the organisation in the North and West Yorkshire area.

Steve is a big fan of the John Storey and I don't blame him because it is a fly I am very fond of also. He ties his version a little differently from the original so I asked him to explain:

I was introduced to the John Storey around 30 years ago when I joined the Pickering Fishery Association. It was a popular fly with many of the members there; hardly surprising as the fly was originally devised by John Storey, the first generation of "Storey" river keepers for the Ryedale Anglers' Club, and the dressing was later adapted by his son. Many of the Pickering members must have fished the Ryedale Anglers' water and vice versa. Three consecutive generations of the Storey family were eventually river keepers on the Ryedale Anglers' water.

At the time parachute-style dry flies were becoming increasingly popular and the majority of the dry flies I dressed used this method of tying. I simply replaced the forward-slanting mallard breast feather

## John Storey Paradun
*Fly tied by Steve Rhodes*

**Materials:**

**Hook:** Tiemco 103 BL in sizes 13 to 19.
**Silk:** Danville's Spiderweb white.
**Tail:** Ginger or red game cock hackle fibres – seven or eight.
**Body:** Bronze peacock herl.
**Wingpost:** White Antron yarn.
**Hackle:** Genetic cock, medium ginger or red.

**Tying Instructions:**

1. Take the silk down to the bend and tie in tail fibres.
2. Tie in the peacock herl and take the silk forward to the thorax region.
3. Tie in the antron for the upright wing and tie the yarn down tightly onto the hook shank towards the bend.
4. Cut off the waste yarn ensuring you cut it off at an angle to avoid a bulky body.
5. Run a few turns of silk around the base of the wing to raise it upright.
6. Take the peacock herl up to the back of the wing and tie off with a couple of turns.
7. Tie in the hackle so that it can easily wind around the base of the wing.
8. Wind the hackle up the wing three or four turns and back down.
9. Tie off the hackle around the base of the wing and remove the waste.
10. Take the peacock up to the eye, tie off, form a small head and whip finish.

**Fishing Method:** Steve uses this in hatches of any upwinged fly or sedges and says, with justification, that this dry-fly has caught fish everywhere and at any time – even in the depths of winter.

*wing with an Antron post and added a tail to create, for want of a better term, a John Storey Paradun.*

*The fly is very effective for both trout and grayling no doubt due to the fact that it contains that seemingly magical trout-, and in particular, grayling-attractor peacock herl. It will catch fish when fish are taking various species of mayflies but is also on occasions effective when fish are taking midges or terrestrials.*

*Many years ago I was fishing with Malcolm Greenhalgh on the River Wharfe and introduced this pattern to him. Malcolm, unusually, was struggling a little that day but I was getting fish on this pattern. Of course I gave him one and he also had some success. Since then it has become one of his favourite dry flies and was later featured in his book,* The Floating Fly.

Praise indeed. If both Steve and Malcolm approve then there is no more to be said. If I was you I would parachute some into your box pretty quickly!

## 18  CdC & Elk – *Hans Weilenmann*

To anyone who is even vaguely interested in fly-tying Hans Weilenmann needs no introduction. A prolific designer of flies – simple but effective are his watchwords – for both grayling and trout, and a specialist in using CdC, he is to be seen regularly on the fly-tyer's podium at major shows in Europe and North America including the British Fly Fair International held at Stafford in February each year. Another Dutchman – how is it that the Netherlands produces so many excellent fly-tyers? – he is also a superb photographer and his flies shown on the website www.flytierspage.com are a joy to behold. He also has a YouTube channel which has clear and thoughtful instructional videos, including a particularly good demonstration of the tying of this fly.

His CdC & Elk fly has achieved worldwide acclaim for its effectiveness, not only as a sedge/caddis dry-fly but also as an emerger or even fished wet and is a true all-rounder.

Here is what Hans himself has to say about its versatility:

*"The CdC & Elk is a very versatile pattern. While originally designed to be a dry caddis imitation, it has proven to be much more than just a 'better' caddis pattern! It is by far my most productive dry to use during mayfly(!) hatches, as well as my staple search pattern during hatchless periods. Fish it as an emerger in the film. Or as a straight wet. It has proven to cover the full spectrum of dry, 'damp' and wet. As an extremely effective 2-materials 2-minutes-to-tie this is one hard to pass up pattern. I suggest you try it!"*

I have used this pattern for some time and would not be without it in my box, although I doubt I tie it quite as neatly as Hans does!

Like many, apparently, simple flies – it only uses two materials. It does require some care when tying because it is so easy to get it wrong. Do read Hans' tying instructions most carefully especially with regard to feather selection and tying in the CdC and deer hair.

Have fun with this one!

## CdC & Elk
*Flies tied by Hans Weilenmann*

**Materials:**

**Hook:** Tiemco 102Y #11 – #17 (or equivalent dry-fly hook).

**Thread:** Brown 6/0.

**Body/hackle:** Type 1 CdC feather. This feather has the shape and structure of a partridge body feather. It is fairly short, with a tapered stem, round tip, and barbules set at about 60 degrees from the stem. I use this feather to wrap around the shank in such a manner that it produces both body and trailing filaments to suggest a multitude of interesting options.

**Wing/head:** Fine tipped deer hair.

**Tying instructions:**

1. Select a Type 1 CdC feather of the required colour and size. (The longest barb approx. two times shank-length). Hold the CdC feather at the butt with the fingers/thumb of your left hand, and draw the feather between thumb and index finger of your right hand towards the tip, bunching the tips together.

2. Tie in the bunch at the tip with the butt pointing backwards over the bend of the hook. Tie down with two tight turns of thread, then slip a third turn under the tips (i.e. towards the eye), effectively forcing them upwards, and follow with a fourth turn over the tips, just forward of the third turn. You have now locked the CdC barbules in place and have ensured the feather will not pull out during fishing. Spiral the thread forward to the eye, then wrap back one touching turn away from the eye of the hook.

3. Clamp the butt with hackle-pliers and wind the CdC feather towards the eye in touching turns. You will find that the rear

half of the body will resemble a dubbed body, but as you progress towards the eye, more and more free barbules will stand out. Stroke these backwards with each turn. A little practice will enable you to arrive at the eye with only the bare part of the stem left.

4. Tie off with one or two tight turn(s) of thread, unclip the hackle but do not trim yet. Tighten with another two turns of thread. You will see that the CdC butt will move with the thread, tightening a fraction further at the tie-off point. Trim the CdC butt.

5. Take a small amount of straight, fine-tipped deer hair (I use early season mule deer). Even the tips in a stacker. Lay the bunch on top of the hook, parallel to the shank. Measure the tips so the wing will be just long enough to reach the outside bend of the hook, and no longer. Trim the butts square (perpendicular to the strands) with the front of the eye of the hook prior to tying in the wing.

6. Tie down the wing with two tight wraps of thread over the hair stubs. Make a third wrap with the thread, through the stubs, at a 45 degree angle. Fourth wrap goes under the stubs. Complete the fly with a whip finish under the stubs, and a little varnish.

**Fishing Method:** Well, all I can say is that Hans has this absolutely right so go out and fish with it in any of the alternative ways that work for you!

# 19  Little Red Sedge – *G E M Skues*

George Edward MacKenzie Skues (right) has long been a hero of mine. Not because of the similarities of our names but because he was a thinking angler and fly designer supreme. He was a rebel, and most certainly one of the greatest trout fishermen ever. I think it was a great travesty that he was so badly treated in that infamous Nymph Debate at the Flyfishers' Club in 1938.

It is a regret of mine that he didn't have a better attitude to grayling. To him, and many others of his time, they were at best a distraction and at worst a plague in the chalkstreams. I have no doubt, however, that he was the kind of man who would have changed his opinion and looked upon grayling more favourably in these more

## Little Red Sedge

*Fly tied by the author*

**Materials:**

**Hook:** Dry-fly hook, size 14.

*Skues was fond of sneck hooks with their square bend and used a 'new scale' size 1.*

**Silk:** Hot orange waxed with brown wax.

**Body:** Darkest hare's ear.

**Rib:** Fine gold wire, binding down body hackle.

**Body Hackle:** Long deep-red cock, with short fibres.

**Wings:** Landrail wing, bunched and rolled, and tied in sloping well back over the tail.

*Use cinnamon partridge tails as a substitute.*

**Front Hackle:** Like body hackle, but larger and long enough to tie five or six turns in front of the wing.

**Tying Instructions:**

1. Run the well-waxed silk down to the bend in neat touching turns.
2. Tie in the rib.
3. Take the silk back to the eye and tie in the body hackle sufficiently well behind the eye to have room for the wing and main hackle.
4. Take the silk back to the bend and then dub the body back to where the body hackle is tied in.
5. Wind the body hackle down to the bend in open turns – Skues says three or four – and leave it hanging with the hackle pliers attached.
6. Rib back to the eye with the gold wire in the opposite direction to that in which you wound the hackle. Again use three or four turns. Tie off at the eye and 'worry' it to break off. Then remove the waste body hackle.
7. Take a long strip of wing material from the quill. Skues says to take nearly all the wing but that seems a bit over the top. However, you do need a reasonable amount. Then roll it gently and finally bunch it by squeezing it lightly with thumb and finger.
8. Tie in this wing just behind the eye leaving enough room for the main hackle.
9. Cut off any waste and tie in the main hackle.
10. Wind about five or six turns of hackle. Tie off, remove the waste and form a neat head.
11. Varnish the head and go sedge fishing.

**Fishing Method:** Fish as a normal dry-fly whenever there are sedges about. It will also bring up fish when there aren't any sedges about!

Typical Medium Sedge
*Photo: Dr. Cyril Bennett MBE*

enlightened times. I hope so because I want him to continue to be my hero!

His Little Red Sedge must have been his top standby fly – he stated that it was his most killing fly when there were no hatches of upwinged duns. While he never claimed any originality in the use of the materials in this dressing it is certainly a pattern specifically developed to suit his needs. I have used Skues' dressing from his book, *Silk, Fur and Feather*.

Skues used this pattern throughout the summer months and considered it ideal for trout nosing around weed beds or for 'bankers' and trout in ditches and drains.

It is also great for grayling and is, to my mind at least, one of the all-time great fly patterns, never mind just sedges.

Unfortunately, like some other older patterns, it requires the use of a material which is not legally obtainable any more. The wing is 'landrail bunched and rolled' which you will not now be able to buy. The landrail, usually called corncrake nowadays, is an endangered and secretive species found mainly in the West of Scotland or Ireland, much more likely to be heard than seen. However, there are substitutes. When I first started tying this fly many years ago I managed to buy some dyed starling wing quills from Geoffrey Bucknall when he had a shop near St Pauls in London. Landrail wing is a very deep ginger or orangey red and the dyers had managed to reproduce this colour. Steve Cooper, who owns Cookshill Fly Tying, recommends using cinnamon partridge tails, and these have proved a very good substitute for the real thing.

# 20  May Franglais

What! A mayfly in a book of grayling flies! How can this be when the grayling close-season, in England and Wales, doesn't end until the 16th of June? I know it sounds a bit like poaching but the point is that, certainly in the south, the mayfly usually arrives in late May, or even in June itself on some of the more western chalkstreams. On the adoption of the Gregorian calendar in England in 1752 the year was shortened by eleven days. So, for example, the 21st of May became the 1st of June and the mayfly edged towards being the junefly!

There are often mayfly hatches on the chalkstreams in the second half of June or even later. In fact, I once had a memorable day with the fly in mid-August and have even used an artificial successfully

Entente Cordiale avec les May Franglais. English to the left, Français à droite!

## May Franglais

*Flies tied by the author*

**Materials:**

**Hook:** A long-shanked, lightweight, dry-fly hook, size 10 or 12. After much experimenting I now always use Grip 11801BL hooks which are light, barbless, and very strong.

*Perfect for mayflies.*

**Silk:** Brown or tan.

**Tail:** Up to 6 herls from a cock pheasant centre tail feather. You need enough to hold the fly up on the surface.

**Abdomen:** Fine cream dubbing. I use Fly-Rite #12 or 25.

**Thorax:** Fine brown dubbing. I use Fly-Rite #6 or 42.

**Body Hackle:** Cree, honey dun or ginger, very short in the flue – say a hackle suitable for a size 18 or 20 fly palmered along body. *A saddle hackle is best.*

**Stiff Hackle:** Cree, honey dun or ginger, larger in flue – say a size 12 or 14. Used behind partridge hackle to stiffen it and give it kick.

**Main Hackle:** Flank feather from a French (red-legged) partridge. Only this feather will do for a genuine French Partridge Mayfly! There is NO substitute in Europe. In the USA use a chukar feather as an alternative. Of course, not everybody is a Francophile. So, if you aren't then tie it with a flank feather from an English or grey partridge (known in the USA as a Hungarian partridge), and it will still work. So, whether you tie the English or French version you will have an effective, and authentic May Franglais.

*See photos below for feathers and preparation.*

*The correct flank feathers – English on left, French on right*

**Tying Instructions:**

1. Run the silk down to the bend and tie in the tail feathers. Make the tail about the same length as the hook.
2. Also tie in the body hackle at the bend.
3. Dub a cream abdomen and leave the silk at the eye end of the abdomen.
4. Run the body hackle up to the silk in even open turns. Tie off and remove the waste.
5. Tie in the stiff hackle at the end of the abdomen.
6. Dub a thorax with brown dubbing finishing it about an eighth of an inch short of the eye.
7. Wind the stiff hackle over the thorax two or three turns, tie off and remove the waste.
8. Tie in the French or English partridge hackle by its tip. To do this, prepare the feather by removing the fluff at the base. Then hold feather by its tip and stroke back fibres from about a quarter of an inch from the tip to create a V shape at the end of the feather. Tie in the feather at the point where the V is joined to the main feather. It is the same way you would tie in a partridge feather for a soft hackled wet spider fly. It is done this way so that the finest part of the feather is used as the hackle and the thickest part of the quill is removed and does not clog up the eye end of the fly. Make a couple of turns then tie off and remove the waste.

*French feather prepared for tying in*

9. Make a small head then whip finish, cut off the silk and varnish.

**Fishing Method:** This is a dun imitation and should be used when the fish are taking the hatched duns, although it can take fish at the start of the hatch, and even when spinners are falling on the water. When tied on a lightweight hook and well-greased it will float forever, even though the partridge hackle may be considered to be more appropriate for a wet-fly and start to look a bit bedraggled after a while.

in October! So I feel quite justified in including May Franglais (my version of the French Partridge Mayfly) in this book. It is, frankly, my 'go to' mayfly whenever there is a hatch in progress. Sure, I use emergers and nymphs and spinner patterns when the time is right but, for an everyday dun imitation, I think that this simple approach is excellent. I have several different mayfly dun patterns in my box but, invariably, this is the one I tie on and it works very well most times. I could become a one fly only man during a mayfly hatch with this pattern.

I am sure it must be the general messiness and broken outline that the combination of the partridge and palmered body hackle creates on, and just under, the surface which makes it so reliable.

Incidentally, if you have ever suffered from mayfly patterns spinning like propellers as you cast and twisting your tippets into a real old mess then try an idea I came up with a few years ago. I am a very keen user of furled leaders and I just tied a tiny swivel onto the business end and then tied my tippet to that. When I first started buying the swivels they were called size 24, from Preston Innovations, but have now been re-classified as size 14 apparently although they still seem to be the same size – which is minute! Gone was the tendency for the tippet to twist as the fly 'propellered' its way towards the fish. And you needn't worry about the weight of the swivel because they are very light indeed and, when matched with the heavier tippets we tend to use during mayfly time, they do not cause the leader/tippet joint to sink at all. Furled versions of this leader, called the 'Grayling Dry Anti-twist' are currently (2016) available from the Grayling Society (www.graylingsociety.net).

# 21  Aphid – *Steve Rhodes*

I mentioned earlier that my friend Mike and myself were refused a day-ticket to fish the Nidd some years ago. What I didn't say is that the week before we had actually managed to blag a ticket off the nice lady who ran a little shop in Pateley Bridge and did, in fact, go grayling fishing. It was only on the subsequent visit that we were shown the red card! I have often thought back and hoped the lady did not get into any trouble over the situation. In defence of the club I should point out that my recent research shows that you now can buy a day-ticket for grayling fishing on their waters after the trout season closes. Another club has seen the light.

So what is the point of digging up this story? Well, the greenfly, or aphid, is the point.

The day that we got our ticket we hotfooted it to a part of the river which I believe is known as Dacre Banks and started fishing. It was a lovely autumn day and things went fine for a while. Then they slowed down and, although fish were rising, we stopped getting any takes. I think we were probably using olive or sedge dry flies. It took some time and a degree of head scratching before we finally worked it all out – they were taking aphids. Fortunately I had a couple of very small green dry flies lurking at the back of one of my boxes so we gave them a shot and, hey presto, that was the winning recipe. That was the day I realised the importance of the aphid as a source of food for grayling. Obviously it is dependent on the local conditions but they were definitely aphid orientated on that day in that place.

Steve Rhodes knows a lot about aphid

# Aphid
## Flies tied by Steve Rhodes

**Materials:**
**Hook:** Tiemco 103 BL, size 21.
**Silk:** Danville's Spiderweb white.
**Body:** Chartreuse Ice Dub.
**Hackle:** Cream or light ginger cock, very short in the flue.

**Tying Instructions:**
1. Run the silk down to the bend in neat touching turns.
2. Dub very lightly with the Ice Dubbing, making sure it is quite short and not straggly and take back to just short of the eye.
3. Tie in the hackle and wind two or three turns.
4. Tie off, remove the waste, form a small head, whip finish and varnish.
5. The hackle can be trimmed at the bottom if required to help the fly sit right down in the surface film.

**Fishing Method:** Keep your eyes peeled and, whenever it looks like there are aphids about, tie on one of these!

fishing, and rates the fly very highly, pointing out that lots of anglers overlook the importance of this apparently insignificant little creature. He tells us, rightly, that aphids are important to grayling right through from late in the summer to around mid-October when it starts to get cold and the leaves are falling from the trees. Leaf-fall is a prime time for aphids as they are being deposited onto the surface. Here is what he told me:

> Both brown trout and, especially, grayling love aphids and an old friend of mine, Bernard Benson, was convinced that he had seen grayling 'sucking' aphids off the leaves floating down the river during the autumn. Bernard has a great sense of humour so believe that if you will. I think it's more likely that the grayling were taking aphids that had been washed off the leaves along the leaf and bubble lines amongst the leaves.
>
> Apparently there are more than 500 species of aphid in the UK and they are generally present from spring through until autumn, probably August, September and until around mid-October are the peak times for fishing aphid patterns.
>
> Like the majority of the flies I use it's a very simple but effective pattern. Bernard Benson used a similar version but I replaced the floss body with a dubbed body of Ice Dub in chartreuse; I believe the added sparkle makes it more effective.
>
> Aphids are small and have a low profile on the water and are therefore difficult to spot; look at the water very

*closely, ideally in a bubble line, and you will be surprised just how often aphids are present.*

Aphid patterns are not difficult to develop but it is always reassuring if someone whose opinions you respect has a pattern which he believes in. This is why I am showing here the Steve Rhodes pattern in which I have a lot of faith and which sits in that corner of my box reserved for aphid time.

# 22  Red Tag

Many of the old traditional flies are still brilliant at catching grayling. Just because they were conceived a hundred or more years ago does not make them any less efficient now. The rivers still run, the flies still hatch and the fish still eat. The Red

### Red Tag
*Fly tied by the author*

**Materials:**

**Hook:**  A suitable dry-fly hook, size 14 - 18.
**Silk:**  Black or green.
**Tag:**  Bright red wool or scarlet ibis.
**Body:**  Two or three bright green herls from a peacock eye feather.
**Hackle:**  Stiff bright red game cock hackle.

**Tying Instructions:**

1. Run the silk down to the bend in neat touching turns.
2. Tie in a tail of bright red wool, not too long but 'fluffy'.
3. Tie in the peacock herls.
4. Wind the silk back towards the eye in neat touching turns.
5. Carefully, because it is not the strongest material, wind the peacock herls towards the eye – you can twist them together to get more strength – and trap them just behind the eye leaving enough room for the hackle and head. This is very important or you will have difficulty in forming a head and tying-off when completing the fly.
6. Tie in the cock hackle.
7. Wind the hackle for about three or four turns, tie off and remove the waste.
8. Form a small head, whip finish and varnish.

**Fishing Method:** Wait until the sun thinks of setting, say 'Hmmm, Red Tag time, I think', and off you go!

Tag is perhaps the most famous of these traditional flies. Using simple and easily obtainable materials it is a fly that can be tied dry, wet, or as a nymph or gold-head, and it will work in all those ways.

Although often thought of as being a classic Yorkshire fly the Red Tag is most likely to have been invented in Worcestershire, probably by a man called Flynn in the mid-1800s, and was known originally as the Worcester Gem. Walbran introduced it into Yorkshire and it soon became a favourite of the northern grayling men.

Red is often cited as a colour that excites grayling and many successful flies incorporate it. Its use on this fly may play to that or it may be that the continued success of the fly over many, many years has actually created the concept that grayling like red.

Certainly it is a distinctive and attractive fly and just looks very 'fishy.'

The red wool needs to be quite striking – a bright Post Office red is a good guide. However, if you have such a thing, and it is quite a rare beast these days, then a bit of scarlet ibis feather, or a substitute, will also work well.

My great friend Mike, when we used to fish together on a regular and frequent basis some years ago, would stop as the sun was thinking of setting, sniff the air and proclaim "Hmmm, Red Tag time I think." On would go his Red Tag and up would come the fish! Uncanny, but it became a predictable event.

Tie one and try it. Mr Walbran will give you a friendly smile from on high, and a grayling or two will, no doubt, come up to have a look as well.

## 23  Sturdy's Fancy – *Tom Sturdy*

This is, essentially, a derivative of the Red Tag and uses exactly the same body and tail material. It was designed by Tom Sturdy to fish on the River Ure, near Masham in North Yorkshire. It has worked wherever I have used it.

Apparently, it was designed to represent spinners, and it certainly does perform best in an evening when you would expect to see them on the water.

It is an excellent fly and, like the Red Tag, can be fished wet simply by replacing the cock hackle with a soft one from a hen. Reg Righyni rated it highly as a grayling fly and included a rib of crimson silk on his variant.

### Sturdy's Fancy
*Fly tied by the author*

**Materials:**
**Hook:** A suitable dry-fly hook, size 14 - 18.
**Silk:** Crimson.
**Tag:** Bright red wool or scarlet ibis.
**Rib:** Crimson silk – optional.
**Body:** 2 or 3 bronze peacock herls.
**Hackle:** Stiff bright off-white cock hackle.

**Tying Instructions:**

1. Run the silk down to the bend in neat touching turns.
2. Tie in a tail of bright red wool, not too long but 'fluffy'.
3. Tie in the crimson silk rib – if used.
4. Tie in the peacock herls.
5. Wind the silk back towards the eye in neat touching turns.
6. Carefully wind the peacock herls towards the eye – you can twist them together to get more strength – and trap them just behind the eye leaving enough room for the hackle and head. This is very important or you will have difficulty in forming a head and tying off when completing the fly.
7. If using, rib with the crimson silk in the opposite direction to which you wound the herl. Tie off at the eye and remove the waste.
8. Tie in the off-white game cock hackle.
9. Wind the hackle for about three or four turns, tie off and remove the waste.
10. Form a small head, whip finish and varnish.

**Fishing Method:** Pop one on whenever the fancy takes you!

## 24 Grayling Fiddler – *Eric Horsfall Turner*

Eric Horsfall Turner, author of *Angler's Cavalcade*, was the Town Clerk of Scarborough and a past President of the Pickering Fishery Association (which kindly supplied the caricature self-portrait featured here), as well as being a pioneer of tuna (or tunny) fishing in the North Sea. He is credited with the invention of many successful patterns for trout and grayling including Eric's Beetle, the Daily Dun and John Titmouse.

But of most interest to us as grayling anglers is his excellent pattern the Grayling Fiddler and we should all carry this pattern in our dry-fly boxes because it really works well. This is another fancy fly that bears no real relationship to any natural but Eric came up with a great formula when he designed this one.

Grizzle, or Plymouth Rock, hackles have a superb ability to create a somewhat blurred and broken up outline. This confused image gives the impression of lots happening around the legs and wings of the fly. And the red body? Well, the Red Tag and countless other flies have demonstrated the effectiveness of this colour when fishing for grayling.

I have found it to be a fly that works best in the smaller sizes – is it taken for a midge then? – and in the evening. It can certainly bring fish up to the surface when there is nothing apparently happening.

## Grayling Fiddler
*Fly tied by the author*

**Materials:**

**Hook:** A suitable dry-fly hook, size 16 to 20, although I prefer size 18.

**Silk:** Brown – preferably reasonably dark.

**Dubbing:** Teased out red wool, or seal's fur, or as an alternative I use shade 20 Midge Red Pupa from a Davy Wotton Masterclass Dubbing Cube.

**Hackle:** Sharp grizzle cock hackle, not too long in the flue.

**Tying Instructions:**

1. Run the silk, in neat touching turns, down to the bend.
2. Return the silk back towards the eye, for about four turns, leaving the silk exposed as a butt.
3. Dub sparsely with the teased out red wool and wind up the hook shank forming a slightly tapered body ending just before the eye with enough space to tie in the hackle.
4. Tie in the grizzle hackle, wind on three or four turns, tie off and remove the waste.
5. Form a neat head and varnish.

**Fishing Method:** This fly can be particularly deadly in the evening when there is nothing, apparently, happening on the surface. Thanks Eric for such a super fly.

# 25  Grayling Steel Blue – *Roger Woolley*

I have a small very nicely printed and bound book in my fly-tying library which I have almost destroyed because of the number of times I have opened it and pressed it flat to look at whilst tying a fly from its pages. It is called *Modern Trout Fly Dressing* by Roger Woolley, published by *The Fishing Gazette* in 1932.

Amongst its 202 pages of detailed instructions and fly patterns is a section on grayling flies containing 31 dressings. Oddly, the fly destined to become a classic grayling fancy fly is not within these pages, but is found in the section called Fancy Wet Flies. That is the Steel Blue or, as we universally call it these days, the Grayling Steel Blue. Originally designed as a wet-fly it is also highly effective in a dry version and this is how I tie and use the fly.

There has long been a tradition in Derbyshire for palmered flies and this follows that, although yet again my friend Bob Lomax has cast the traditional approach into the air and it has come down, like thistledown, with a paraloop hackle! I will, therefore, give both the traditional and paraloop dry-fly dressings here.

This is a very good fancy fly and one that, to my mind, fits in alongside the Red Tag, Sturdy's Fancy and Grayling Fiddler as must-haves in any grayling fly box.

## Original Fly – Dry-fly Dressing
*Fly tied by the author*

**Materials:**

**Hook:** Dry-fly hook, size 14, 16 or 18.
**Silk:** Bright orange.
**Tag:** Fine flat silver tinsel – optional in my view.
**Rib:** Fine gold wire.
**Body:** Peacock herl – only one or two herls.
**Hackle:** Well-grizzled bright blue cock.

*A standard grizzle hackle works well here also, and one from a saddle, rather than a cape, is the best for a palmered fly such as this because it does not taper.*

**Tying Instructions:**

1. Run the silk down to the bend and tie in the rib.
2. Tie in the flat silver tinsel (if using) and form a small tag on the hook at the bend.
3. Take three turns of silk as a butt, come back to where you tied in the rib and tie in the grizzle hackle. These turns of silk must show clearly behind the peacock.

4. Tie in the peacock herl.
5. Take the silk to just behind the eye and wind the peacock herl to that point before tying off and removing the waste.
6. Take the hackle forward in a palmered manner to the eye, tie off and remove the waste.
7. Wind the rib forward in the opposite direction to the herl and hackle and 'wiggle' it as you do so to stop it trapping the hackle fibres.
8. Tie off at the eye, remove all waste, form a small head, whip finish and varnish.

## Bob Lomax Paraloop Version
*Fly tied by Bob Lomax*

**Materials:**

Hook:   Dry-fly hook, size 14, 16 or 18.
Silk:   Veevus Black 14/0.
Tag:    Fine flat silver tinsel.
Butt:   Orange silk or fine floss.
Body:   Peacock herl – only one or two herls.
Hackle: Grizzle cock.

**Tying Instructions:**

1. Ensure you have a gallows tool or alternative attached to your vice. This is essential to hold two loops of silk around which you will tie the hackle.
2. Run the silk down to the bend in neat touching turns.
3. Tie in the flat silver tinsel and form a small tag on the hook at the bend.
4. Tie in a small length of orange silk or fine floss and form a small butt forward of the silver tag.
5. Tie in the peacock herl.
6. Wind the peacock herl to a point where you would normally form a thorax and tie it off but leave it hanging.
7. Take two loops over the gallows tool.

*Note: See fly no. 5 Grey Duster for details on forming loops on the gallows tool.*

8. Tie in the hackle so it lies alongside the hook shank where you have created the loops.
9. Wind the hackle up the silk loops for about four or five turns and then back down again.
10. Tie off the hackle with a few turns of silk around base of the silk loop post and remove the waste. The hackles can be stroked back towards the bend, doubling them, if required. This allows the hackles to form a more 'V' shape when pulled over towards the hook eye.
11. Continue winding the peacock herl to form a small thorax in front of the hackle leaving enough room to fold over the hackle and tie off behind the eye. Remove the excess herl.
12. Leaving the silk at the eye now fold the hackle over towards the front of the hook

and tie down. Tie off and remove the waste.

13. Form a small head, whip finish and varnish.

**Fishing Method:** Whenever you think of using a fancy fly, think about this one.

All the dry flies you need ...

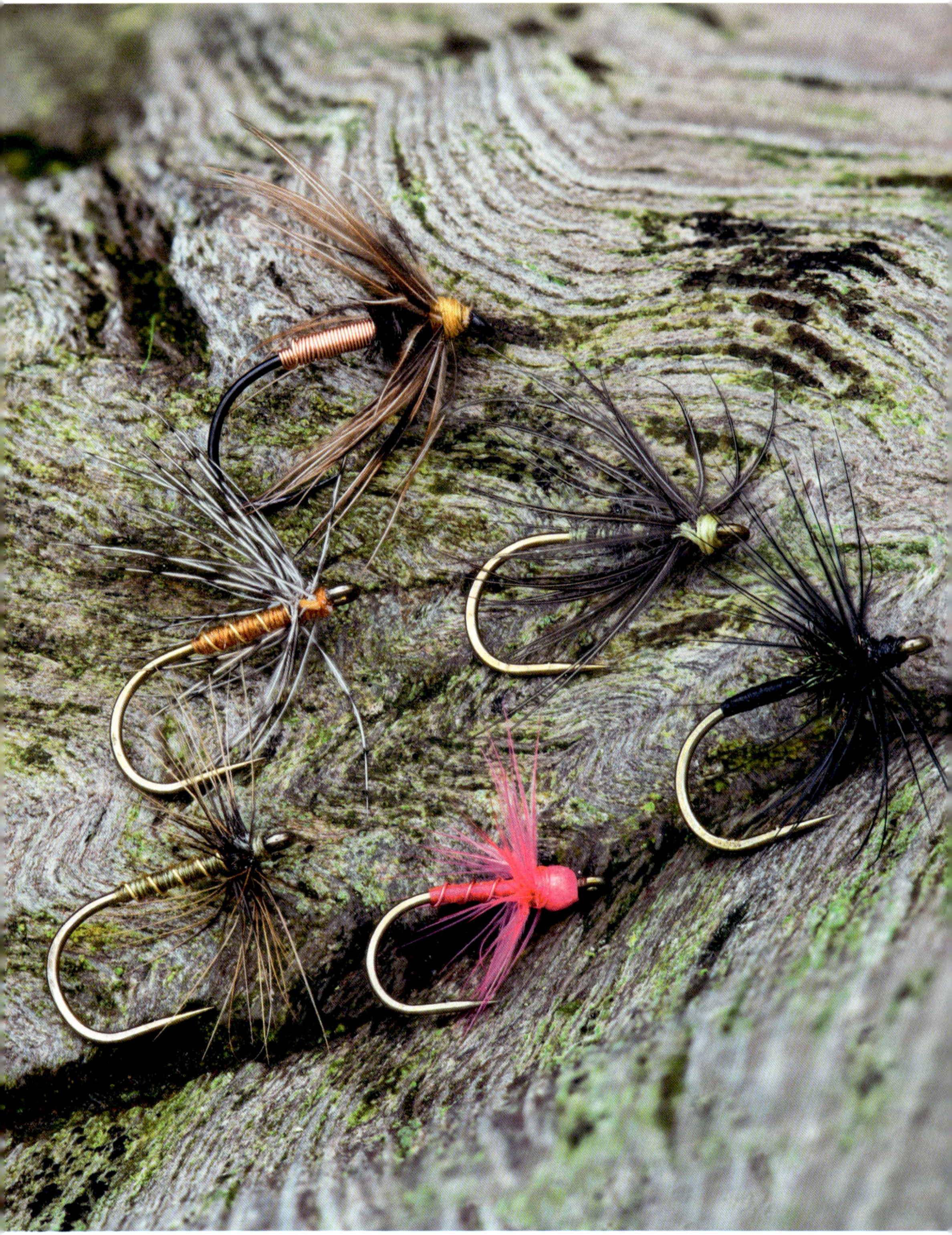

# Chapter Five

# Wet Flies

Wet flies have been used in flyfishing since the dawn of time. Well, even if not quite that far back, certainly as long as men have used flies to catch fish they have fished them underwater.

Famous anglers in the past like Dame Juliana Berners, John Dennys, Isaac Walton, Charles Cotton and Colonel Robert Venables, as well as all those well-known northern spider men would have used the wet-fly regularly and, probably exclusively.

Authors much more competent and diligent than I have researched the history of wet flies in great detail and have shown much more resolve and patience in ploughing the furrows of the past to uncover information about the origins of flyfishing and its most important element – the thing on the end of the line – and I don't propose to even attempt to emulate any of their works here.

Let's just say that there is an almost endless list of wet-fly patterns available to the fly fisherman. Many of these are designed for, and used in, quite different situations from that in which the grayling angler will find himself. We are not really interested in, for example, flies designed for loch fishing in Scotland, but we are very interested in patterns originating and perfected in the north of England where grayling fishing has been popular for centuries.

And it is probably because of my northern background that the wet flies I like, and have used successfully, all had their origins in that part of the country, and are all of the spider type. Winged wet-flies will work for grayling without a doubt, but I prefer spider patterns, or soft-hackles as they describe them on the other side of that large pond to the west of Ireland.

I use relatively few wet-fly patterns, which I think is probably a result of spending much of my fishing life on chalkstreams where still to this day the use of a wet-fly fished downstream is considered a hanging offence! The other reason I use few patterns is because the ones I do use work well and I haven't found it necessary to add to their number. No doubt if I moved back up north then I would start to fill my box with some more essential patterns.

I can thoroughly recommend every wet-fly in this section for use on any type of river – including chalkstreams where allowed, or where the keeper is too lazy to patrol!

# 26  Partridge & Orange

This has been a staple spider pattern for more years than anyone can remember, especially in its homeland of the north of England, and particularly Yorkshire. Pick up virtually any northern fly pattern book from the 19th or early 20th century and you will find this fly, often called the Orange Partridge.

I have used this fly ever since I started flyfishing and it can be fantastically successful. It always has a place on the three-fly cast I put up to start my grayling autumn season on the first day after the trout season ends on the Wylye. Fished as a spider it can be successful throughout the year and especially, in my experience, when there are olives about. It has been variously described as a fly which can represent caddis pupa, sunken spinners, olive nymphs, etc., although I think Malcolm Greenhalgh hit the nail on the head when he suggested that grayling, and trout just like the orange body because it is a colour to which they respond. Considering how many other orangey flies there are which are known grayling catchers I can go along with that idea quite happily.

Edmonds and Lee, in *Brook and River Trouting*, stated that the fly should be 'hackled with a brown mottled (not barred) feather from a partridge's neck or back.'

There are differing opinions as to whether it should have a rib or not. I like mine to be ribbed and use a very fine gold wire to do that job. I think it helps with the segmentation look and helps to make the fly a bit more robust.

And, finally, if you want to be authentically 'northern' in your tying, make sure the body is not too long. Tie this in the Clyde style, for instance, and you would keep the body very short. In Yorkshire it would be longer but still should not take up the whole shank of the hook.

*Suck the Silk!* Among wet fly aficionados the colour of the silk for the P&O is absolutely critical. Edmonds & Lee state quite precisely that is must be 'orange silk, No. 6a' and I was always taught to use Pearsall's Gossamer 6a. when it is wet this silk develops the deep orange-mahogany shade that is so important to the fly. Apparently back in the late 1980s or early 1990s Pearsall changed the nature of the dye they used for 6a such that the deep orange-mahogany colour didn't develop anymore when the fly was wet. Consequently 'old' dyed 6a gossamer silk was, and I think still is, much sought after by spider-men!

And so it was that, one day some years ago, I picked up Russell Murray, who is a better friend than I deserve, from his house in Rawtenstall, Lancashire, for a day's fishing on the Wharfe at Bolton Abbey. Driving through the village of Earby, Russell told me that he had heard, on some secretive spider fly-tying grapevine, that the local tackle shop had a stock of 'old' 6a and we should go and get some. Into the shop we went to find a little old lady behind the counter, the mother of the owner. Russell got her to open every drawer in the shop until we found the Pearsall's spools, then he had her put the drawer on the counter while he then proceeded to pick up and suck every single spool of 6a until

# Partridge & Orange

*Fly tied by the author*

**Materials:**

**Hook:** A suitable wet-fly hook, size 14 to 18, or one made especially for spider flies with a straight eye such as the excellent Partridge L3A/S, currently available (2016) only down to size 16.

**Silk:** Pearsall's Gossamer shade 6a, or another orange silk which goes darker when wet.

**Rib:** Fine gold wire.

**Body:** Tying silk.

**Hackle:** Brown mottled (not barred) feather from a partridge's neck or back.

**Tying Instructions:**

1. Run the silk down the shank in neat touching turns, but do not run all the way down. Choose the length of the body to suit yourself – and your critical friends! Don't wax the silk or the colour will not develop properly when wet.
2. Tie in the fine gold wire rib.
3. Wind the silk back towards the eye in neat touching turns again stopping just short.
4. Rib in the opposite direction to that you have wound the silk and tie off at the eye and remove the waste.
5. Tie in the partridge feather ensuring you tie it in by the tip not the butt. To do this pull backwards a few of the fibres at the tip and tie in using the fine quill which is now exposed. Cut off the waste tip.
6. Wind the hackle for only one or two turns, tie off and remove the waste.
7. Form a small head, whip finish and varnish.

**Fishing Method:** A truly great spider pattern. As well as all the normal wet-fly fishing methods it can be surprisingly good treated with a little floatant and fished upstream in the surface film as an olive emerger.

**Note:** All things considered I guess the 'new' 6a silk works OK and if that is all you can get, then use it. Alternatively, go online and visit www.pearsallsembroidery.com to buy some Langley Superfine silk, shade LT1089 Antique Orange, which is their 6a equivalent. It was dyed specifically to match a sample of 6a given to them by Louis Noble. This is an excellent company who exhibit at the British Fly Fair International each year and have a fantastic range of 53 shades of gossamer silks for fly-tying.

Russell approved 'old' 6a plus a rogue 'new' 6a on upper right

it was thoroughly soaked and he could see exactly what colour it had turned. Those he judged to be 'old' dyed ones he put on one side and the others he threw back into the drawer. The old lady was speechless, but Russell was totally oblivious to her reaction to his strange behaviour. As I followed him out of the door I could see the lady's mouth going but no words were coming out. The moral being that you should be very picky about the silk you use to tie your P&O's and give it a real good sucking first it check it out!

## 27 Waterhen Bloa

The use of yellow silk and a very light dubbing of mole, matched with the dark smoky waterhen feather, creates a very edible looking morsel for a grayling. The mixture of yellow and blue-grey is a great combination in a fly, creating that overall impression of olive that can make such an effective fly. This can also be seen, for example, in the Greenwell's Glory with its olive hue caused by the brown wax on yellow silk.

Born in 'Tykeland,' the Waterhen Bloa is highly regarded by Yorkshire anglers. It is another traditional fly that got the Edmonds & Lee treatment and it must, as

## Waterhen Bloa
*Fly tied by the author*

**Materials:**

**Hook:** A suitable wet-fly hook, size 14 to 18, or one made especially for spider flies with a straight eye such as the Partridge L3A/S, currently available (*2016*) only down to size 16.

**Silk:** Pearsall's Gossamer shade 4 yellow or a substitute yellow silk. Again Langley Superfine comes to the rescue with shade LT1084 Old Yellow.

**Body:** Tying silk.

**Overbody:** Extremely light dubbing of mole's fur.

**Hackle:** Underwing covert feather from a waterhen, picked from near the shoulder or knuckle part of the wing.

**Tying Instructions:**

1. Run the silk down the shank in neat touching turns but do not run all the way down. Choose the length of the body to suit yourself.
2. Dub the silk extremely lightly with mole fur. Pinch this from the skin, don't cut it. The dubbing must be just a whisper so that the silk colour shows through clearly.
3. Wind the dubbed silk back towards the eye in moderately open turns stopping just short.
4. Tie in the waterhen feather ensuring you tie it in by the tip not the butt. To do this pull backwards a few of the fibres at the tip and tie in using the fine quill which is now exposed. Cut off the waste tip.
5. Wind the hackle for only one or two turns, tie off and remove the waste.
6. Form a small head, whip finish and varnish.

**Fishing Method:** A truly great spider pattern which I will happily fish with anywhere there are grayling.

they tell us, be tied with Pearsall Gossamer No. 4 Yellow. Personally I find Gossamer a little thick for much of my tying but on spiders where it forms the body I use it all the time. Fortunately, unlike 6a, the No. 4 silk seems to have maintained its true colour over the years – so no need to go sucking any spools in back street tackle shops!

# 28 Greenwell's Glory Spider

Several flies are equally successful if fished dry or wet and, like the Red Tag or Sturdy's Fancy, the Greenwell's Glory makes a great wet-fly. It is often tied in classic wet-fly fashion, with a wing sloping backwards, but I prefer it dressed as a spider. Simply substitute a furnace or Greenwell's hen hackle for the normal cock one.

Make sure you only take 1 or 2 turns of the hackle to avoid over-hackling and reducing the ability of the hackle to flow over the body.

## Greenwell's Glory Spider
*Fly tied by the author*

**Materials:**

**Hook:** A suitable wet-fly hook, size 14 to 18, or one made especially for spider flies with a straight eye such as the Partridge L3A/S, currently available (2016) only down to size 16.

**Silk:** Yellow silk, well-waxed with brown cobbler's wax to create a light olive hue.

**Rib:** Fine gold wire.

**Body:** Tying silk.

**Hackle:** Good quality furnace or Greenwell's soft hen hackle.

**Tying Instructions:**

1. Run the waxed silk down the shank in neat touching turns but do not run all the way down. Choose the length of the body to suit yourself.
2. Tie in the fine gold wire rib.
3. Wind the silk back towards the eye in neat touching turns again.
4. Rib in the opposite direction to that you have wound the silk and tie off at the eye and remove the waste.
5. Tie in the hen hackle ensuring you tie it in by the tip not the butt. To do this pull backwards a few of the fibres at the tip and tie in using the fine quill which is now exposed. Cut off the waste tip.
6. Wind the hackle for about one or two turns only, tie off and remove the waste.
7. Form a small head, whip finish and varnish.

**Fishing Method:** A truly great olive pattern which works well when used with any of the methods of spider fishing.

# 29 Pink Spider

I was standing talking with Steve Rhodes three or four years ago at the British Fly Fair International when the subject got around to pink as a useful colour for grayling flies, and to the general value of spider patterns as well. Inevitably we ended up at pink spiders! The Chevron Hackles stand was close by so we spoke to Christina, the very nice lady who runs the business, and subsequently each ordered a hen cape to be dyed in a bright pink.

A few days later our capes arrived and we separately started tying flies. My version was constructed as shown below, with a pink fluorescent bead – only a small one – added in front of the hackle to encourage

## Pink Spider
*Fly tied by the author*

### Materials:

**Hook:** A suitable wet-fly hook, size 14 to 18, or one of the Partridge Spider L3A/S hooks which are only currently available (2016) down to size 16.

**Silk:** Bright fluorescent pink, e.g. Danville shade 508.

**Rib:** Extra fine pink wire.

**Bead:** Fluorescent pink – tungsten or brass.

**Hackle:** Bright pink hen hackle.

### Tying Instructions:

1. Put the bead onto the hook ensuring the rebated side is towards the back.
2. Tie on the silk and run it down to the bend in neat touching turns. This is important because the silk will form the body and we want as neat an underbody as possible.
3. At the bend tie in the pink wire.
4. Take the silk back to the back of the bead in neat touching turns.
5. Rib with the wire in the opposite direction to the one you wound the silk and, at the back of the bead, tie off and remove the waste.
6. Tie in the hen hackle behind the bead, wind on just one or, at most, two turns, tie off and remove the waste.
7. Whip finish behind the bead and varnish the whippings. Here is where an acupuncture needle will help because we are dealing with a very small area to be varnished.

**Fishing Method:** Fish either on its own or as part of a team of three, either upstream or down.

the fly down a bit lower in the water column.

Fished on its own or with other spiders it has proved pretty successful and can be a fly to use in those days when a bit of extra brightness seems like it might help.

I understand Steve also had success with the patterns he produced from this colour of cape.

# 30 Black Magic

Black, or nearly black, wet flies can work very well for both trout and grayling. I use such flies as the Snipe & Purple, Fog Black and Stewart's Black Spider. But for this book I have chosen the Black Magic because it is well-named and I have had good experiences with it. It is a favourite of Harry Vallack, the well-known resident of Middleton-in-Teesdale, author of the booklet, *Fishing Flies for Upper Teesdale*, and the best wet-fly fisherman I have ever had the pleasure of fishing with.

Although probably of indeterminate provenance, it was publicised in the 1960s by Frederick Mold in his book *Presenting the Fly to the Trout*.

The tying is simplicity itself, a feature common in many of the very best flies, and I can recommend it either fished alone or in a team of three.

## Black Magic
*Fly tied by the author*

**Materials:**

**Hook:** Any suitable wet-fly hook, size 12 to 18.

**Silk:** Black.

**Body:** Tying silk.

**Thorax:** Peacock herl, two or three strands. Mold added a few turns of copper wire under his thorax and this could be a useful option if the fly needs to go deeper than normal.

**Hackle:** Black hen, very soft.

**Tying Instructions:**

1. Run the silk down the hook shank, in neat touching turns, as far as you feel you want to. Normally it is tied, in common with most spider patterns, with a short body.

2. Bring the silk back about half of its length and tie in the peacock herl. If using copper

wire under the thorax tie it in now and wind to just behind the eye.

3. Take the silk to a point just short of the eye to allow room for the hackle and wind the peacock herl to that point.
4. Tie off and remove the waste.
5. Tie in the hen hackle ensuring you tie it in by the tip not the butt. To do this pull backwards a few of the fibres at the tip and tie in using the fine quill which is now exposed. Cut off the waste tip.
6. Wind the hackle for about one or two turns only, tie off and remove the waste.
7. Form a small head, whip finish and varnish.

**Fishing Method:** Fish to suit your own particular style of spider fishing.

# 31 Copper Bodied Spider – *Brian Clarke*

It is great to have talented friends, even if it does show up your own inadequacies. There are some things you just know you could never do yourself and so it is reassuring to have someone around who can demonstrate the talents you wish you had but will never possess. My friend Brian Clarke is like that. When it comes to working with wood he is a Michelin-starred artisan! What he cannot do with a bit of oak or other hardwood isn't worth getting out of bed for. I have two beautiful hexagonal oak rod cases he made for my cane rods some years ago plus a set of extremely attractive and very practical fly-tying tools that I wouldn't part with for anything.

Fly-tying is another of his talents and I wonder how a man with such big hands manages it so well. He does though and is one of those tyers who can turn out flies as though they were peas from the same pod – my own creations are usually recognisable but not exactly perfect clones of each other! Brian's Copper Bodied Spider is just superb and is a welcome resident in my box. Here is the story behind the fly as told by Brian:

*Over the years I have found that successful flies are generally born in two ways, the first is through observation, knowledge of the species to be represented and great tying skill. The second is from coincidence, a little inspiration and a little tying skill. Sadly I can only claim my Copper Bodied Spider came from the second method, unlike the flies devised by my old friend Stuart Crofts whose flies are very much born from observation, knowledge and tying skill.*

*My Copper Bodied Spider happened through a series of coincidences, the first being the finding, while visiting a property at work, of a beautiful iridescent green/black feather from a black muscovy duck, kept as a pet in the back garden of the house, the length of the feather fibres almost two inches long. Knowing some North Country Spider patterns used the shorter fibres of the iridescent magpie's tail I thought the muscovy feather may just come in useful. I learned long ago to never refuse a gift of fur or feather. The second coincidence*

## Copper Bodied Spider

*Fly tied by Brian Clarke*

### Materials:

**Hook:** TMC 103BL, size 15 or 17.

**Body:** Fine copper wire.

**Thorax:** Three muscovy duck fibres twisted together. An acceptable substitute is herl from a magpie centre tail. It must be a centre-tail to get sufficient length.

**Hackle:** Barred neck feathers from a hen pheasant.

**Thread:** Pearsall Gossamer silk 6a.

### Tying Instructions:

1. Wind on the copper wire in touching turns down the hook from about 2 mm behind the eye and then back up again to the starting point and break the wire off.
2. Wind on the thread from behind the eye and take it just over the copper wire to secure it.
3. Catch in the muscovy duck fibres, twist into a rope and build up a small thorax. Leaving enough space for the hackle and whip finish.
4. Catch in the hackle (method of your choice) and wind on two turns and tie off.
5. Whip finish to form a neat head.

**Note:** The Black Muscovy duck feathers are hard to come by and to my knowledge these feathers are only available from time to time at a few good fly tying material stockists. Sadly my last supplier had a rather unfortunate encounter with an admirer - Mrs Waddle was eaten by Mr Fox. *(I have a small supply of these feathers although they are not as long as those from Mrs Waddle. I got mine from around an ornamental pond at some gardens in Cornwall where the resident muscovy ducks seemed to shed their feathers – Author)*

**Fishing Method:** It's a spider – so fish it like one. You can also fish this as an upstream nymph very successfully.

---

*was, when a shooting friend offered me a handful of hen pheasant neck feathers. The third coincidence happened while staying with the then Bolton Abbey river keeper, Charlie Hoyle, who mentioned an old spider pattern which had a copper-coloured body, but he could not give me the tying as he only had a vague knowledge of the fly.*

*This is where the inspiration comes in; I decided to use the two materials, muscovy duck and hen pheasant neck feathers, which as far as I knew were not being used in any of the traditional patterns of spiders.*

*At that time I was ribbing small flies*

*with fine copper wire rescued from an old telephone, I thought I would use this for the body, two or three fibres from the muscovy duck feather twisted together and wound on as a thorax and the hen pheasant neck feather as the hackle, all tied together with Pearsall's silk shade 6a. The fly looked the part so off I went to try it and to my pleasure and a little amazement it worked!*

*I have successfully used this fly for trout and grayling on the chalkstreams of the south and the rivers of the Yorkshire Dales, as a single fly or as point fly as part of a team. Friends who I have given it to try have also found it to be successful, indeed one friend, being invited as a guest to fish the River Wharfe at Kilnsey, when submitting his catch return at the end of the day, was so embarrassed at the number of fish caught using the Copper Bodied Spider he recorded a lesser number of fish.*

*I do not claim that the Copper Bodied Spider is the answer to an angler's prayer but what I would say is try it and see.*

Wow, so there we are! Isn't this how many great flies have come together – inspiration and chance merging to create something unique and worthwhile. Let's just gloss over who the Kilnsey friend might be though. I know and I ain't telling!

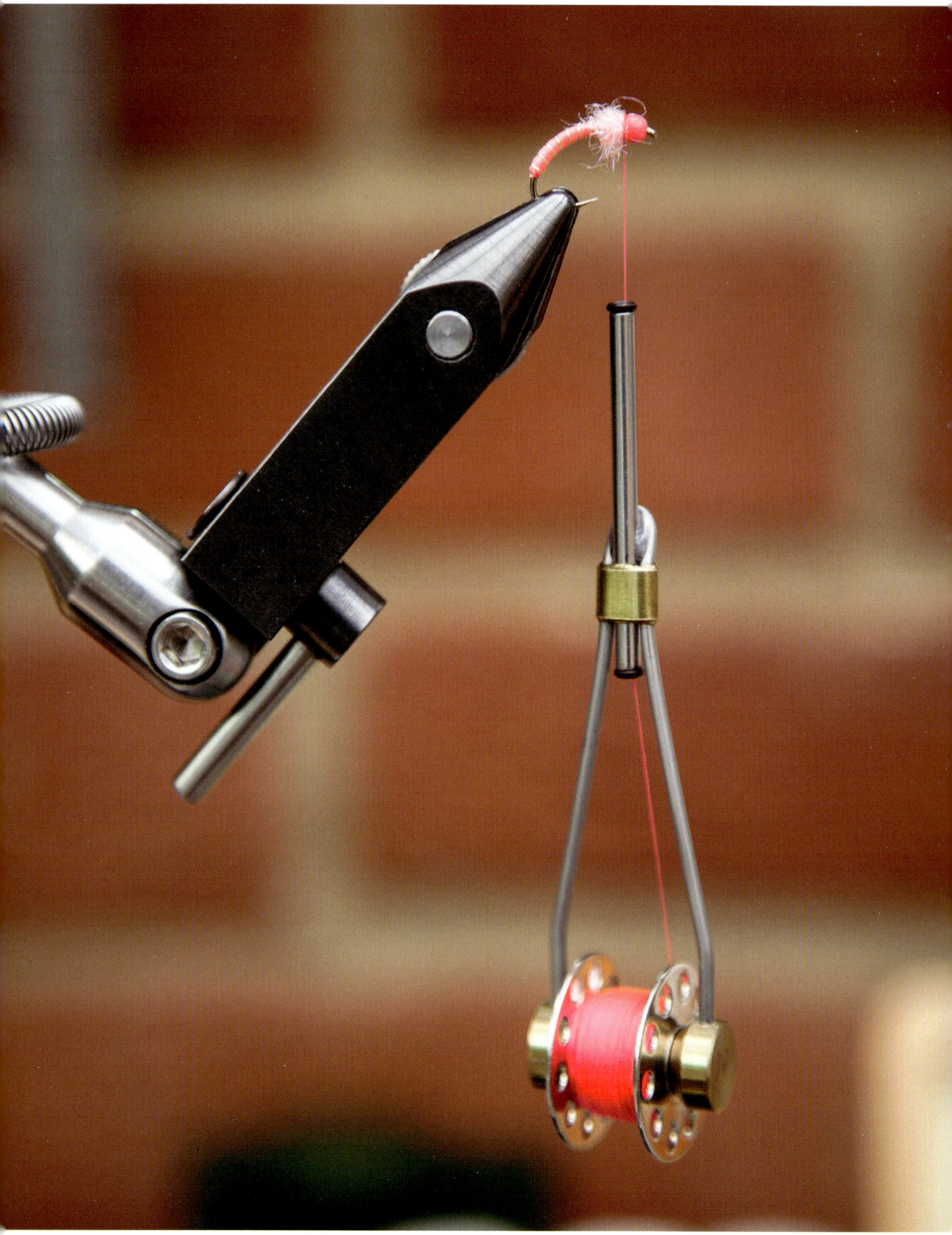

# Chapter Six

# Nymphs

I keep my fly-tying materials in a set of drawers in our conservatory. Yes, my wife is very understanding and lets me have a permanent fly-tying set-up with the drawers and a desk and shelves etc. It helps that she likes to fly fish also, of course, although it doesn't help that she is not a fly-tyer herself, so I have to keep her boxes filled as my fee for being allowed such a super tying set-up. Anyway, each one of these drawers is about three feet wide by about eight inches tall and there are six drawers in the unit. They are jam-packed to bursting with materials and I even have to keep my capes and saddles in a separate fly-tyer's travel bag because the drawers are just so full of stuff. I told you before I was a squirrel. Now just how much stuff is there and what it has cost me over the years I dread to think, but I am just happy that fly-tying materials do not come with a best-before date on them. At least most of those items I bought 30 years ago can still be used today. So I don't feel quite as bad about the cost because I can see it, quite rightly, as an investment.

Now, if I was to raid that unit to find materials for bodies, tails, ribs etc. for nymphs I am sure I would find 30 or 40 different items which could all be incorporated into a fly. Of course, I will never do that because the number of patterns would be astronomical.

The number of nymphs in this section is just 39. These are the ones I like and which catch fish. Now, there are many, many other nymphs which have been designed, or are going to be designed, which will also catch fish but there has to be a start point somewhere and this is it for me.

Let's just think of the types of nymph we use. There are those which are designed to imitate parts of the life cycle of waterborne flies such as the Pheasant Tail Nymph or Skues Nymphs for the upwinged flies. Then we have flies such as the Caseless Caddis or Peek-a-boo Caddis for the larval form of the sedge fly, Killer Bug and Gammy Shrimp for freshwater shrimps and several more all designed to imitate some form of living creature that inhabits grayling filled waters and which grayling like to eat.

Then there are those which we dreamt up one day! And there are lots of those patterns with most anglers having their own favourites, many of which look like the inventor had been on something when he dreamt them up!

This book does not, indeed could not, even attempt to include all those invented patterns of nymphs. In fact, I doubt you could ever write such a book because, even as you were writing it, more patterns would be continually being designed to make your book obsolete before it was even printed.

Let's look at the numbers game:

Take five materials for tails; five for ribs; five for abdomens and five for thoraxes.

With just these 20 items you can tie 625 completely unique flies.

Now, add five types of bead to those other materials and the combinations rise dramatically.

You can now tie 3125 separate and quite unique nymphs – and that is with just 25 items from your materials store.

Heaven knows how many unique flies I could tie with my materials mountain!

So, obviously, we have to be much more discerning when we decide to tie flies for our boxes. And until they invent clothing materials and threads that are as strong, relatively, as those which a spider uses to create its web and we all increase our body strength tenfold and get stronger boots, we will not be carrying 3 of each of 3125 nymph patterns in 3 sizes in our fly vests!

That, therefore, is part of the reason why there are just 39 nymph patterns in this section. But they are 39 designs which catch grayling regularly.

Fishing and designing nymphs to catch grayling is the one area that has seen the most significant development in the last 50 years and this has been somewhat logarithmic, with the last 15 or so years seeing massive changes in the designs of flies and their methods of use.

Long may the process of inventive nymph design continue ...

Iron Blue Dun
*Photo: Dr. Cyril Bennett MBE*

# 32 & 33   Skues Nymphs – *G E M Skues*

G E M Skues, often referred to as the father of nymph fishing, was one of the most influential anglers of all time. There is no doubt that he made the most significant contributions to flyfishing of anyone in the late 19th and early 20th centuries.

He fished for 56 years on the Abbots Barton stretch of the River Itchen above Winchester before moving to the Nadder in Wiltshire. It is believed that he caught his last trout on the Wylye waters of the Wilton Fly Fishing Club. I have had the massive pleasure of once fishing at Abbots Barton as a guest of my good friend Robin Mulholland, and I took great delight in fishing Duck's Nest Spinney which has always stuck in my mind as a classic stretch of the water which Skues regularly mentioned in his books. The other place I wanted to fish was McCaskie's Corner, but this, alas, is no longer part of the fishery. Happily I caught 21 grayling in Duck's Nest Spinney and some were, indeed, caught on Skues nymphs. I flew home ten feet above the ground!

Although Skues is known as a chalkstream expert he did not confine himself to those waters and for some years made an annual pilgrimage to Bavaria as well as fishing in Yorkshire. The accounts of the numbers of trout and grayling he caught in a typical day's fishing have me writhing with envy that those numbers just don't seem to be about anymore, whilst also

Duck's Nest Spinney on the Itchen at Abbots Barton

# Skues Nymph No. VI
*Fly tied by the author*

**Materials:**

**Hook:** Wet-fly, size 14 or 16.
**Silk:** Pale orange.
**Tail:** Two strands of darkish unfreckled cock guinea fowl neck – short.

*Blue dun hen or cock hackle fibres could be used, and although Skues says two, I think you really need four or six for a noticeable tail.*

**Abdomen:** Three or four strands of dyed olive heron herl (or substitute).
**Thorax:** Squirrel fur or dark hare's ear.
**Hackle:** Darkish blue dun cock hackle, one or two turns at most – very short.

**Tying Instructions:**

1. Take the silk down to the bend and tie in the tail fibres making sure they are short.
2. Tie in the heron herl or substitute and wind up to a point behind the eye where you will start the thorax.
3. Dub a thorax with the squirrel or hare's ear fur.
4. Tie in the hackle and wind one or two turns only then remove the waste.
5. Form a small head, whip finish and varnish.

**Fishing Method:** I have found this a useful fly at any time in the season and especially when small medium olives are hatching.

---

cringing with horror at the perfunctory manner in which he appeared to kill his captives. Still, in those days life was different and I am sure none of the fish went to waste, or to cats!

The fact that most of his fishing was on clear chalkstreams must have been instrumental in enabling him to develop his approach and ideas of nymph fishing. He was a natural observer, despite having only one properly functioning eye, and this stood him in good stead as he observed the ways trout rose and took nymphs.

His experiments encompassed many materials and tying methods until he arrived at his standard patterns of which there were several and included such novel ideas as using the herl from a blue and yellow macaw feather to form both body (yellow side) and rib (blue side) of one of his patterns. I have tied a similar nymph with some success.

He was, of course, at the very centre of the, now infamous, debate at the Flyfishers' Club in London on the 10th of February 1938. By all accounts he was quite badly treated in this debate. Supported by Dr Walshe who opened the debate, Skues and

## Skues Nymph No. X
*Fly tied by the author*

**Materials:**

**Hook:** Wet-fly, size 16 or 18.
**Silk:** Crimson.
**Tail:** Three strands of soft white hen hackle – short.
**Body:** Tying silk with mole fur dubbed, very lightly, and exposing two turns of silk at the tail.

*With our modern, finer, silks I would expose four to six turns.*

**Hackle:** Shortest hackle from throat of a cock jackdaw – one or two turns at most.

*A substitute could be a blue-grey hen hackle – very short.*

**Tying Instructions:**

1. Take the silk down to the bend and tie in the tail fibres making sure they are short.
2. Dub the silk with mole fur ensuring it is very light and wind up to just behind the eye. Taper the body so that the thickest part is at the thorax.
3. Tie in the hackle and wind one or two turns only then remove the waste.
4. Form a small head, whip finish and varnish.

**Fishing Method:** Although it is an Iron Blue Dun nymph, I have found this fly can work well irrespective of the presence of IBDs. It may be taken for any small dark nymph or even a drowned terrestrial. Whatever it is taken for it does work well at times.

---

his ideas were then attacked by several individuals but, in particular, by Sir Joseph Ball who attempted to systematically pick apart most of his theories relating to the behaviour of natural nymphs and fishing methods using artificials. Some of the arguments put forward against nymph fishing we would find laughable today, but I guess we should recognise that these were less liberated times than we enjoy now and concepts of what constituted gentlemanly behaviour were narrower and more rigid in their implementation.

Thankfully, neither Skues nor his devotees were muzzled or inhibited by this ill-judged debate and so nymph fishing increased in popularity and scope to that which we see and enjoy today. But George Edward Mackenzie Skues was 'the daddy!' In *Nymph Fishing for Chalk Stream Trout*, published in 1939, he listed 20 nymph patterns taking us on a journey from April to the end of the trout season. In particular I like his Medium Olive No. VI, marked for use in June and July, and his Iron Blue Dun No. X and these are the patterns I use now and are listed here.

# 34 BBWON – *Peter Hayes*

Now, Peter Hayes is a thinking angler and fly-tyer. If you haven't read his book *Fly Fishing Outside the Box: Emerging Heresies*, published by Coch-y-Bonddu Books in 2013, then you should do so right now! It does what it says on the tin – expounds heretical theories about flyfishing and offers thoughts to improve your performance without being too dogmatic or aiming to force any ideas upon you. I like it because it is a left field approach which, when my American employers tried to educate me some years ago, was called 'lateral thinking' (and they even brought the main man Edward de Bono along to teach us how to do it. I can't say I learned all that much!).

Peter puts a lot of thought and observation into his fishing, and experiments until he gets flies just right. His Better Blue Winged Olive Nymph or BBWON is just such a fly. The nymphs of the Blue Winged Olive are an important food source for both trout and grayling but devising a suitable artificial has dogged many an angler. Peter has produced one which works well and is a worthy occupant of this slot in the book. Here is what he has to say about its development:

> *The larvae of many ephemerid species, worldwide, cock their abdomens and tails up like a scorpion when at rest, and between bursts of swimming. It has always seemed worthwhile to me to tie some nymph patterns with bodies that curve round the bend of the hook, weighted so as to fish 'upside down', hook point upwards, to imitate this feature. This is a particularly strong characteristic of Ephemerella and Seratella species (in the UK, the BWO). They swim poorly, with many 'rocking horse' kicks and rests, rather than with an animated continuous wriggle as do, for example, Baetis nymphs. It has the added advantage of your being able to fish the fly close to the riverbed with fewer hitch-ups on rocks and weed. My 'BBWON' (Better Blue Winged Olive Nymph) pattern is now tied to achieve these results. Interestingly, many of the PTNs tied by Frank Sawyer were tied more than somewhat round the bend, and depending on the amount of copper armature wire used, may well have fished upside down and mimicked the BWO nymph rather well (although he thought himself that to imitate it was impossible). The upside down hook attitude and the animal's body shape can be reinforced, if you use a heavy sproat bend hook like the Kamasan B175, tie the body and tails round the bend, and add a bead head.*
>
> *BWO nymphs have distinctly marked legs and tails, with contrasting small light and dark bars, so it is in my view worth imitating these with suitably marked squirrel hair. The nymph's colour, incidentally, varies according to where it is living and feeding—green on weed, brown on a brown-algaed river bed. Definitely tie some in alternative colours.*
>
> *The first version of this I published in* Fly Fishing & Fly Tying *magazine in 2002. But it is a fluid design which has been continually improved as my understanding of how artificial nymphs work underwater has developed. In its original shape it was responsible for some amazing catches of trout and grayling*

## BBWON

*Flies tied by Peter Hayes*

### Materials:

**Hook:** Kamasan B175 (but a heavy wire grub hook or jig hook would not be wrong), size 14 or 16.

**Silk:** Uni-thread 8/0, olive dun.

**Bead:** Black, tungsten or brass depending on the desired sink-rate. This nymph is simpler to tie with the bead at the head, but I often move the bead down the shank to form the rear of the thorax rather than the front of it, with the advantage of an even more definite upside down presentation.

**Tail:** Six or eight guard hairs of brown squirrel back, clearly barred with the light markings over dark brown. Not pheasant tail fibres as they will break off.

**Rib:** Darkish, reddish copper wire, not too bright

*I like Flybox micro wire, brown, 0.09 mm.*

**Abdomen:** Purplish, olive-dyed pheasant tail, three or four fibres, so as not to be too fat;

**Thorax & Legs:** Brown squirrel back as for the tail, spread out to an inch length in a dubbing loop and spun, wound on, and then clipped very tightly on the inside of the hook. The clipped area coloured black with waterproof marker. Two sequentially cured layers of UV resin.

### Tying Instructions:

1. Put the bead on the hook ensuring the countersunk side is to the back of the hook.

2. Carry the thread well round the bend of the hook to halfway round it, spin the thread and form a small ball to splay the tail fibres.

3. Tie in the copper wire ribbing, tail fibres of squirrel, and pheasant tail for the abdomen. Have the copper wire project underneath and make sure that the tail fibres splay in the direction of the hook curve.

4. Wind the abdomen without twisting the pheasant tail fibres, and rib in the opposite direction with the copper wire, finishing off behind the bead.

5. Wind the thread back about an eighth of an inch to where the rear of the thorax will be, remembering that the BWO

nymph has a long thorax relative to its abdomen compared with other nymphs.

6. Form a dubbing loop, cut a long sparse crosswise slice of squirrel back off the skin and insert it into the dubbing loop prior to spinning it.

7. Wind the thread to behind the bead and then wind the spun dubbing loop up to the bead to form the thorax and legs, and tie off securely.

8. With very fine sharp scissors snip off all the dubbed fibres down to the thread on the curved side of the hook.

9. Colour this area black with a black waterproof marker pen.

10. Apply and cure with UV the first coating of varnish.

11. Apply and cure with UV a second coating of varnish to form a bulging wing case.

**Fishing Method:** BWO nymphs can be grazing on the bottom, on a structure of any kind, or on weed. Their colour will be that of their grazing grounds so if you are finding them on weed, tie this pattern in green. The main objective is to get down to the feeding area whilst maintaining the ability to spot a take, without hanging up all the time – but strike at any hesitation of the leader or indicator. Fish with confidence.

*on the rivers Wylye and Frome – big fish and lots of them. My friend Owain Mealing read the article, tied some up and took them to the Usk where he caught a succession of big trout to over 4 pounds. He came to thank me at the Fly Fair and we became fishing partners both in the UK, and in Ireland and New Zealand.*

*The next version was published in my book, Fly Fishing Outside the Box, and this has proved to be an even greater success, especially on the Derbyshire Wye.*

*Further refinement has come with the current version which uses a black tungsten bead and is tied on a Kamasan B175 hook with its exaggerated Sproat bend.*

See what I mean about the thinking fly-tyer and the experimentation to get it just right? And it is a very good fly which will always be in my box.

# 35 & 36   Sawyer Killer Bug – *Frank Sawyer*

If ever a fly was well named it is the Sawyer Killer Bug. Of course, in these days where our approach is normally one of catch and release for grayling then its name could be said to be just a touch non-PC! Yet, in defence of Frank, at the time he invented the fly the killing of grayling was quite common. It is just most unfortunate that, in those unenlightened days, much of that killing was down to a misguided idea of vermin control. However, I'll step down from my Grayling Society soapbox for a moment and discuss the fly.

Frank Sawyer, shown in action in the picture opposite, was, for many years, keeper of the Officer's Fishing Association waters on the Upper Avon near Netheravon, Wiltshire. It is interesting to note that in 1967 a more egalitarian approach from the organisation saw it opened to other ranks and it then became known as the Services Dry Fly Fishing Association, which is the name it still carries. In angling circles Frank is best remembered for his excellent books *Nymphs and the Trout* and *Keeper of the Stream*, and for the creation of the Pheasant Tail Nymph. Amongst his other well-known flies is the Killer Bug.

Frank was a man who earned his living from managing a river for the benefit of the anglers of the Association. At that time there was a general feeling that grayling offered some form of unfair competition to trout and that their numbers should be controlled. Subsequent scientific research has shown that this belief is flawed and that the biggest dangers to a healthy trout population in a chalkstream are water conditions and other environmental factors, rather than the presence of grayling.

Stocked trout undoubtedly adversely affect wild populations also. Although Frank seemed not to advocate wholesale culling of grayling, nevertheless, as part of his work, he removed grayling from the river.

In inventing the Killer Bug he was solely focussed on producing a fly that worked very well in extracting grayling. Being a country lad, and not a wealthy man, he naturally looked to use easily obtainable, low-priced materials. A practical fly-tyer, tying flies for his personal use to catch fish and not to gain praise or win fly-tying competitions. he therefore looked to tie simple flies that could be reproduced quickly and easily with the minimum of materials. He also pioneered the use of copper wire instead of tying silk, thus using just one item for two purposes – weight and binding. Like his other nymph patterns, his Killer Bug uses just two materials – moderately heavy reddish copper wire, usually obtained by taking solenoids out of electrical equipment, and Chadwick's 477 wool which was sold at haberdashers for darning socks in the days when clothes were repaired and not just replaced. Simple, quick to tie, low priced and deadly, it is an essential fly for anyone fishing the chalkstreams and works well in many other types of river and in lakes. As well as being a deadly grayling fly it has also accounted for many brown and rainbow trout, and Frank even caught salmon on one!

A word about Chadwick's 477. I believe it was made at the mills located in the tiny village of Eagley near Bolton in Lancashire, and probably elsewhere. The three Eagley Mills were originally built by James Chadwick & Brother in the early 19th century. I grew up nearby and went to the junior school directly opposite them. I used to fish for sticklebacks in one of the mill lodges that was sited alongside the boundary

Chadwick's 477 and 33 cards plus Scanfil shade 61 and one of Mum's 'tennis balls'!

railings. (A mill lodge was a small pond which was used to provide water originally for steam power but also, I think, to help humidify the mills to prevent breakages of cotton when spinning). Eagley Brook, a source of power and water, was one of those waterways you did not want to fall into. If you didn't die from drowning you would certainly have died from poisoning since there were bleach works, dye works and a paper mill in the couple of miles above the mills. Thankfully, in common with many other rivers in parts of the old industrial landscape, Eagley Brook is now much healthier and sustains a population of trout. In fact, it was the subject of a major fish kill in 2006 when an estimated 10,000 trout up to 3lbs in weight were killed in a pollution incident. Chadwicks were eventually taken over by J & P Coats of Paisley in 1896 and the mills continued to operate until 1972. They are still standing, having been converted into rather nice apartments.

As all Killer Bug fans know, Chadwick's 477 is in extremely limited supply, having not been made for over 40 years. I have seen full cards advertised for anything from £50.00 to over £100.00! It has become almost mystical in its appeal and has spawned several substitutes, some of which are, frankly, useless as copies of the original. I obtained my supply of 477 by just asking my mother one day in the 1980s if she had any darning wool. You see, for a time she worked as a cook at the nursery set up in Eagley Mills for the worker's children and, like many of the employees had a rather large supply of different wools which had been 'acquired' at some point or other. I was presented with several cards of shade 33 but no cards of 477. However, she also gave me several balls of wool which looked remarkably like the real thing. As it happened I had a small piece of 477 which

Dry & wet shade 33 (*left*) & 477 (*right*) KB's. Nothing in it as far as colour is concerned is there?

some kind soul had once given to me so out came my microscope and I went to work establishing which of these 'tennis balls' was 477 and which wasn't. Let's just say I will never have to trawl the internet to get any genuine material! And no, I don't sell it, although if you ever happen to bump into me at a show or on the riverbank I am sometimes known to give a bit of it away.

What is the secret of 477? Well the most important feature of the Killer Bug is that it changes colour once it is thoroughly wet. In fact, I always feel it never starts working until it has been cast and re-cast about half a dozen times. The wool, which has a distinct beige look when dry, once wetted acquires a pinkish hue over the beige undercolour. Is this the trigger? Who knows and, frankly, who cares as long as it is successful in fooling Her Ladyship.

I think that there is too much mysticism attributed to the 'real' 477. If you look at it closely under a strong lens you will find it consists of many fine almost colourless fibres, which I guess are the wool in the 70% wool / 30% nylon mix. It also has several reddish fibres which are probably the nylon. What seems to separate shade 33 and shade 477 is the number of these reddish fibres: there are less of them in the 33. However, accepting that the pinkish hue is critical to the fly's success I can vouch for the fact that shade 33 also produces this colour change although not quite so pronounced as 477. I have no problems at all in using flies tied with 33 as opposed to 477 and, although I have never carried out any form of quasi-scientific analysis, I am sure that 33s are so close in terms of success to 477s that I have no reservations in wholeheartedly recommending them to anyone. And, importantly, I have seen cards of shade 33 in charity shops for pence and on-line for reasonable sums. I also recently found a very good 477 substitute in a haberdasher's shop in Bognor Regis: a mending wool called Scanfil is a 55% wool / 45% nylon mixture, and shade 61 is a little darker than 477 but turns a very good pinky colour when wet.

Whatever the reason for the success of the Killer Bug, it will always find a place in my chalkstream fly box.

# SAWYER KILLER BUG SIZE 10

## Killer Bug – Original Version
*Originals supplied by Margaret Sawyer*

**Materials:**

Hook: Standard wet-fly hook, in size 10 to 16 – yes it does work in a 16!

Underbody: Reasonably thick copper wire dependent on hook size.

Body: Chadwick's 477 or 33 or substitute

**Tying Instructions:**

1. Place the hook in the vice and run copper wire from the bend to the eye in neat touching turns.
2. Then, again using neat touching turns, take the wire back to the bend and leave it hanging there.
3. Lap on the wool at the eye and run it, in neat touching turns, down to the bend.
4. Run the wool back up to the eye, then back down to the bend.
5. Tie off the wool with the copper wire using four or five turns.

You may find that a tiny drop of Superglue will help to secure the wire more firmly when you tie off at the bend. Alternatively a couple of half hitches will do the job. Please note that the finished fly should be cigar/sausage shaped.

Good luck – it is the world's easiest fly to tie – you don't even need a vice!

**Fishing Method:** This fly was devised to be fished in the classic chalkstream style of upstream nymph. Once cast upstream of a spotted fish or likely lie it is allowed to drift back towards the angler without any drag. Obviously, you need to retrieve line to keep in touch with the fly, but you must not retrieve so fast that you move the fly more quickly than the current. This is a form of drag, and may discourage fish. The Killer Bug also works well, in a small size, as the nymph in a Klink & Dink set up. In fact, I have even bait fished with it successfully using a trotting rod and centrepin reel.

# Sawyer Killer Bug – My Version
*Flies tied by the author*

*I have often thought that if Frank Sawyer had possessed some of the materials we have nowadays his flies would have looked a little different. I particularly think this in relation to the Killer Bug.*

*I usually tie mine on a grub hook which is also my standard shrimp hook. In fact I often tie KB's on gold grub hooks which seem, to me, to emphasise the shrimpiness of the fly – see the Gammy Shrimp pattern and my views on shrimp colouring. I feel certain that Frank would approve and would have even tied them on these hooks himself if they had been readily available in his day.*

*Certainly I feel that the combination of the pinkish wet Chadwick's, copper wire underbody just adding to the colour, and the gold hook making a further contribution all adds up to a shrimp imitation juicy enough to fool any fish.*

## Materials:

**Hook:** Standard grub hook such as Kamasan B100 or B100G, size 10 to 16.

**Underbody:** Reasonably thick copper wire, dependent on hook size.

**Body:** Chadwick's 477 or 33 or substitute.

## Tying Instructions:

*These are basically the same as those for the original Killer Bug shown earlier. However, here is a tip to save some of that precious Chadwick's 477.*

1. Start your copper wire at the bend and take it up to the eye and back to the bend.
2. Then tie in your Chadwick's wool at the bend with a couple of turns of wire to secure it.
3. Take the wool in touching turns to the eye and back again.
4. Now you can tie off as the earlier instructions and you have your fly, except this has used just two layers of wool, not three.

*And it looks pretty well the same once it is in the water because the curve of the hook helps convey the chubbiness of the original tied on a straight hook with its extra layer of wool.*

*Crumbs! There must be some Yorkshire blood in me to be so thrifty. A frightening thought for a Lancastrian!*

**Fishing Method:** As opposite

# 37 Utah Killer Bug – *David Southall*

This is another highly successful pattern used and recommended by Dave Southall. It was developed in the USA and, like the original Killer Bug, uses a very specific wool – although fortunately this one is still readily available.

Here are Dave's words about the development of this fly:

*In 2012 Utah Tenkara Guides mentioned on their website a variant of Frank Sawyer's Killer Bug using pink Uni thread, pink UTC wire and Shetland Spindrift wool in oyster colour. I wanted a heavier fly than one with a wire underbody so used a lead wire underbody overlaid with Globrite pink floss (used also as tying thread) for my version.*

*A lot of grayling have succumbed to my variant.*

*I also tied up a variant with Globrite orange floss that has accounted for several grayling over 3 lb and numerous smaller fish. Both colours are also good for trout.*

## Utah Killer Bug

*Fly tied by David Southall*

**Materials:**

**Hook:** Grub or heavy wire wet-fly hook.

**Silk:** Globrite floss, pink or orange.

**Underbody:** One or two layers of lead wire (second layer shorter than the first).

**Underbody Coating:** Globrite floss, pink or orange.

**Overbody:** Shetland Spindrift wool in Oyster colour. Coat the underbody with wet Superglue before tying in the overbody.

**Tying Instructions:**

1. Run the Globrite down to about halfway around the bend.
2. Wind lead over this layer of Globrite in touching turns, either one or two layers, and remove the waste.
3. Tie in the Spindrift wool at bend after leaving a small tag of Globrite.
4. Take the Globrite back to the eye.
5. Apply Superglue to the underbody and, whilst it is still wet, wind the Spindrift wool up to the eye. This does not need to be in touching turns as you can leave a little of the underbody showing up the length of the fly.
6. Tie off with Globrite, remove the waste, form a small head, whip finish and varnish.

**Fishing Method:** Whatever you would do with a Sawyer Killer bug, do with this one!

*With just one layer of wool the colour of the floss shows through giving a wonderful translucent effect when wet. I like to leave a coloured tag at the butt end of the fly.*

My own experience with this fly has been very good and it is truly a useful addition to the Killer Bug family even if it does look quite different from Sawyer's original. And, let's face it, any fly that can account for 3 lb grayling has just got to be in your box!

# 38  Frank Sawyer's Pheasant Tail Nymphs

In the past 30 years I must have seen hundreds, if not thousands, of Sawyer-style Pheasant Tail Nymphs or PTNs. Some were well tied and reasonably true to the original whilst others were, sad to say, abominations whose only resemblance to one of Frank Sawyer's was in the material used!

Although it is a simple fly, it is not easy to tie well. Like many successful flies it is important to consider the proportions when tying a PTN. How often have we looked at PTNs in shops and seen them with tails that are too long, bodies too short or fat, and thoraxes which are completely disproportionate to the rest of the fly?

I have never seen a PTN that looks as good as those I bought from Frank's widow Margaret in the late 1980s. For some years after Frank passed away there appeared in *Trout & Salmon* magazine a small advertisement offering Sawyer nymphs. Mrs Sawyer sold these from her cottage in Compton, near Enford, just a short distance up the Wiltshire Avon from Netheravon, at prices we would now consider to be silly. I remember writing to her to say that I thought her flies were worth much more than the 19p she was charging! I was pleased to see that she eventually raised the price to 25p but the flies were still a steal even at that price.

I corresponded with her for a while and, most notably, received a very nice letter from her in 1989 advising me that she was getting orders from the USA – South Dakota, California, North & South Carolina, New Mexico, Connecticut and New York – all mentioning my name. This was the result of me having read an article on tying Sawyer PTNs in the American magazine *Fly Fisherman* in which the author mistakenly, and rather stupidly, stated that the body material was peacock herl. Peacock herl on a fly called the Pheasant Tail Nymph – what a numpty!  Anyway, the English passion in me was aroused and I wrote a letter to the magazine outlining the error of the writer's way and advising readers that the correct material was, of course, herl from the centre tail feather from a male common pheasant. I also advised readers to contact Mrs Sawyer if they wanted the world's best Sawyer nymphs.

Anyway, I digress. The point is that the flies bought from her show most clearly all those features Frank sought in a successful nymph.

- Slim to cut through the water quickly
- Realistic profile

# SAWYER PHEASANT TAIL

## Frank Sawyer Original Pheasant Tail Nymph

*Originals supplied by Margaret Sawyer*

The dressing for the traditional, as originally conceived and as many feel the best, PTN.

**Materials:**

Hook: Any suitable wet-fly hook, size 14 to 18.

Frank used old sizes 1, 0 and 00, which translate to 15, 16 and 17.

Wire: Fine dark-coloured copper wire – adjust thickness for hook size.

Tail: Four cock pheasant centre tail herls.

Abdomen: Same.

Thorax: Same.

**Tying Instructions:**

1. Wind on the copper wire at the bend and take to the hook eye in touching turns.
2. Form a small thorax with the wire then run the wire from the thorax down to the bend and let it dangle.
3. At the bend tie in the herls with the ends pointing back to form tails about 3 mm long.
4. Twist together the pheasant tail herls and copper wire.
5. In close turns wind the herls/wire together to about 1 mm behind the eye.
6. Untwist the herls and wire so they are separated again.
7. Take a single turn of the wire to trap the herls.
8. In an open turn take the wire back to the back of the thorax.
9. Pull the separated herls over the top of the wire thorax and trap with a single turn of the wire at the back of the thorax.
10. In an open turn take the wire back to a point 1 mm behind the eye.
11. Take the herls to that point and tie off with half a dozen turns of wire.
12. Remove the waste herls and wire.

**Fishing Method:** This is THE fly for the classic upstream nymphing technique, including the induced take.

> 19 Compton, Enford
> Pewsey, Wilts SN9 6AZ.
>
> Dear Mr. Skuce,
>
> Thank you for your order for nymphs and enclosed cheque for $15.
>
> Actually our price has increased to £9.50 per card of ten so that your cheque is exactly correct.
>
> I am pleased to know that you consider the nymphs worth that amount.
>
> At 81 I am still fit and well and able to keep my interest in all things pertaining to fish and fishing, so yes thank you 1989 is proving pretty good for me.
>
> Yours sincerely,
> Margaret Sawyer.

A note from Mrs Sawyer about prices, sent in 1989

- Some weight, but not such that it adversely affects the profile
- Short tail like real nymphs
- Well-proportioned thorax
- Realistic colouring

As you will see from the photographs the flies were tied on what may now appear to be rather old-fashioned-looking hooks but there is no doubt that they are terrific-looking flies and are also, in my experience, superb catchers of both grayling and trout.

It only remains to say, when tying a PTN, please make sure that:

1. The hook is long enough to represent the longish and thin body of a natural.
2. The tail is not too long.
3. The copper wire is thin enough to perform its function of tying silk but thick enough to have sufficient weight.
4. The pheasant tail herls are long enough. Be fussy when you buy, or salvage from road kills or a shoot, centre tails and make sure you get ones that have the longest herls you can find.
5. The thorax is small enough to aid the overall slimness of the fly.
6. You finish the fly by half a dozen turns of wire at the eye, says Frank, although there is a short video (on YouTube in 2016) called, appropriately, *Frank Sawyer tying a Pheasant Tail Nymph* in which he appears to finish the fly with a single half hitch at the eye. This is generally how I do it also.

# 39 Pearly PTN – *Roger Smith*

This fly has gone through a period of development by my friend Roger Smith who represents the Grayling Society in the Welsh Marches. Roger is a remarkable man: slight, modest and quietly spoken, you wouldn't think that this retired biology teacher is a man who has led expeditions climbing the North Col of Everest and

## Pearly PTN
*Fly tied by Roger Smith*

### Materials:
**Hook:** Size 16 or 18 Partridge Patriot barbless jig hook SUJ or similar.
**Silk:** Brown.
**Bead:** Copper slotted tungsten bead 2.8 mm for size 16 and 2.5 mm for size 18 hook.
**Tail:** Six cock pheasant tail fibres.
**Rib:** Fine copper wire (fluorescent coating optional).
**Abdomen:** Four cock pheasant tail fibres.
*Don't use the six tail fibres for the abdomen because it will make it too fat.*
**Thorax:** Dark hare's ear dubbing.
**Thorax cover:** 2 mm clear Mylar tied onto each flank.

### Tying Instructions:
1. Put the bead onto the hook ensuring the slot is to the back so that the bead sits down correctly.
2. Take the silk down to the bend and tie in the tail fibres and remove the waste.
3. Tie in the rib and the abdomen fibres.
4. Take the silk to the back of the bead and wind the pheasant tail abdomen fibres to form the abdomen. Remove the waste.
5. Take the rib to the back of the bead in open turns, say about four or five, tie off and 'worry off' the waste.
6. Tie in short lengths of Mylar on the flanks of the fly alongside the thorax area. Remove the waste at the front end.
7. Dub a thorax with the hare's ear.
8. Pull each Mylar flank to the back of the bead and tie off then remove the waste, whip finish and varnish.

**Fishing Method:** Roger always fishes this using the 'Duo' or 'Klink & Dink' method, and if it works for him it will work for you too!

following Shackleton's route across South Georgia! He is also the author of that fine book, *Flyfishing the Welsh Borderlands*.

I asked Roger to tell me how he developed the fly and here is what he told me:

*The story behind the evolution of the Pearly PTN began when I started, a number of years ago, using the 'Duo' set up as my principal searching technique on the rivers and streams of the Welsh Borderlands that I frequent. Initially I used a heavily dressed Deer-hair Sedge or a Western Olive Klinkhåmer as the dry fly on a short dropper with a Gold-head Nymph suspended beneath to represent a darting or stone-clinging nymph. The results were most rewarding, and my catch rate increased noticeably. Then after completing the training for the Riverfly Partnership and starting to take regular samples from my local brook the first change I made to the nymph was to drastically reduce the size of hook to 16, 18 or even 20!*

*The advent of the heavier tungsten beads on the market meant that smaller beads could be used to advantage and I replaced the Gold-heads with slightly smaller copper-coloured tungsten beads. The copper colour seemingly more attractive to the fish!*

*I was aware that as the nymph falls through the water the fish need to be alerted by the material tied on the flanks and ventral (underside) of the nymph. Most of the patterns I originally used had a thorax cover on the dorsal (upper) side which was not visible to the fish until it had fallen below it in the water. Using clear 3/16th Mylar as thorax cover-material, I experimented by tying it to the ventral side of the thorax. The next move was to tie the Mylar into the flanks and I found that there appeared to be some benefit in this with many more takes by fish.*

*I noticed that the nymph frequently snagged on material close to or on the stream/river bed. To overcome this, the most significant change to the nymph occurred. I experimented by tying the nymph onto jig hooks which were just becoming popular and with their use I significantly reduced the frequency of snagging.*

*Evolution is a dynamic on-going process and so as new materials become available and my experimenting continues I expect there will be further changes!*

The fly is similar to a pattern devised some years ago by Simon Robinson called the Mary Copperhead Nymph. However, Roger has quite clearly spent a lot of time and effort in independently developing his fly and his idea of tying the Mylar on the thorax flanks is inspirational and, good scientist that he is, based on experimentation. It was experimentation well-spent as it is a superb catcher of grayling and is one of my own top patterns. I believe it accounted for over 200 of Roger's grayling catch in the Autumn of 2014 so that is praise indeed.

# 40 Copperbonce

This is a fly that I first tied in 2012 in an attempt to overcome a problem on the River Test. During the traditional grayling season, between mid-October and mid-March, there can be very high fishing pressure on those chalkstreams which offer reasonably priced day-ticket fishing. This, in turn, can mean that finding the right fly is not always easy.

Some of us who fish or guide on these rivers reached the conclusion a while ago that one of the most effective approaches was to fish Klink & Dink, Duo, Hopper & Dropper or New Zealand Style. (Any of those names will do – they all refer to the same method). This is, of course, the technique where you fish a small weighted nymph underneath a larger, buoyant, dry-fly. The dry-fly acts both as a lure and also as an indicator should a fish take the nymph.

The favourite nymph in this set up was a small Pheasant Tail or similar and I developed the Copperbonce as a variation on the standard with a copper bead and some twinkle around the thorax.

It has proved to be not only a great grayling fly but also a superb fooler of trout, and many a fat *Salmo trutta* – and even *Oncorhynchus mykiss* – has fallen for its charms.

## Copperbonce
*Fly tied by the author*

### Materials:

**Hook:** Any suitable wet-fly hook, size 14 to 18, but make sure the shank is not too short.

*Size 16 is the best all-rounder.*

**Silk:** Brown – make sure it is very fine to ensure build up behind the bead is not too excessive.

**Tails:** Cock pheasant centre tail herls – three or four.

**Bead:** Copper-coloured tungsten bead – adjust to suit hook size, fishing depths and river conditions. I normally use a 2.8 mm for size 14, 2.5 mm for size 16 and 2.0 mm for size 18 on UK chalkstreams.

**Rib:** Fine gold wire – adjust thickness for hook size.

**Body:** Same materials as Tails, above.

**Thorax:** Hends Spectra Dubbing No. 2 Orange, or Ice Dub.

### Tying Instructions:

1. Put the copper bead onto the hook and push up to the eye – with the countersunk section to the back of the fly.
2. Lap on the tying silk behind the bead

and run a few turns onto the hook shank. There is no need to ensure the bead is fixed at this stage.

3. Run the silk down to the bend and tie in fine gold wire for the ribbing.
4. Then tie in three or four herls from a cock pheasant centre tail feather with the ends pointing back to forms tails about 3 – 4 mm long.
5. Run the silk up the hook shank to behind the bead.
6. In close turns wind the herls together (you can twist them together to help this stage) to the back of the bead. Tie off, cut off and dispose of the waste.
7. Wind the gold wire up the hook shank in open turns, about four or five, in the opposite direction to the herls and secure at the back of the bead. Break off and dispose of the waste.
8. Build up some silk at the back of the bead to secure it – but not too much.
9. Dub a very small amount of the Spectra No. 2 Orange dubbing at the back of the bead.
10. Whip finish behind the bead and cut off.

**Fishing Method:** Use as you would any small weighted nymph. The common methods are, of course, the upstream nymph technique of the UK greats, Frank Sawyer or Oliver Kite, or alternatively, use the fly as the dropper on the Klink & Dink approach of a buoyant dry-fly and a nymph dropper. Lengthen the dropper tippet to suit conditions.

## 41  Black Bead CJ Ant – *Bo Cash*

When John Zimmerman came to the UK in 2014 and I guided him and his three students on the River Test he had asked if he could borrow a cane rod. I lent him a 7 foot 6 inch 5 weight impregnated cane rod which I had made up from a Partridge blank back in 1988, still as straight as a die and with a nice dry-fly action. He soon wandered off on his own, happy as a pig in you know what.

Later in the day when comparing notes, and after the furtive glancing around which accompanied the whispered tales of the Squirmy Wormy effectiveness – lest Halford should rise from his grave and marmalise us both – he told me about the Black Bead CJ Ant. In this instance I should point out that the CJ in this instance, refers to Copper John because it is a variant of that great fly.

The fly was designed by John's old friend and fishing mentor, William 'Bo' Cash, who until his retirement owned a flyfishing shop in Morganton, North Carolina. Bo had, for some years, enjoyed fishing with a plain black Copper John and also, at different times with a black ant pattern. Basically, he melded the two together and up came this fly.

It has been extremely successful in the area of its birth and, although it was never even contemplated that it could be a good grayling fly, especially since grayling in North Carolina are as abundant as bonefish in the Big Ditch (Manchester Ship Canal to non-Lancastrians), it has proved to be just that.

## Black Bead CJ Ant
*Fly tied by John Zimmerman*

**Materials:**

**Hook:** Daiichi 1710 size 14.
**Silk:** Black 6/0 thread.
**Bead:** Black 1/8" (3 mm) tungsten bead.
**Tails:** Black cock pheasant centre tail – four herls which are then split to form two tails each composed of two herls.
**Abdomen:** Black medium copper wire.
**Thorax:** Black Ice Dub.
**Hackle:** Black cock or hen hackle wound, then trimmed top and bottom.

**Tying Instructions:**

1. Put the bead onto the hook ensuring the rebated side is towards the back.
2. Run the silk down to the bend and tie in the pheasant herls. Then split the four herls into two by taking silk between them. This should create two splayed tails each with two herls.
3. Tie in black copper wire.
4. Take silk back to the back of the bead.
5. Wind copper wire up to the back of the bead in touching turns forming a nicely segmented body. Tie off and 'worry' off the waste.
6. Dub a thorax with the Ice Dub. This can be fairly chunky.
7. Tie in a small black hackle and wind just one turn.
8. Trim off the top and bottom of the hackle.
9. Take the silk to the back of the bead, whip finish and remove the waste. Varnish if you wish.
10. Pick out the Ice Dub a little but not too much.

**Fishing Method:** This is a fairly chunky fly and can be used with any nymphing technique.

When John Z used it over here that day it accounted for 17 of his 39 fish haul of trout and grayling. Not a bad bit of cut and shut fly welding then!

I have had many a good day with this fly since being introduced to its deadly charms.

Bo put its development like this:

*This pattern is basically a Black Copper John with modifications. I experimented with 8 previous flies and #9 was the first one that satisfied me. Each one prior to this one was slightly different. For lack of a better name, I am calling it a Black Bead CJ Ant. I think the small stream fish will eat it up. I had some success about 2 months ago with a plain old black Copper John and I used to love to fish sinking Black Bead Ants. The sink rate on this ought to be good with both wire and bead pulling her down. The black Ice Dub adds a lot of sparkle which actually reflects several different colors.*

# 42  Green Genie

I like green. It is one of my favourite colours. That means I wear a lot of green and I like green flies. It is good thing then that this green fly works really well.

Following on from the Pheasant Tail Nymph I have often played around with small nymph patterns which take on the principles that Frank Sawyer established yet have some distinctive elements to them. The use of green is part of that, but so is the use of a bead, pretty common these days of course, and turkey biot as a body material.

I am very fond of turkey biot, and that of goose which is shorter but tougher, because of the way they can form a very attractive segmented body, with a small ridged edge to each segment, and have a natural sheen which is so commonly seen in real nymphs. They are not that robust as a body material so I usually add a rib which, unusually for me, I wind in the same direction that I wound the biot. This is because it is not performing a role of creating segmentation, the biot does that already, but is giving some form of protection to the biot itself and sits neatly on the flat part of that material.

I was on the River Test one Autumn day with a novice Australian lady client, and we had caught some fish on Ginger Toms and Copperbonces but I thought there was a chance to improve our catch rate and decided to give this fly a go. Wow, I just hit on the dish of the day! The fish, both trout and grayling, just could not get enough of it. The fun ended when we lost the last fly up a tree but it was great while it lasted.

Since then I have had many successes with this PTN-inspired fly and it is a definite permanent resident in my nymph box.

## Green Genie
*Fly tied by the author*

**Materials:**

**Hook:** Any suitable wet-fly hook, size 14 to 18, but make sure the shank is not too short.

*Size 16 is the best all-rounder.*

**Silk:** Green – make sure it is very fine to ensure build up behind bead is not too excessive.

**Tails:** Green dyed cock pheasant centre tail herls – three or four.

**Bead:** Green painted tungsten bead – adjust to suit hook size and fishing depths and river conditions. I normally use a 2.8 mm for size 14, 2.5 mm for size 16 and 2.0 mm for size 18 on UK chalkstreams.

**Rib:** Fine gold wire – adjust thickness for hook size.

**Body:** Green turkey or goose biot – one strand.

**Thorax:** Any dark green dubbing material – say dyed hare's ear or squirrel.

### Tying Instructions:

1. Put the green bead onto the hook and push up to the eye – with the countersunk section to the back of the fly.
2. Lap on the tying silk behind the bead and run a few turns onto the hook shank. There is no need to ensure the bead is fixed at this stage.
3. Run silk down to the bend and tie in the three or four herls from a green cock pheasant centre tail feather with the ends pointing back to forms tails about 3 or 4 mm long.
4. Then tie in the fine gold wire for the ribbing.
5. Run the silk up the hook shank to behind the bead trapping the pheasant tails which are then cut off.
6. Take the silk back to the bend and tie in the turkey or goose biot by its tip. Be careful because they can be a bit brittle. Wetting them may help. Try to tie it in so the 'raised notch' is to the back when you wind the biot up the hook. It is quite obvious what this is and it will stand proud of the body to give a superbly segmented look.
7. Take the silk back to just behind the bead.
8. Wind the biot in neat touching turns, or even overlapping slightly if you have managed to keep the notch to the back, to where the silk is hanging then tie off and remove the waste.
9. Wind the gold wire up over the biot ensuring it sits in the flat part of each segment and secure at the back of the bead. Break off and dispose of the waste.
10. Build up some silk at the back of the bead to secure it – but not too much.
11. Dub a very small amount of the green hare's ear or squirrel dubbing at the back of the bead.
12. Whip finish behind the bead and cut off.

**Fishing Method:** Use exactly as you would a Sawyer Pheasant Tail Nymph.

# 43 Ginger Tom

Every so often you come upon a fly that is just sheer magic. The Ginger Tom is such a fly and, at the risk of appearing to be immodest, it's one of mine, a pattern which I developed on the River Wylye in Wiltshire. I was, at the time, devising some nymph patterns for an upcoming trip to France to fish the Dordogne at Argentat in the Corrèze department. I put half a dozen patterns together but this is the one which worked best by far on both the Dordogne and the Marrone. In its first week on the Wylye, when I returned home, it accounted for over 100 grayling and about 30 brownlings in the hands of myself and a friend.

Subsequently, I have tried it on rain-fed rivers in the North, Midlands, Wales

# Ginger Tom
*Fly tied by the author*

**Materials:**

**Hook:** Grub-type hook or similar size jig hook, size 14, 16, 18.

**Silk:** Brown or tan.

**Bead:** Copper-coloured bead – either tungsten or brass dependent on the rate of sink you need. I use one about 2 mm for size 18, 2.4 mm for 16 and 2.8 mm for 14. If tying on a jig hook use a slotted bead.

**Tail:** Four or five herls from a cock pheasant centre tail feather.

**Rib:** Pale-coloured copper wire – thickness to match hook size.

**Abdomen:** Light ginger dubbing. My favourite is Wapsi Rabbit. Other dubbings – Life Cycle Nymph Ginger, Fly-Rite #36 Ginger Cream, SLF #40 etc., will work but, whatever you use, make sure it is a light ginger in colour. The 'ginger' colour is key.

**Thorax:** Any suitable dark brown dubbing. I have used Life Cycle Nymph Dark Brown or Fly-Rite #6.

**Tying Instructions:**

1. Put the bead on the hook ensuring the countersunk side is to the back of the hook.

*Use a slotted bead if tying on a jig hook.*

2. Run the silk down to the outside of the bend and catch in the cock pheasant tail fibres to form a short tail.
3. Tie in the copper wire ribbing.
4. Run the silk up to the back of the bead trapping the cock pheasant tail fibres and tag end of the ribbing wire. Cut or break off the waste.
5. Run the silk back to the bend and dub with ginger dubbing. Dub an abdomen leaving enough room to dub a thorax behind the bead.
6. Rib the abdomen with the wire turning it in the opposite direction to that of the silk so it doesn't bed in. About four to six turns dependent on hook size. Tie off and remove the waste.
7. Dub on a short thorax with dark brown dubbing.
8. Whip finish behind the eye, tie off, cut off the waste thread and varnish the whipping.
9. Pick out a few fibres of the thorax dubbing.

**Fishing Method:** Fish this as you would any small weighted nymph. It is particularly effective as the nymph in a Klink & Dink set up although I generally fish it as an upstream nymph on its own, possibly with an indicator if the old eyes are struggling!

and Scotland and it has never failed to produce fish. Many friends have also used it – mainly by begging ones from me! They have generally been extremely complimentary and I hope you'll pardon me including a few of the testimonials below.

I mainly tie it in size 16 or 18, but 14 works also, as do jig hooks of the same sizes.

So there you are – a cracking fly that I cannot recommend highly enough.

Oh, and no, I didn't molest next door's tomcat to get the abdomen dubbing. It is rabbit. I just thought Ginger Tom was a good name!

## *Ginger Tom Testimonials ...*

*Hi Steve*

*Just had a few hours on the Avon and took 12 fish – 9 of them to the Ginger Tom in size 18 – it really is a good pattern. I did not have the ginger material you suggested so I used Davy Wotton SLF number 40 ginger – it works fine and matched the one you gave me.*

*Thanks for a great pattern.*

*Richard*

(*Richard Ellis* – Fly Dresser's Guild)

*Hi Steve,*

*Well, what a cracking little fly that's turned out to be (even when I have tied it). Today on the Churnet it accounted for 11 ladies and 3 OOS Brownies.*

*Thank you for the pattern ... suppose it will cost me at some point!*

*Regards,*

*Paul*

(*Paul Deaville* – Grayling Society Area Secretary)

*Hi Steve*

*Fished Wherwell yesterday with Mick and a friend and pulled out some crackers on the Tom. Mick had one of your flies and in comparison mine was rather more orange than ginger but when wet toned right down. Certainly is a 'killer fly'. Thank you.*

*Cheers,*

*Stephen*

(*Stephen Wright* – Flyfishing guide for Go Flyfishing UK)

(*Right*) A 'glaring' of Ginger Toms – on both grub and jig hooks

(*Left*) Honor fights a huge Annan grayling which took a size 16 Ginger Tom

*Hi Steve*

*I have always been sceptical about the value of individual fly patterns, presentation comes first, but there have been many occasions over the last two seasons when the 'GT' has made a real difference. Grayling will often take this fly when other 'stand-by' patterns are refused. It is now a feature of my fly box and will remain so.*

*Bob*

(*Bob Male* – Grayling Society Editor & Secretary Wiltshire Fishery Association)

*Steve*

*The Ginger Tom is a super fly. Very successful on all chalkstream and freestone waters I have fished including Test, Wylye, Itchen, Wharfe and Wye (Afon Gwy). A very easy fly to tie and great durability. Top marks on all counts and a 'must have' in my fly box.*

*Mike Shaw*

(*Mike Shaw* –Trout & grayling angler from Wakefield)

*Hi Steve*

*The Ginger Tom is excellent, thanks also for that gem!*

*See you soon.*

*Louis*

(*Louis Noble* – APGAI and Orvis accredited Flyfishing Guide)

*Hello Steve,*

*The last two Saturdays have seen a pal and I looking for ladies on the Wylye at Eastleigh Farm. This very wild fishery did not disappoint. On both occasions we had around fifteen each together with a trout of about two pounds. One or two were taken on a shrimp but by far the majority fell to your Ginger Tom. What a fly that is!! All three sizes had their place. Eighteens in the shallower runs, sixteens in most of the pools, and the fourteens in the deeper runs and pools. While my pal had one or two on a Sturdy's Fancy during a very light hatch of olives, I stuck to the Ginger Tom and kept up the catch rate. Two very enjoyable days made perfect with a new fly. Thank you!*

*Needless to say, I am now at the bench tying up one or two more ready for later this month.*

*Thanks Steve, talk soon,*

*Regards, Rod*

(*Rod Dibble* – Furled Leader & Cane Rod maker)

# 44  Juicy Tom – *Peter Buckey*

Well I don't know, but it seems that no sooner do you think you have created a cracking fly than someone who likes it wants to create a variation. Just before Christmas 2015 a card and small present landed on my front door mat. I thought, since the present was gift wrapped, I should open the card first and, maybe leave the present until Christmas Day. It was from a young man called Peter Buckey who lives in the village of Hanging Langford a little lower down the Wylye valley. I had taken Peter fishing on the Wylye in the Autumn and we had some great sport nymphing for grayling. The Ginger Tom was used a lot during this session and worked very well.

Peter must have been impressed by the Ginger Tom and decided to have a bit of a play and develop a variation. Thus was born the Juicy Tom and when, on Christmas morning, I opened the present there were several of them (plus lots of other nymphs) just ready to tie on and go fishing.

Here is how Peter describes its birth:

*This nymph came to fruition in the way that so many do; you go fishing and get given a fly, that fly catches lots of fish then you get home and try to tie some up but find you haven't got the exact materials used, so you cobble together something similar, tweak it a bit and end up with something quite different, classed as a variant. Steve took me fishing and offered me a couple of his Ginger Tom flies. I've been given a few flies in the past. Always they are promised to be something special but never seem to out-perform any of my other flies, so I tucked them in my fly box and tied on one of my own very trusted patterns. Steve let me fish just ahead of him and have a few casts before he started to fish. There were no grayling in that lovely deep hole, obviously, so I looked back to see Steve take his first cast of the day and with that, his first fish. Then his second, then his third until he suggested we moved along the river a bit. Perhaps there were grayling in that hole after all! I immediately took my fly off and tied on a Ginger Tom! Soon like Steve, I was catching fish after fish. It wasn't long before I lost that fly to a submerged tree root, so I saved the other as a tying reference.*

*As mentioned above, I didn't have the main ingredient for the Ginger Tom – the ginger rabbit fur. As I pored over my materials for something similar, Steve's earlier words from the day rang out in my head "there's something about that orangey/ginger colour that grayling find irresistible." He certainly isn't wrong!*

*The D-Rib used in my variant struck me as almost having the right orangey colour but I experimented a bit with the colour of the thread underneath it. Orange, purple, and fluorescent pink threads all yielded interesting results, but when I tried a yellow thread I knew I was getting close to the look I wanted. The chartreuse thread was a bit of a wild gamble; not a colour thread I would use for river fishing normally! The effect however was better than I could have imagined and instantly had something that looked like a fly that would just 'work.' I had to give the new creation a suitable name, – and it does look rather juicy* – so as a nod to Steve's original, settled on the Juicy Tom.

I suppose it is best described as a very good fly based on a very good fly! Since it is very different in its materials one should say it was 'influenced' by the Ginger Tom but is an original and very good idea in its own right.

## Juicy Tom
### Fly tied by Peter Buckey

**Materials:**

**Hook:** Partridge K4AY size 14 (but any barbless or de-barbed grub hook will do).
**Bead:** 2.8 mm copper tungsten.
**Thread 1:** Uni 8/0 – chartreuse.
**Thread 2:** Sheer 14/0 – brown.
**Abdomen:** UTC Vinyl D-Rib (Nymph) – rust.
**Thorax:** Wapsi Life Cycle Nymph Dubbing – brown.

**Tying Instructions:**

1. Put the bead on the hook ensuring the countersunk side is to the back of the hook.
2. Start the chartreuse thread tight behind the bead and take about six to eight touching turns rearwards then trim away the tag end.
3. Catch D-Rib on your side of the hook, round side facing you and allow the D-Rib to turn on the hook as you tighten the thread so that the rib is on top of the hook.
4. Run the silk up to the back of the bead then back to the tying-in point of the D-Rib. This will be the makings of the taper we are after in the fly.
5. Keeping the D-Rib on top of the hook, make touching turns towards and around the bend of the hook, gradually increasing tension to stretch the D-Rib as you go – again helping with the taper.
6. Then with touching turns take the thread towards the bead and stop at the start of the thorax section.
7. Next, wind the D-Rib up the fly, but this time reverse the stretching so that maximum stretch is applied at the first turn, gradually decreasing the tension until none is applied for the last turn or two until you tie off the D-Rib with a few tight turns of thread.
8. Stretch the D-Rib tag end as you cut the excess away so that as small amount as possible protrudes from the last turns of thread.
9. Whip finish the chartreuse thread in the thorax area and cut away.
10. Start the brown thread behind the bead

and take turns rearwards then forwards over the thorax area, trim the tag end then take turns to the rear of the thorax area. There shouldn't be any chartreuse thread visible now – if there is cover it with the brown thread.

11. Finally, dub a noodle of Life Cycle brown dubbing towards the bead and whip finish while there is still some dubbing on the thread, so that there isn't a visible build-up of thread turns behind the bead. Trim the thread away and if you like, pluck a few fibres out with a touch of a Velcro pad.

**Fishing Method:** Fish this as you would any small weighted nymph. It is particularly effective as the nymph in a Klink & Dink set up although I generally fish it as an upstream nymph on its own, possibly with an indicator if the old eyes are struggling!

# 45 Gammy Shrimp

This is another pattern which I have developed on the River Wylye. It is a shrimp representation which has worked well on all the chalkstreams where I have tried it, and on some rain-fed rivers also. It is a relatively standard shrimp pattern but the body material is fairly critical in its colour. The body is a creamy pale gingery colour and, having observed chalkstream shrimps several times this seems to be a good colour, especially when matched with a slightly brownish shellback.

I have had some quite magical moments on chalkstreams, especially the Wylye, with this pattern. Since grayling are big shrimp eaters – yes 8 out of 10 grayling prefer gammarus! – it is often on the end of my leader.

There are days when this is just the fly you need. One day, in February on the River Test, I was fishing with some friends who also guide on the chalkstreams. I had done OK but not that great. I stopped to talk to one of the other guys to compare notes and he must have said something to give me the inspiration to pop on a Gammy Shrimp and fish it with the standard upstream method. Well, in the next hour I had 15 grayling! Just the right fly at the right time – and a lot of luck of course! I often tie this fly on a gold hook which I think adds to its appeal.

Gammarus pulex
Photo: Dr. Cyril Bennett MBE

# Gammy Shrimp

*Fly tied by the author*

**Materials**

**Hook:** Grub hook such as Kamasan B100 or B100G, size 10 to 16.

**Weight:** Flat lead 0.2 mm or 0.3 mm thick, or square lead or lead sheet.

**Silk:** Brown or tan.

**Body:** Amber or cream hare/Antron mix. Mine is an Orvis version from some time ago and is probably not available anymore. Whatever you use it should have a creamy/amber look and be capable of being teased out to simulate legs.

**Back:** Shellback material about 3 mm wide. I have used several including disposable gloves but I now use some tan-coloured material which I acquired somewhere. Jiri Klima Body Stretch in a brown, rusty or sandy might do fine, or his Live Body in tan. If you don't have any suitable material then have a look on the internet for retailers.

**Rib:** 4 lb nylon or fine gold wire.

**Tying Instructions:**

1. Lay up to about eight to ten turns of flat lead from the bend towards the eye – 0.2 mm if using 16 or 14 hooks or 0.3 mm if using 12 or 10 sized hooks. Do not wind the lead right up to the eye since there is a need to leave a space behind the eye until the final tying off and head forming. Lock this onto the hook with a little Superglue.
2. Lap on the tying silk behind the eye and run down to the middle of the bend covering the lead.
3. Tie in the nylon or wire for the ribbing.
4. Then tie in the shellback about halfway down the hook ensuring it is aligned on top of the hook. Hold down on the hook with your left forefinger, if right handed, whilst tying it down to where you previously finished the silk round the bend. By holding it under tension against the hook this way you can easily ensure it stays on the top of the hook. Ensure you have enough length of shellback material behind the hook to easily fold it forward to the eye to form the shrimp back.
5. Dub the hare/Antron mixture onto the thread and wrap up to about 1 mm behind the eye.
6. Pull forward the shellback material and tie down tightly behind the eye and cut off the waste. Make sure it is tight because if it comes off after you have cut off the waste you will not be pleased! When pulling forward and tying down make sure it still sits on top of the hook.
7. Rib the nylon/wire in open turns up to the eye. Take about six to eight turns. Then tie off and cut or break the wire by 'worrying' it or cut the nylon with scissors. When wrapping the wire or nylon jiggle it backwards and forwards to ensure

it doesn't trap too many of the dubbing fibres.

8. Form a neat head, tie off, cut off the waste thread and varnish the head.
9. Finally, tease out some of the fibres to look like legs.

*Then go catch some grayling! It works on brownlings too!*

**Fishing Method:** This can be fished using several different methods. Pitched upstream on its own and allowed to dead drift back to you – as part of a Czech Nymph or French Leader rig – as the nymph on a Klink & Dink set up – or just down and across. I have caught fish using all of these methods. And don't be afraid of using the smaller, 14 and 16, sizes because they will work especially in thin water.

# 46 Gammy Parasite Shrimp

If the standard Gammy Shrimp isn't working, or if you are aware of shrimps with a small orange spot near the centre, then this is the time to tie on a Gammy Parasite Shrimp.

The acanthocephalan, *Pomphorhynchus laevis*, is a parasite which attacks the *Gammarus pulex* amphipod. (Yes, our freshwater shrimps aren't actually shrimps – they are amphipods!). The parasite infects the individual gammarus and appears as a bright orange spot near the centre of the creature. I have often heard it said that this spot indicates the gammarus is in its mating colours but it is definitely the parasite which causes the orange spot.

It is also felt that the presence of this parasite induces a behavioural change within the gammarus which becomes more active and more prone to enter shallower water. Can it be that this is what induces the fish to take a parasitic one instead of a healthy one, or does the orange just act as a target for a fish to attack, bearing in mind that grayling seem to like bright colours?

Try the Gammy Parasite Shrimp because it can be very successful in the right situation. The tying is, basically identical to the Gammy Shrimp but with the addition of a fluorescent orange spot, and I also often tie this using a gold hook.

Freshwater shrimp with parasite

## Gammy Parasite Shrimp

*Fly tied by the author*

### Materials

**Hook:** Grub hook such as Kamasan B100 or B100G, size 10 to 16.

**Weight:** Flat lead 0.2 mm or 0.3 mm thick, or square lead or lead sheet.

**Silk:** Brown or tan.

**Body:** Amber or cream hare/Antron mix. Mine is an Orvis version from some time ago and is probably not available anymore. Whatever you use it should have a creamy/amber look and be capable of being teased out to simulate legs.

**Parasite:** Small, and I mean small, amount of bright orange Ice Dub or Hends Spectra No. 2 Orange.

**Back:** Shellback material about 3 mm wide. I have used several including disposable gloves but I now use some tan-coloured material which I acquired somewhere. Jiri Klima Body Stretch in a brown, rusty or sandy might do fine or his Live Body in tan.

**Rib:** 4 lb nylon or fine gold wire.

### Tying Instructions:

1. Lay up to about eight to ten turns of flat lead from the bend towards the eye – 0.2 mm if using 16 or 14 hooks or 0.3 mm if using 12 or 10 sized hooks. Do not wind the lead right up to the eye since there is a need to leave a space behind the eye until the final tying off and head forming. Lock this onto the hook with a little Superglue.

2. Lap on the tying silk behind the eye and run down to the middle of the bend covering the lead.

3. Tie in the nylon or wire for the ribbing.

4. Then tie in the shellback about halfway down the hook ensuring it is aligned on top of the hook. Hold down on the hook with your left forefinger, if right handed, whilst tying it down to where you previously finished the silk round the bend. By holding it under tension against the hook this way you can easily ensure it stays on the top of the hook. Ensure you have enough length of shellback material behind the hook to easily fold it forward to the eye to form the shrimp back.

5. Dub enough of the hare/Antron mixture onto the thread to go halfway towards the eye and dub to this point.

6. Clear any excess dubbing from the silk and dub with the small amount of orange dubbing – just a couple of turns.

7. Re-dub with the hare/Antron mixture and continue to just behind the eye.

8. Pull forward the shellback material and tie down tightly behind the eye and cut off the waste. Make sure it is tight because if it comes off after you have cut off the waste you will not be pleased! When pulling forward and tying down make sure it still sits on top of the hook.

9. Rib the nylon/wire in open turns up to eye. Take about six to eight turns. Then tie off and cut or break the wire by 'worrying' it or cut the nylon with scissors. When wrapping wire or nylon jiggle it backwards and forwards to ensure it doesn't trap too many of the dubbing fibres.
10. Form a neat head, tie off, cut off the waste thread and varnish the head.
11. Finally, tease out some of the fibres to look like legs.

**Fishing Method:** This can be fished using several different methods just like the Gammy or Pink Shrimp. Pitched upstream and allowed to dead drift back to you – as part of a Czech Nymph or French Leader rig – as the nymph on a Klink & Dink set up – or just down and across. I have caught fish using all of these methods. And, again, don't be afraid of using the smaller, 14 and 16, sizes because they will work especially in thin water.

# 47  Phil White Shrimp – *Philip White*

This shrimp pattern is one of Phil White's: it must be good because he won't mess about with stuff that doesn't work!

I first met Phil one sultry and spooky summer's night on the Derbyshire Wye over 25 years ago. I was fishing a bend in the river, near Rowsley, at about 9.30 pm with my back to the A6. Suddenly I felt a presence behind me and there he was. Phil was the keeper on the Haddon Hall Estate in those days and, once he had checked that I wasn't poaching, bang went the fishing – because we both know how to talk!

Phil has a great approach to his flyfishing – bridge leaning. It is something he and I talked about when I moved to Wiltshire 11 years ago and he encouraged me to do lots of it. Watching the water and the air

### Phil White Shrimp
*Fly tied by Phil White*

**Materials:**

Hook:     Standard, not curved, heavy wet-fly hook, size 10 to 14.

Silk:     Olive.

Weight:   Flat lead.

Rib:      Copper wire. Gold or other wires also work well so experiment to suit the water.

**Body:** Mixed seal's fur – 40% hot orange, 60% medium olive.

**Back:** Olive or orange Bustard Thin Skin or olive or brown raffine (Swiss Straw). Raffine swells when wet so open the strand and use only 1 narrow strip.

**Legs:** Body material picked out.

**Tying Instructions:**

1. Lay on a thread base from the eye to the bend. Catch in the flat lead and tie down the lead strip almost to the eye.
2. Fold it and then tie it back down the body nearly to the bend and then back again almost to the eye to create a hump. Repeat as necessary to give the shape and weight required. Make sure you leave room at the head to complete the fly. Take the thread back to the bend covering the lead as you do so. Varnish.
3. Take a strip of raffine, Thin Skin or similar material about 2 to 4 mm wide or so depending on hook size, taper it a little at the end and catch it in on top of the hook. Also catch in the rib.
4. Thoroughly mix the seal's fur dubbing and dub the thread. Form the body almost to the head.
5. Pull the back material forward over the back and tie down behind the head. Wind the wire forward in even, open turns to segment the body making sure the back material 'skirts' down over the upper body and tie off. Form a neat head. Whip finish.
6. Pick out the dubbing between the ribs underneath the hook to suggest legs. I usually trim these legs level with the point of the hook so they are not too long but this is a personal choice as some people like them long and straggly.

**Fishing Method:** As Phil says – fish this pattern dead drift on rivers.

and the weather whilst gently leaning on a bridge parapet is probably as good a reason as any to call this angling malarkey the 'contemplative man's recreation,' as Walton so neatly put it.

Anyway, from his vast collection of original patterns I have taken this particular one to heart because it adds another dimension to the shrimp portfolio in my nymph box and it works really well, especially on rain-fed rivers.

The tying instructions are Phil's own.

# 48 Normal Pink Shrimp

Every serious grayling angler has a Pink Shrimp! Or, should I say, every serious grayling angler should have a Pink Shrimp.

Heaven knows why, but grayling just love them. How can that be when grayling could never have seen a shrimp that was pink? Freshwater shrimps aren't pink. In fact, most marine shrimps aren't pink either.

As far as I know, a shrimp, irrespective of its colour when alive, only becomes pink when it has been cooked.

It is one of life's intriguing mysteries that the Pink Shrimp works so well. No doubt it is all connected with the theory that red (and shades of red) is a killer colour for grayling flies.

Anyway I, and many other grayling anglers, can vouch for the fact that Pink Shrimps do work and I encourage you to have some in your box.

It is a fly that usually has some weight on it because it is often fished in deep holes and in the depths of winter when a fly needs to cut through the water column quickly. However, do be careful about the weighting of the fly because it should still have a relatively slim body. This is where flat lead, or square lead, or lead sheet can be useful.

And don't be scared of tying it small. It may not be used as regularly as the larger sizes but sometimes, as all grayling anglers know, they can be very selective and only a small fly will do the job.

## Normal Pink Shrimp
*Fly tied by the author*

### Materials:

**Hook:** Grub hook such as Kamasan B100 or B100G, size 10 to 16.

**Weight:** Flat lead 0.2 mm or 0.3 mm thick, or square lead or lead sheet.

**Silk:** Fluorescent pink such as Danville Flymaster shade 508.

**Rib:** Fine silver wire.

**Body:** Sow Scud pink dubbing with a few strands of hot pink seal's fur.

**Shellback:** Opalescent shellback material about 3 mm wide. e.g. Hends Pearlescent Shrimp Foil in pink or Hends Flashback in white pearl or Virtual Nymph Waterwing or even a wide sized Uni Mylar Pearl.

### Tying Instructions:

1. Lay up to about eight turns of flat lead from well down the bend towards the eye (0.2 mm if using 16 or 14 hooks or 0.3 mm if using 12 or 10 sized hooks). Do not wind the lead right up to the eye since there is a need to leave a space behind the eye until the final tying off and head forming. Lock this onto the hook with a little Superglue.

2. Lap on tying silk behind the eye and run down to just past the end of the lead.

3. Tie in the wire or nylon for the ribbing.

4. Then tie in the shellback about halfway down the hook ensuring it is aligned on top of the hook. Hold down on the hook with your left forefinger, if right handed, whilst tying it down to where you previously finished the silk round the bend. By holding it under tension against the hook this way you can easily ensure it

stays on the top of the hook. Ensure you have enough length of shellback material behind the hook to easily fold it forward to the eye to form the shrimp back.

5. Dub the Sow Scud and seal's fur mixture onto the thread and wrap up to about 2 mm behind the eye.

6. Pull forward the shellback material and tie down tightly behind the eye and cut off the waste. Make sure it is tight because if it comes off after you have cut off the waste you will not be pleased! When pulling forward and tying down make sure it still sits on top of the hook.

7. Rib the wire in open turns up to the eye. Take about six to eight turns. Then tie off and cut or break the wire by 'worrying' it or cut with scissors but, please, not your best ones! When ribbing wire jiggle it backwards and forwards to ensure it doesn't trap too many of the dubbing fibres.

8. Form a neat head, tie off, cut off the waste thread and varnish the head.

9. Finally, tease out some of the fibres to look like legs.

**Fishing Method:** This is a fly that works best in the depths of winter when the grayling have moved into the deeper pools. Drop one in amongst a shoal and who knows what might happen!

# 49 Fatbelly Pink Shrimp

Of course, there are those times when you need to get down really deep if you are to have any hope of catching a grayling. In the depths of winter when they have shoaled and headed for the deeper holes you will have to prospect for them with heavier flies than normal.

Following the Pink Shrimp theme here is a version designed for searching deeper holes. It is, essentially, a normal Pink Shrimp but with the addition of a pink fluorescent tungsten bead in the middle of the hook.

Do mind your head when casting – or wear a tin helmet!

**Fatbelly Pink Shrimp**
*Fly tied by the author*

**Materials:**

Hook:   Grub hook such as Kamasan B100 or B100G, size 10 to 14.

Silk:   Fluorescent pink or any pale-coloured silk.

**Bead:** Pink fluorescent painted or anodised tungsten bead. 3 mm for size 10 – adjust accordingly.

**Rib:** Silver wire.

**Body:** Sow Scud Pink dubbing with a few strands of hot pink seal's fur.

**Shellback:** Opalescent shellback material about 3 mm wide. e.g. Hends Pearlescent Shrimp Foil in pink, or Hends Flashback in white pearl, or Virtual Nymph Waterwing or even a wide sized Uni Mylar Pearl.

**Tying Instructions:**

1. Put the pink bead onto the hook and leave in the middle.
2. If extra weight is needed lay four or five turns of 3 mm flat lead behind and in front of the bead to add weight and help lock it in place. Do not wind lead right up to the eye since there is a need to leave a space behind the eye until the final tying off and head forming. Lock in place with a small amount of Superglue.
3. Lap on the tying silk behind the eye and run a few turns onto hook shank to cover the lead, if using, then take one wide turn over the top of the bead and trap down the lead behind it. Continue the thread down to the middle of the bend.
4. Tie in the silver wire for the ribbing.
5. Then tie in the shellback just behind the bead ensuring it is aligned on top of the hook. Hold down on the hook with your left forefinger, if right handed, whilst tying it down to the middle of the bend. By holding it under tension against the hook this way you can easily ensure it stays on the top of the hook. Ensure you have enough length of shellback material behind the hook to easily fold it forward to the eye to form the shrimp back.
6. Dub the Sow Scud and seal's fur mixture onto the thread and wrap up to the back of the bead. Clear the dubbing off the thread and take one wide turn over the back of the bead. Re-dub the thread and continue winding to just behind the eye.
7. Pull forward the shellback material and tie it down tightly behind eye and cut off the waste. Make sure it is tight because if it comes off after you have cut off the waste you will not be pleased! When pulling forward and tying down make sure it still sits on top of the hook.
8. Rib the silver wire in open turns up to the eye. Take about eight to ten turns with an open one over the bead. Then tie off and cut or break off the wire waste. When wrapping wire jiggle it backwards and forwards to ensure it doesn't trap too many of the dubbing fibres.
9. Form a neat head, tie off, cut off the waste thread and varnish the head.

**Fishing Method:** This is a fly that works best in the depths of winter when the grayling have moved into the deeper pools. Drop one in amongst a shoal and who knows what might happen! But watch your head as you cast – it is a wee bit heavy!

# 50 UVSP Shrimp – *David Southall*

The last of Dave Southall's trio of flies in this book is the UVSP Shrimp – or the Ultra Violet Shrimp Pink Shrimp!

It was designed by Dave following a trip to Montana some years ago. Here he tells us of his discovery:

*This Gammarus variant evolved thanks to my seeing ultra violet shrimp pink Ice Dub in a fly shop at Ennis on the Madison River in Montana in September 2009.*

*It was just what I was looking for to tie up some shrimps with a bit of subtle exaggeration of the natural carotenoid enhanced pigmentation, plus a hint of pink, so loved by grayling.*

*My new pattern met with immediate success, including a 3 lb-plus Driffield Beck grayling. I gave some to Stuart Crofts who had equally good results whilst guiding a client on one of the southern chalkstreams. On his return he informed me that I had been banned from all southern chalkstreams, as the UVSP Shrimp was too devastating!*

All good stuff and the fly certainly catches grayling whether on a chalkstream or not. In fact, it is such a good fly that I think we will really let David back on the chalkstreams any time he likes because such inventiveness should be congratulated and rewarded!

## UVSP Shrimp
### Fly tied by David Southall

**Materials:**

**Hook:** Grub hook, size 8 to 16.

**Silk:** 8/0 orange, pink or tan. I use tan.

**Rib:** Fine gold or copper wire.

**Underbody:** One or two layers of lead wire, flattened vertically to give a thin natural profile and to aid sinking. If two layers of wire are used the top layer needs to be shorter than the bottom one.

**Body:** Ultra Violet Shrimp Pink Ice Dub.

**Back:** Tan or grey Scud Back or similar.

**Tying Instructions:**

1. Lay on the flattened lead from well down the bend towards the hook eye. Do not wind the lead right up to the eye since there is a need to leave a space behind the eye until the final tying off and head forming. If using a second layer then wind this so it is shorter than the first and is centred on the middle of the hook. You can lock the lead onto hook with a little Superglue.

2. Lap on the tying silk behind the eye and run down to just past the end of the lead.
3. Tie in the wire for the ribbing.
4. Then tie in the Scud Back or similar material about halfway down the hook ensuring it is aligned on top of the hook. Hold down on the hook with your left forefinger, if right handed, whilst tying it down to where you previously finished the silk at the bend. Holding it under tension against the hook this way you can easily ensure it stays on the top of the hook. Ensure you have enough length of this material behind the hook to easily fold it forward to the eye to form the shrimp back.
5. Dub the Ultra Violet Shrimp Pink Ice Dub onto the thread and wrap up to about 2 mm behind the eye.
6. Pull forward the back material and tie it down tightly behind eye and cut off the waste. Make sure it is tight because if it comes off after you have cut off the waste you will not be pleased! When pulling forward and tying down make sure it still sits on top of the hook.
7. Rib the wire in open turns up to the eye. Take about six to eight turns. Then tie off and cut or break the wire by 'worrying' it or cut with scissors but, please, not your best ones! When ribbing wire jiggle it backwards and forwards to ensure it doesn't trap too many of the dubbing fibres.
8. Form a neat head, tie off, cut off the waste thread and varnish the head.
9. Finally, tease out some of the fibres to look like legs.

**Fishing Method:** Fish this as you would any shrimp pattern, especially in those deep holes where grayling love to lie as the winter sets in.

# 51 Czech Nymphs

'Get down, deeper and down.' The opening words from a classic hit, *Down, Down*, by Status Quo, surely the finest rock band ever – and who said there are more than 3 chords on a guitar then! And that is what Czech Nymphs are all about – getting down deep and quickly.

Born in the hotbed of competition flyfishing; supposedly devised by the Poles; perfected by the Czechs; used by everyone! What really put them on the scene was the 1986 World Flyfishing Championships where the individual winner was Slavoj Svoboda, fishing for what was then the communist state of Czechoslovakia and using the now well-known short-lining technique.

Invariably linked to the short line, or Czech method of fishing, it is essential for the flies to sink quickly yet not be too bulky. Thus, and this was before bead-heads came along, lead wire was used for the weight and originally this was added in layers to standard wet-fly hooks. Of course, things have changed somewhat as the flies and fishing technique have become more popular so that just about every hook manufacturer has a Czech Nymph range of curved heavy hooks in their range. In addition there have been advances in lead and tyers will now often use square or flat lead to add weight without bulk. I don't wish to bore anyone with mathematics but let me assure you if you can get square lead, which is available from some fly-tying materials suppliers, it is a good idea since it adds 27% extra weight for the same number of wraps and thickness of wire than normal round lead.

The flies are pretty well streamlined and are really caricatures of food sources such as caddis or shrimps. The emphasis is to get the flies to the feeding zones and not to look for exact imitation. And it seems to be a good theory because the flies do work really well.

In my experience they work best on a rain-fed rivers and I don't use them all that often on the chalkstreams except when I need to get a fly down quickly into deep water such as a weir pool or something similar.

There are lots of varieties one can tie and the one shown here is a relatively simple version which works well for me. Incidentally the Czechs themselves call these flies Bobeš or Bobesh.

## Czech Nymphs
*Flies tied by the author*

**Materials:**

**Hook:** Czech Nymph type hook, size 8 to 12.

**Silk:** Brown or black.

**Weight:** Flat, square or round lead or lead sheet cut to size.

**Rib:** Gold or silver wire or 4 lb nylon.

**Shellback:** Any of various shellback materials available – I get mine from the Jan Siman range.

**Abdomen:** Various dubbing materials can be used from hare, rabbit, squirrel, seal, Sow Scud, SLF, etc., but not too long in the fibre.

**Thorax:** Bright coloured SLF, Ice Dub, seal, etc., such as hot orange or red.

**Head:** Dark, black or brown say, longer fibred material such as seal or man-made equivalents.

**Wing Case:** Marker pen in black or brown.

**Tying Instructions:**

1. Apply the lead to the hook. Make sure you apply enough for the intended use of the fly. Normally two layers of flat lead work well although you may prefer one layer of square or round lead.

2. Run silk all over the lead to secure it and do this several times. You can add a drop of Superglue if you wish.

3. Take the lead down to the bend and tie in the rib material.

4. Then tie in the shellback about halfway down the hook ensuring it is aligned on top of the hook. Hold down on the hook with your left forefinger, if right handed, whilst tying it down to where you previously finished the silk round the bend. By holding it under tension against the hook this way you can easily ensure it stays on the top of the hook. Ensure you have enough length of shellback material behind the hook to easily fold it forward to the eye to form the fly's back.

5. Dub the abdomen material mixture onto

the thread and wrap up to about 4 mm behind the eye.

6. Dub on the bright coloured thorax material and take that about 2 mm towards the eye.
7. Dub on the head material and take to just short of the eye.
8. Pull forward the shellback material and tie down tightly behind eye and cut off waste. Make sure it is tight because if it comes off after you have cut off the waste you will not be pleased! When pulling forward and tying down make sure it still sits on top of the hook.
9. Rib the nylon/wire in open turns up to the eye. Take about six to eight turns. Then tie off and cut or break the wire by 'worrying' it or cut the nylon with scissors. When wrapping wire or nylon jiggle it backwards and forwards to ensure it doesn't trap too many of the dubbing fibres.
10. Form a neat head, tie off, cut off the waste thread and varnish the head.
11. Take your marker pen and colour the shellback over the head and thorax region.
12. Finally, tease out some of the fibres in the head section to look like legs.

**Fishing Method:** How about using the Czech Nymph technique?

# 52 Hare's Ear Goldhead

The hair from a hare's ear is such a brilliant dubbing material that it was an obvious candidate to be one of the first and best gold-beaded flies. This great combination of hair and bead has accounted for more grayling than I can even contemplate counting over the years I have used this fly.

It is simple to tie, and the body colour can be varied by judiciously picking the hair from different parts of the ear. Alternatively, hare's ear dubbing can be bought, ready plucked as it were, in a variety of colours. And, to make it completely daft, the Hare's Ear Goldhead works well with squirrel as the dubbing material!

This is a super fly and one that seems to produce fish when others fail. I have often fished with some of my flashier nymphs without success only to reverse my fortunes once I changed to this fly.

## Hare's Ear Goldhead
*Fly tied by the author*

**Materials:**

- **Hook:** Wet-fly hook, size 12 to 18.
- **Silk:** Brown.
- **Tails:** Several guard hairs from a hare's ear.
- **Bead:** Gold tungsten bead – adjust diameter to suit hook size, fishing depths and river conditions. (I normally use a 3.0 mm for size 12, 2.8 mm for size 14, 2.5 mm for size 16 and 2.0 mm for size 18 on chalkstreams).
- **Rib:** Gold wire.
- **Body:** Hair picked off the hare's ear by thumb and finger nails – not cut off.
- **Hackle:** Guard hairs picked out with a dubbing needle.

**Tying Instructions:**

1. Put the gold bead onto the hook and push up to the eye – with the countersunk section to the back of the fly.
2. Lap on the tying silk behind the bead and run a few turns onto the hook shank. There is no need to ensure the bead is fixed at this stage.
3. Run the silk down to the bend and tie in the fine gold wire for the ribbing.
4. Pluck some longish guard hairs from the ear and tie in as a tail.
5. Dub the silk with the hare's ear hair back towards the bead and don't bother too much about how rough it is because you want it to look 'hairy.'
6. Rib in the opposite direction to that you

have wound the silk and tie off at the back of the bead and remove the waste.
7. Run the silk back to the point at which to start a thorax.
8. Dub the silk with the guard hairs and wind a 'hairy' thorax.
9. Pick out the guard hairs with a dubbing needle or by giving them a gentle brush with a piece of the hooked part of some Velcro stuck to a wooden stirrer from a coffee shop – a lot cheaper than buying a dubbing teaser!
10. Whip finish at the back of the bead and remove the waste. Varnish if you want to.

**Fishing Method:** This fly can be fished successfully with all the nymphing techniques known to man!

# 53  Pedro's White Bead Nymph – *Pedro Guridi*

I have never met a man as enthusiastic as Pedro Guridi. He is the Area Secretary in Belgium for the Grayling Society and so keen on grayling, flyfishing and, most importantly, fly-tying, that it is tiring just watching him! I first met him at the Belgian Fly Happening in 2012 which I visited with Brian Clarke on behalf of the Society. Pedro had organised a stand for us and we had two wonderful days there, meeting many friends and new acquaintances not only from Belgium but also France, Germany and the Netherlands. A great show organised by the Flemish Federation of Fly Fishers and held in November in the small town of Putte near Mechelen.

Soon after setting up the stand Brian and myself got our fly boxes out and opened them for visitors to look into. Pedro also opened his boxes. Brian and myself took one look at his flies and closed our own boxes! His beautiful flies put mine to shame. Brian is a better tyer than me but even his flies were hard-pressed to compete with Pedro's. In fact he is such a good tyer that, at the time, his local tackle dealer swapped flies for goods and saved Pedro having to dole out his Euros every time he needed new flyfishing tackle!

One of the more amusing incidents was when Brian got out a UV torch and shone it into Pedro's box. The flies just lit up and so did Pedro's eyes. He, amazingly, had not realised that so many of the materials he was using were fluorescent!

He is actually Chilean by birth and lived there until he was 24. Then his studies took him to Belgium where he did a masters and a specialisation in classical and classical contemporary music. He also studied to be a chef as a hobby with no intention of actually working as such. However, since the recession hit the cultural sector hard he ended up cooking in a very good restaurant. So he combines working some days a week in the restaurant and playing concerts at other times!

Oh, and on top of this and fly-tying, he is also, with his friend Eddy, carrying out a comprehensive river restoration project! He is some versatile and energetic boy!

His nymphs are real winners and I have

chosen just two of his many patterns to show here. Both are always in my own box and have proved themselves on English, Welsh and Scottish grayling since 2012.

The first one, the White Bead Nymph, is Pedro's own favourite when he fishes in the Ardennes for trout and grayling.

## Pedro's White Bead Nymph
*Fly tied by Pedro Guridi*

**Materials:**

**Hook:** Any suitable wet-fly hook, size 16 or 18.

**Silk:** Spiderweb or ultra fine GSP such as Veevus 30 denier Dyneema. Pedro is very keen on the use of GSP.

**Bead:** White fluorescent bead, say 2 mm for size 18 and 2.4 mm for size 16. The fly is best with a fluorescent white bead but they are not always easy to obtain. A normal white bead is the substitute but try to get the fluorescent version if possible.

**Tail:** 4 or 5 'grizzled' mallard or teal fibres.

**Abdomen:** Gold tinsel about 1 mm wide.

**Thorax:** Peacock Black Ice Dub.

**Tying Instructions:**

1. Put white bead onto hook and push up to eye – with countersunk section to back of fly.
2. Lap on tying silk behind bead and run a few turns onto hook shank. There is no need to ensure the bead is fixed at this stage.
3. Run silk down to bend and tie in the mallard or teal fibres to forms tails about 3 or 4 mm long.
4. Tie in fine gold tinsel for abdomen.
5. Run silk up hook shank to behind the bead.
6. In close turns wind the tinsel to the back of the bead. Tie off, cut off and dispose of waste.
7. Build up some silk at the back of the bead to secure it – but not too much.
8. Dub a thorax of the peacock black ice dub at the back of the bead.
9. Whip finish behind the bead and cut off.

**Fishing Method:** Use as you would any small weighted nymph.

# 54  Pedro's Pink & Grey Nymph – *Pedro Guridi*

Another of Pedro's great nymphs is his Pink & Grey. This takes up a familiar theme of pink for grayling flies and does so very well. It also incorporates a copper bead which I am very partial to using on my bead headed nymphs. The pink material is fluorescent which I think helps a lot.

I do like using this fly and it usually produces the goods!

## Pedro's Pink & Grey Nymph
*Fly tied by Pedro Guridi*

**Materials:**

**Hook:** A jig hook, size 14 or 16.

**Silk:** GSP – Roman Moser Power Silk or equivalent.

**Bead:** Copper slotted tungsten bead – 3 mm for size 14 and 2.5 mm for size 16 hook.

**Tail:** 4 or 5 'grizzled' mallard or teal fibres.

**Rib:** Copper wire.

**Abdomen 1:** Ice Dub UV Pink – tightly dubbed.

**Abdomen 2:** Any pale grey dubbing.

**Thorax:** Dark hare's ear or squirrel with lots of guard hairs.

**Tying Instructions:**

1. Put copper bead onto hook and push up to eye – with slotted section to back of fly.
2. Lap on tying silk behind bead and run a few turns onto hook shank to trap bead.
3. Run silk down to bend and tie in the tail fibres to leave a tail about 5 or 6 mm long.
4. Then tie in copper wire for the ribbing.
5. Dub silk with the UV Pink Ice Dub and dub towards eye stopping at about 1/3rd the distance. Try to create a taper when dubbing.
6. Now dub the silk with the pale grey dubbing and dub up to the back of the bead. Again create a taper but do not leave it too fat behind the bead.
7. Take your copper wire and rib up to the back of the bead in even turns – about 6. Remove waste.
8. Dub a thorax behind the bead using the dark hare's ear or squirrel. Pick out guard hairs if necessary to give a hackle like appearance.
9. Whip finish behind the bead.

**Fishing Method:** Like most jig hooked flies this one works well when fishing with the Czech Nymph or French Leader approach or in classic upstream nymph style.

# 55 G G G (Green Grayling Grabber)

Another one of my patterns that has proved its worth time and time again. The combination of bright green and orange shows clearly in the water and offers a target for the grayling. There are several successful patterns of nymph which use similar colouring and this is my version.

I have tied it with a silver bead because I sometimes feel that gold is so often used that maybe fish get used to it. Often I will use silver or copper to be different.

## GGG
*Fly tied by the author*

**Materials:**

- **Hook:** A jig hook, size 14 or 16.
- **Silk:** Green.
- **Bead:** Silver slotted tungsten bead – 3 mm for size 14 and 2.5 mm for size 16 hook.
- **Tail:** Tiemco Aero Dry Wing No. 03 Flo Orange or equivalent fluorescent orange polyyarn.
- **Rib:** Reddish copper wire.
- **Body:** Hends Spectra Dubbing No. 39 olive.
- **Hackle:** Small dun-coloured CdC feather.
- **Thorax:** Hends Spectra Dubbing No. 239 dark green.

**Tying Instructions:**

1. Put silver bead onto hook and push up to eye – with slotted section to back of fly.
2. If extra weight is needed lay 4 or 5 turns of flat lead behind bead to add weight and help lock in bead.
3. Lap on tying silk behind bead and run a few turns onto hook shank to trap lead, if using.
4. Run silk down to bend and tie in copper wire for the ribbing.
5. Then tie in tail comprised of a couple of thicknesses of Aero Dry Wing (it comes a 4 separate strands laid alongside each other so take one strand and double it.) leaving it about 5 mm long.
6. Dub silk with Spectra Dubbing No. 39 and run up to back of bead to form body.
7. Wind on rib up to back of bead in 4 or 5 open turns in the opposite direction to the dubbing. Tie off and cut or break off waste.
8. Tie in CdC hackle by tip and wind

maximum of 2 turns. Tie off and trim waste

9. Dub a small thorax in front of the hackle using Spectra Dubbing No. 239.
10. Whip finish behind the bead and cut off

**Fishing Method:** Like most jig-hooked flies this one works well when fishing with the Czech Nymph or French Leader approach. It also performs perfectly fished on its own in classic upstream nymph style. Alternatively use the fly as the dropper on the Klink & Dink approach of a buoyant dry-fly and a nymph dropper. Lengthen the dropper tippet to suit conditions.

# 56 P P P (Purple & Pink Peril)

In much the same way that red is a known attractor of grayling, so, in my experience, is purple.

I developed this particular fly after watching a friend, Mick, have great success with a nymph that incorporated purple. He and I had been employed as instructors for a father and son who were novices to flyfishing. I looked after the grown-up son and Mick looked after the father. The weather was not kind and the river was fairly full but running clear enough. In fact, it had rained so much that winter that we had to put on our waders just to

## PPP
*Fly tied by the author*

**Materials:**

**Hook:** A jig hook, size 14 or 16.
**Silk:** Black or brown.
**Bead:** A pink anodised tungsten bead – preferably the slotted type because it sits better on the jig hook. A pink fluorescent painted bead would probably work also. Try a 3 mm for the size 14 version and a 2.5 mm for the size 16.
**Tail:** Tiemco Aero Dry Wing No. 04 Flo Pink or equivalent fluorescent pink Poly Yarn.
**Rib:** Dark copper wire
**Body:** Single strand of peacock herl.
**Hackle:** Small feather from back of a grey partridge.
**Thorax:** Hends Microflash dubbing Nos. 13 shrimp pink, 17 purple & 18 dark purple mixed together in equal amounts.

**Tying Instructions:**

1. Put pink bead onto hook and push up to eye – with slotted section to back of fly.
2. If extra weight is needed lay 4 or 5 turns of flat lead behind bead to add weight and help lock in bead.
3. Lap on tying silk behind bead and run a few turns onto hook shank to trap lead, if using.
4. Run silk down to bend and tie in copper wire for the ribbing.
5. Then tie in tail material and leave it about 3 – 5 mm long.
6. Tie in peacock herl and wrap up to back of bead to form body.
7. Wind on rib up to back of bead in 4 or 5 open turns in opposite direction to that which you wound on the peacock herl. Tie off and cut or break off waste.
8. Tie in a small grey partridge hackle by tip and wind maximum of 2 turns. Tie off and trim waste
9. Dub a small thorax in front of the hackle using the Microflash dubbing mixture.
10. Whip finish behind the bead and cut off.

**Fishing Method:** Like most jig hooked flies this one works well when fishing with the Czech Nymph or French Leader approach. It also performs perfectly fished on its own in classic upstream nymph style. Alternatively use the fly as the dropper on the Klink & Dink' approach of a buoyant dry-fly and a nymph dropper. Lengthen the dropper tippet to suit conditions.

get through the water meadows to the riverbank! However, it was the River Test which is, in my experience, the best of the chalkstreams when it comes to staying clear and fishable after bad weather. Even in the wettest of winters you can generally rely on being able to flyfish the Test.

Anyway, after lunch my student caught a few fish but nothing of any size. We met up with the others, talked about our success and asked how they had got on. They were particularly modest and said they had just done alright. Then, of course, out came the iPhone and we were shown the extremely large grayling which the father had caught. My friend just grinned and showed me the fly – which I subsequently stole from him!

The PPP is pretty close to this fly of Mick's and I have used it very successfully ever since! It is a good fly for both clear and coloured water.

# 57 Dove Bug – *John Roberts*

When I first started grayling fishing I read John Roberts book, *The Grayling Angler*, from cover to cover. In fact I actually owned two copies of the book, one of which I donated to the Grayling Society auction some years ago, so I must have been keen on it. I suspect one was a downstairs copy and one an upstairs one – how lavish!

Anyway, in this super book with lots of valuable advice and fly patterns there was one fly in particular which really took my interest. That was John's own pattern the Dove Bug. I tied some straightaway (I was in my fly-tying infancy at that time so I doubt if they looked much like John's original), and set off to fish with them on the Wiltshire Avon. The fly worked for me then, and it works now. I have caught grayling on this fly all over Britain, and in Sweden and Denmark also. It is one of the two or three patterns which have been in my fly box ever since I started serious grayling fishing and it will always be in there.

John is the author of a number of books on trout and grayling fishing and on flies, of course, and he has kindly penned below the history of this smashing fly and brought us up to date with the latest tying. He also tied the example photographed here so we can be sure this one is true to pattern!

*In the late 1970's when I devised this bug there were no alternatives to Sawyer's Grayling Bug for deep lying fish. The Dove Bug was my answer as an alternative if grayling went off the Sawyer Bug. What I finished up with is very simply a weighted seal's fur*

## Dove Bug
*Fly tied by John Roberts*

**Materials.**

**Hook:** Heavyweight wet-fly hook, size 10-14 (e.g. Kamasan B175).

**Silk:** Orange.

**Underbody:** 2/3 layers of wound medium copper wire.

**Rib:** As for the underbody.

**Body:** Mixed seal's fur, usually pink, orange and brown.

**Tying Instructions.**

1. Run 2 or 3 layers – depending on hook size and weight requirements – of copper wire along hook shank and leave wire hanging at bend. Wrap it by bringing it towards you, not away from you, since this will help when using it as ribbing.
2. Take silk down to bend in neat touching turns covering wire underbody.
3. Dub silk with pre-mixed seal's fur mix and wind up towards eye.
4. Rib with copper wire ensuring you rib in opposite direction to the dubbing to avoid wire burying itself into seal's fur body. If you wound the copper wire towards you initially then this process is now easy.
5. At eye tie off and remove waste before whip-finishing and varnishing head.

**Fishing Method:** Fish this as you would a Killer Bug or similar weighted nymph. It will work happily with any nymphing technique and on any water. Have fun!

*bug which can be used in a wide range of colours and hues to great effect as a shrimp imitation, a cased or caseless caddis or general food impression. The original published pattern had a different seal's fur mix for the front and rear body. Now I use only one mix throughout although the mix will vary with the amount of pink, orange and brown seal's fur. Sometimes the pinkier version is more successful, others it's the orangier one. Originally I included a red wool tag in my efforts to be more grayling orientated. On balance, I don't think it adds to any success so I generally omit the tag.*

*Forty years later we are a little clearer as to why colours in the orange-red spectrum appeal to grayling but at the time it was just a bit hit and miss. I had a lucky evolutionary step towards the scores of weighted grayling patterns we currently employ.*

We hear a lot these days about shrimp and nymph flies which have bodies created from mixtures of bright coloured, leggy, dubbing materials. Well, the Dove Bug pre-dated all these whizzo new patterns by some years. So, thanks John, for a great fly.

I should add that the 'Dove' in the fly's name refers to that sweet tributary of the Rye in North Yorkshire, where the fly was devised, and not the Derbyshire/Staffordshire river of the same name.

# 58  Pink Poison – *David Lerche*

This is a fly which came to my attention via my good friend John Machin who does some guiding in the Midlands. One day he guided a very pleasant and experienced South African angler, David Lerche. They had a successful day not the least because David produced from his box a nymph which had travelled about 7,500 miles to worry trout and grayling in the Dove in Staffordshire; and worry them it did. John showed it to me a short time afterwards and I immediately snaffled one, copied it and started throwing it into various chalkstreams. It worked like a charm and many trout and even more grayling have succumbed to its deadly attractions. Poisonous it may be to any unsuspecting fish but it is sheer joy to the angler.

This is how it came into being and should be tied, as described by David himself:

*Regarding the development of the pattern, the basic thought process came from the competitive French/Spanish nymphing scene. The logic was to create a fly that:*

*1) Sinks effectively to get down to the fish in fast water – hence the slim profile and tungsten bead. Something that I have been taught by various competitive fishermen and also learned on my own is that getting the fly into the right zone is often more important than exactly what the fly looks like.*

*2) Rides hook point up so it doesn't get stuck on the bottom.*

*3) Has some movement – CdC.*

*4) Has contrast (black thread, silver segments, pink bead).*

*5) Is easy to tie.*

*Originally, I tied the fly with a gold*

bead and caught plenty of fish. I found pink anodised beads at a local fly store and tried this as a variation. It worked much more effectively in two-fly rigs, irrespective of whether is was the point or dropper fly. I have tested the pink bead extensively side by side with other colours on 1-fly rigs and found that with a gold bead, the fish in any given pool go off the bite after about 5 hook-ups, while the pink is usually good for 10 fish even after having fished a pool with a gold bead (orange about 3 fish and brown about 2 fish). By having a thin profile, the fly does not need to be very heavy to get down deep. It works best with thin tippets that have low drag.

The key development was done in the Rhodes area of the North-Eastern Cape in South Africa, in the mountains near the Lesotho border. In these clear streams (generally fast flowing, mostly freestone), trout have been breeding naturally for over 100 years and peacefully co-exist with the indigenous yellowfish population. The fly has been proven to work in all SA trout streams (both brown and rainbow trout), as well as in Lesotho and the UK.

Thanks, David, for devising such a great fly which is as successful in the Northern hemisphere as it is in the Southern. It is a great nymph for our grayling as well as trout!

## Pink Poison

*Fly tied by David Lerche*

### Materials:

- **Hook:** Hanak H 450 BL, or similar jig hook, size 14.
- **Silk:** Black thread – I prefer 140 denier as it is easy to split.
- **Bead:** Pink anodised slotted tungsten bead – 2.8 mm or 2.3 mm.
- **Tail:** 3-6 Gallo de León fibres.
- **Rib:** Silver wire – extra thin.
- **Thorax:** Black CdC.

### Tying Instructions:

1. Place bead on hook and tie in place, then wrap thread down to the end of the shank and tie in the tail fibres.
2. Tie in the silver wire and wrap the thread forward, keeping the profile of the body slim.
3. Wind the wire forward to create segments and cut off.
4. Split the thread and insert about 10 CdC fibres (a Petitjean clip makes life easier) then spin the thread and wrap a thorax, stroking the CdC fibres backwards.
5. Tie off.

**Fishing Method:** I think David has said it all. Fish it as either fly in a two fly rig or as a single upstream nymph. I have used both methods successfully.

# 59 Grayling Special Pink – *Louis Noble*

Here is a very attractive and successful grayling nymph which plays on the fascination they seem to have for the colour pink. I was introduced to the fly when I hosted the Grayling Society's Public Relations Officer Kris Kent on the Wylye one day. He uses this fly frequently and, having snaffled one off him at the time to use as a pattern, I can only concur that he is right to do so because it is a good 'un! He was introduced to the fly by a mutual friend, Louis Noble who is also an active member of the Society and looks after its interest in the North Wales area. Louis is also a very well-known contributor to *Trout & Salmon* magazine, an Orvis endorsed and APGAI qualified flyfishing guide operating on the Welsh Dee and its tributaries, and a

## Grayling Special Pink
*Fly tied by Louis Noble*

**Materials:**

**Hook:** Kamasan B911 (coarse hook), size 16 or 18.
**Silk:** Fine pink.
**Bead:** Gold tungsten bead, 2.4 mm for size hook and 2.0 mm for size 18.
**Tail:** Badger hackle fibres.
**Rib:** Dark grey thread under thin piece of Polywrap.
**Abdomen:** Fluorescent pink floss Glo Brite No. 2 – exposed at tail, remainder under polywrap.
**Thorax:** Medium brown hare's ear.

**Tying Instructions:**

1. Put bead on hook ensuring the rebated side is towards the bend.
2. Run on a few turns of silk behind the bead to help lock it.
3. Take silk down around bend and tie in tails.
4. Tie in rib and floss.
5. Take silk part way back to eye and tie in thin strip of Polywrap.
6. Take silk to back of bead.
7. Wind floss to back of bead ensuring it does not trap the Polywrap, remove waste.
8. Wind rib to bead ensuring it does not trap Polywrap, remove waste.
9. Wind Polywrap up to back of bead, remove waste.
10. Dub on a small thorax of hare's ear, tie off, whip finish and varnish if you want.

**Fishing Method:** Fish wherever you would use a small nymph. Works very well with the Duo/Klink & Dink technique.

highly experienced and skilled fly dresser and instructor.

Louis is not 100% certain of the fly's origins but feels it was developed for use by the English international flyfishing team some while ago and has since proved its worth for many anglers.

Being cheeky I asked Louis to tie me a couple and the example shown here is one of his as are the tying details. Well, he is a much better tyer than me so why not?

Thank you Kris and Louis and whoever invented it for the English team!

# 60 The Pink Thingy

I think we have already established that pink is a really useful colour when grayling fishing. This one takes it to the extreme! Sometimes you just can't get enough pink. Funnily enough my mum hated the colour but I am quite happy with it – but just for flies you understand! And, since baby grayling are often called 'pinks' it seems appropriate that they should enjoy eating pink flies. And this fly is really pink!

It works very well, especially in slightly coloured water, and is better in the winter than the summer.

## The Pink Thingy
*Fly tied by the author*

**Materials:**

**Hook:** Grub-style hook, size 10 or 12.

**Silk:** Fluorescent pink – I use Danville Flymaster 6/0 shade 508.

**Bead:** Pink tungsten bead either painted or anodised. Size to suit your fishing but you can go up to a size 3.5 mm on a 10 hook. On a chalkstream I generally use a 3 mm on a 10 and a 2.5 mm on a 12 hook.

**Rib:** Silver wire.

**Body:** Fluorescent pink floss – I use Glo Brite shade 2.

**Thorax:** Fluorescent pink dubbing – I use Hends Spectra shade 19.

**Tying Instructions:**

1. Put bead onto hook ensuring that the rebated side is toward the back of the hook.
2. Run silk onto hook and take a few turns behind the bead to help lock it.
3. Run silk along shank to about half way round the bend.
4. Tie in rib.

5. Tie in floss and take silk back to back of bead.
6. Wind floss up to back of bead, tie off and remove waste.

*I always wet the floss a bit before doing this because it can catch so easily on any bit of uneven skin on your fingers and wetting it seem to help prevent this.*

7. Wind rib up to back of bead, and this can be in the same direction as the floss was wound, tie off and 'worry 'off the waste.
8. Form a dubbed thorax with the pink dubbing, tie off, whip finish and varnish if you want.
9. You can then brush out the dubbing a bit to make it more hairy.

**Fishing Method:** Whenever you think there is a need for a bright coloured fly that gets down quickly then call up The Pink Thingy!

# 61  Mr Tangerine Man

When I was younger I was a great fan of Bob Dylan and all his music. In particular, I just loved the way the Byrds performed his great classic *Mr Tambourine Man* with the opening notes, played by Roger McGuinn on his 12 string Rickenbacker, being absolutely magical and surely one of the top ten best ever guitar riffs. I have a Rickenbacker 12 string but struggle to match that jingly, jangly sound he created. I named this fly Mr Tangerine Man for fun and the name just stuck!

Following the old theme that grayling like bright colours it started with a

**Mr Tangerine Man**
*Fly tied by the author*

**Materials:**
- **Hook:** Standard heavy wet-fly hook, size 10 to 14.
- **Silk:** Tan or cinnamon – Sheer 14/0 Cinnamon is the one I use.
- **Bead:** Fluorescent orange tungsten – use a 2.8 mm on a size 12 and adjust for the other size hooks.
- **Tail:** CdC feather tip fibres.
- **Body:** Hareline Micro Tubing orange, UTC Vinyl Rib (Midge) orange or similar.
- **Hackle:** CdC hackle – If possible in a light brown/tan/cinnamon colour.
- **Collar:** Hare's ear or squirrel fur.

**Tying Instructions:**

1. Fix tungsten bead to hook ensuring the rebated side is towards the bend. I usually lay a short bed of silk on the hook near the eye and then whip finish and cut off the silk. Then I slide the bead onto this silk bed which I have coated in a thin layer of Superglue – *Zap a Gap* is good. The bead won't come off then!
2. Wind silk back onto hook behind the bead, run it down the hook after trapping the butt end of a CdC feather with loose open turns and then pulling it forward slightly to compress the fibres and form a tail at the hook bend. Run the silk down to the bend with tighter turns to firmly trap this feather and ensure the tail is firm and fulsome.
3. At the bend tie in the micro tubing or equivalent.
4. Run silk back to behind eye.
5. Wind the tubing up the hook and trap, tie off and remove waste about 2 mm behind the bead.
6. Tie in another CdC, by the tip, at the point where the tubing finished.
7. Take silk up to back of bead.
8. Using hackle pliers wind the hackle forward towards the bead ensuring you fold the fibres backwards as you wind.
9. After a couple of turns tie off and cut off waste.
10. Apply a small amount of hare's ear or squirrel fur dubbing behind the bead as a collar.
11. Tie off, whip finish, and apply a small amount of varnish to secure the whipping.
12. Go to the river and jingle jangle!

**Fishing Method:** It can be used with any preferred nymphing technique but the CdC fibres work best when fished upstream since they are more mobile in this situation.

fluorescent orange bead. I think fluorescence is important in some situations and this was an ideal opportunity to develop a fly that relied on it to some extent. I check out fluorescence in beads, when in a tackle shop or at a fly show, by shining a light on them from a tiny UV light on a key ring. It sounds a bit nerdy I know but at least I always know for sure which are the fluorescent beads! And, of course, it is also ideal for checking out other materials.

Matched to this is the undeniable attraction of wet CdC, which traps minute bubbles of air within the fibres whilst waving seductively in the current. Put the two together with a bit of other stuff and, Hey Presto, you have Mr Tangerine Man.

Go on, hum the tune, sing the song - and cast Mr Tangerine Man to get the jingle jangle!

# 62 Hotspot Nymph II – *Richard Ellis*

Richard Ellis is well-known in the Fly Dresser's Guild and his ebook, *Inspiring Ties: Grayling Flies*, contains some great patterns with complete tying sequences nicely illustrated (although, by some quirk, this particular fly is not in the ebook).

As Richard says:

*This was developed to give a fly with a hotspot for use in coloured water. The coq de leon gives a stiff tail, the black body with red rib a natural appearance and the collar a hotspot for attracting grayling. The silver bead adds further visibility to the fly.*

*A jig hook was chosen to allow the fly to fish upside down and thus minimise snagging. The fly works individually or as part of a team. The colour of the collar can be varied with pink or violet dubbings.*

On the basis of my friend's recommendation I tied a few and stuck them in my nymph box. There was an odds-on chance they would just stay there for some time. However, that was not to be the case!

Let's just say that the first time I used it was on the morning of Sunday 26th of October 2014 on the Dove at Rocester, Staffordshire. We had just held our 38th Grayling Society Symposium at Mickleover in Derbyshire on the Saturday and we all set off on the Sunday to fish various stretches of various rivers. Myself and my Domestic Director were booked to fish on the water kindly donated by the Norbury Fishing Club. I had fished this particular stretch before with a friend who was a member so I had a little bit of knowledge about the river. The river had some colour in it but

## Hotspot Nymph II
### Fly tied by Richard Ellis

**Materials:**

**Hook:** Jig hook, size 14 or 16.

**Silk:** Hends orange 0.05 mm.

**Bead:** Silver tungsten bead – 3 mm for size 14 and, say, 2.5 mm for 16.

*I would normally use a slotted bead on a jig hook but an example I have seen tied by Richard seems to be tied with a normal bead reversed with the countersink side towards the eye and he tells me is happy with either approach. Also, I overheard a conversation between a fly-tying materials retailer and customer at the BFFI where the retailer advised that a slotted bead was 20% lighter than a conventional one. It might be worth thinking about.*

**Rib:** Red wire 0.18 mm.

**Tail:** Gallo de León fibres.

**Abdomen:** Hends Spectra dubbing shade 45 Black Peacock.

**Thorax:** Hends Spectra shade 294 Hot Fluo Orange.

### Tying Instructions:

1. Put bead on hook ensuring the slotted side is to the back of the hook and the slot is vertical. If using a non-slotted bead then it will probably work best of the rebated side is towards the eye.

2. Run silk down to bend and catch in tail fibres to form short tail.
3. Tie in red wire ribbing also.
4. Run silk up to back of bead, trapping tail fibres and tag end of ribbing wire. Cut or break off waste.
5. Run silk back to bend and dub with black dubbing. Dub an abdomen leaving enough room to dub a small thorax behind bead.
6. Rib abdomen with wire, turning it in the opposite direction to that of the silk so it doesn't bed in. About 4 to 6 turns dependent on hook size. Tie off and remove waste.
7. Dub on a small thorax with orange dubbing.
8. Whip finish behind eye, tie off, cut off waste thread and varnish whipping.

**Fishing Method:** I normally fish this on its own in classic upstream nymph style. However, like most jig hooked flies this one also performs perfectly well when fishing with the Czech Nymph or French Leader approach. Richard claims it works best in murky water and that is where you would expect fluorescence to be most useful I guess and this certainly fits in with my experience of this fly.

was eminently fishable with the nymph. I spent about half an hour with one of my Ginger Toms and had a few fish. Then I decided to give the Hotspot Nymph II a try out, encouraged by what my friend had told me.

In one and a quarter hours, fishing it as an upstream nymph with an indicator, I caught 25 grayling! A gobsmackingly good bit of fluff-wrangling then!

I have, subsequently, tried it on many rivers including the chalkstreams and it has proved to be a very good fly although, predictably, it has never managed quite such a good score as it did that first day! I feel it does need a little colour in the water for it to be at its best but, when it is at its best, it is a formidable fly. And, of course, it plays to that familiar theme of using bright colours for grayling to set their sights on.

Thank you Richard for such a great fly.

# 63  Perdigón Style Flies

Perdigón flies are Spanish in origin and are small heavy nymphs that go down like a bullet. Not surprisingly when you consider that *perdigón* is Spanish for pellet – not the floating trout pellet type that creates feeding frenzies on stock ponds. No, this is more like an air gun pellet which is pure lead!

They are not old patterns, as they were probably devised in the 1980's and are, I think, yet another type of fly which was spawned in the field of competitive flyfishing. They have long been associated with the 'French Leader' style of nymphing.

I had heard of them a few years earlier but it was only when guiding some French ex-international fly fisherman that I got to see several and try them out. They are extremely good flies and are all based on the principle of being small and heavy to sink quickly, and are juicy enough in their looks to fool fish into thinking they are food. Nothing new there then! However, they do perform these two roles very well indeed.

As it's a style of fly rather than a unique pattern you can tie many variations but they'll have certain common features:

*Small hooks* – the modern straight-eyed upturned point hooks are very popular, but they can be tied on normal wet-fly hooks with short shanks, or grub hooks or jig types.

*Coq de Leon* – well, being Spanish you'd expect this wouldn't you? And, strictly speaking since they are Spanish feathers we should call them Gallo de León!

*Steeply tapered short bodies* – either of silk, floss, tinsel or whatever takes your fancy providing it is smooth and can be successfully coated with UV resin.

*Oversized bead* – the bead is always larger than you would expect for the size of the hook.

*UV resin coated* – they are almost always encased in a coat of UV resin.

*Black top* – most will have a black top, like a wing case, applied with a marker pen or nail varnish.

I've tried different versions of these flies and they all work to one degree or other.

## Perdigon Style Fly
*Flies tied by the author*

**Materials:** For typical fly

**Hook:** Standard wet-fly or more specialist hook with turned up point, e.g. Hanak H500BL, or a grub or jig type.

**Silk:** Fine – Veevus 14/0 is good.

**Bead:** Tungsten silver, copper, black or gold – say 3 mm on a size 16 hook.

**Tail:** A few fibres of Gallo de León, pardo or indio – Pardo Claro used here.

**Abdomen:** Tying silk, or you can use coloured tinsel.

**Thorax:** Floss, especially fluorescent colours.

**Covering:** UV resin.

**Wing Case:** Black marker pen or nail varnish.

**Tying Instructions:**

1. Put bead on hook and run a few turns of silk behind it for locking.
2. Take silk to bend and tie in tail fibres – no more than 5 mm long.
3. Run silk back and forth up to the bead and back to the bend to build up a steeply tapered body which is thickest at the bead.
4. If you want a tinsel body then tie this in now and take up to bead in touching turns. Tie off and remove waste.
5. Leave silk about 2 mm back from the bead and tie in the floss.
6. Create a thorax with the floss, tie off, remove waste and whip finish.
7. Coat whole fly (you can miss out the bead) with UV resin making sure it is smooth with no blobs.
8. Rotate in vice as you cure resin with a UV torch.
9. Paint wing case on using a black marker pen or nail varnish.

**Fishing Method:** Designed for French Leader fishing, you can use Perdigón flies with any deep nymphing technique.

# 64 Green Caddis – *Aad van der Jagt*

I have some really good Dutch friends as a result of having been a member of the Grayling Society for many years and having visited the Dutch, Belgian and Danish flyfishing shows several times. Dutch grayling fanatics get around a lot. Well, they would have to really when you consider that Holland is the last place you would think of looking for grayling.

Two of these friends visit the UK regularly in October for a week chasing Her Ladyship on the chalkstreams and we all have a great time together and usually catch lots of fish. Aad van der Jagt is one of my 'Flying Dutchmen' buddies and he is probably more accurately described as the 'Fly-tying Dutchman'! He is a prolific inventor and tyer of flies and my fly box, and that of my wife, usually benefits from his talents whenever he and his companion, Wim van Montfoort, come over here on their regular trips.

One year this nice green tungsten beaded fly was amongst the gifts from Aad and it has worked very well for me ever since. I just had to have him tell me about the fly because I have nearly run out of the stock he gave me on that particular visit and I need to tie up some more. So, now we can all benefit from his talent in designing this simple but very successful fly.

Aad says:

*I started to make this nymph when I first came across tungsten beads. Needing a heavy nymph for deep water, I was looking for a real bottom bouncer.*

*I have tried out this nymph in several rivers in Europe and it works very well, not only for grayling but also for brown trout.*

Well, as he and several other friends know, it certainly does work well on UK rivers.

### Green Caddis
*Fly tied by Aad van der Jagt*

**Materials:**

| | |
|---|---|
| **Hook:** | Tiemco 101 or similar, size 8 - 14. |
| **Silk:** | Olive. |
| **Tail:** | Grey squirrel, dyed olive, from the back of the body. |
| **Rib:** | Bright copper wire – size 8 hook 0.30 mm, sizes 10 – 12 hooks 0.24 mm, size 14 hook 0.20 mm. |
| **Underbody:** | Same as rib. |
| **Body:** | Grey squirrel, dyed olive, from the mask. |
| **Hackle:** | Grey squirrel, dyed olive, from the back of the body. |
| **Bead:** | Tungsten bead: size 8–10 hooks, 4 mm, 12–14 hooks, 3 mm. |

*Other variations are also useful such as natural grey, dyed black, ginger or brown.*

**Tying Instructions:**

1. Slide the bead on the hook and place hook in the vice.
2. Select the appropriate diameter copper wire and wrap it around the hook from the bend to the back of the bead. Leave a length hanging at the bend for the rib.
3. Remove the waste wire at the bead.
4. Cover the copper wire with thread.
5. Tie in the tail with a length of 3/4 of the hook shank.
6. Using the direct dubbing technique form the body.
7. Wrap the copper wire, for the rib, through the body.
8. Remove the waste wire at the bead.
9. Make a dubbing loop with the tying silk and place in this loop the squirrel hair.
10. Pull the loop very tight and spin this around.
11. Wind the dubbing loop behind the bead to form a hackle.
12. Tie off, remove waste, whip finish and varnish.

**Fishing Method:** It's essentially a caddis so fish as you would any other weighted caddis larva imitation, either singly or as part of a Czech Nymph or French Leader team.

# 65  SBE Caddis – *Bob Male*

I have a very good friend, Bob Male, who has retired to Wilton, the ancient capital of Wiltshire and renowned historically for carpet manufacture, just a few miles down the road from where I live. He is the editor of the excellent publications of the Grayling Society, and is also a keen member of the Wilton Fly Fishing Club, which is handy because the River Wylye is just a longish stone's throw from his house and he seems to be never out of its waters, whether carrying out some bank work, or as part of the club's fly monitoring team, or just fishing. In fact, he seems to do a lot of 'just fishing!'

His philosophy about flies is to keep them as simple as possible, so it seems appropriate that one of his best caddis creations is called just SBE or Simple But Effective. This is now a mainstay in my nymph box.

Here is what Bob says about his fly:

*This is a direct descendant of many cased caddis patterns, but I did come up with it myself. Riverfly sampling sessions on the River Wylye always showed numbers of small curved caddis whose cases were made from grains of sand and very fine gravel. A white or cream body and a dark head were also characteristic.*

*The SBE works well as a sight-fishing bug, and as part of a team of nymphs. Like the Killer Bug, it needs to be seen in water to appreciate its appeal.*

I have experimented myself with patterns designed to replicate this fine sand and gravel case of the Wylye caddis larva including gluing mixed colours of ballasting material, of the sort made for N gauge model railways, to the body but this fly is a much better option and is also a lot easier to tie.

Bob's tying instructions are featured below.

## SBE Caddis
*Fly tied by Bob Male*

### Materials

**Hook:** Any curved hook, size 18 to 12. I like the Partridge Patriot Czech Nymph fine wire for its length of shank and straight eye.

**Silk:** I use Griffith's Sheer 14/0 white thread, as colour is not really an issue for this pattern.

**Body:** Lureflash Superbug Yarn in grey dun or hare's ear brown. Both colours work well. My stock is ancient but it is still available.

**Thorax:** White or cream wool or fluorescent floss.

**Head:** Black or natural tungsten bead to suit hook size.

### Tying Instructions:

1. Thread the bead onto the hook. Add a few turns of lead wire if you wish to get a deeper fishing bug.
2. Catch the thread in behind the bead and wind down a couple of millimetres.
3. Shred the end of the superbug yarn between thumbnail and finger to taper it a bit, and tie it in.
4. Bind the yarn down on top of the shank to the point roughly opposite where the barb would be. I find this helps to keep the end of the body slim.
5. Take the thread back to the point where you will tie in the collar of wool.
6. Wind the yarn up the shank to make a gentle taper. Superbug yarn doesn't unwind easily, but you can flatten it a bit to start off, then make closer tighter turns as you go up the shank. Leave room for a decent size collar. Trim.
7. Tie in the wool or floss for the collar and wind it closely up to the bead.
8. Tie off, trim and whip finish behind the bead, putting a drop of varnish or Superglue on the last centimetre of thread before whip-finishing.

**Fishing Method:** Caddis live down at the bottom of the river so, obviously, this is the place to fish this fly. It can be fished successfully with any nymphing technique.

# 66 Peek-a-boo Caddis

Many species of caddis, or sedge, fly make houses, or cases, for themselves as a protection from predators. Dependent on the nature of the river in which they live, and also the particular species, these cases can be made of wood, weed, gravel or just about anything lying about which is useful. When kick sampling you frequently find caddis in their cases and it is interesting to see just what materials these are composed of so that you can attempt to copy these naturals with reasonably exact imitations.

As I have said earlier, I have successfully designed and used flies (Ballast Caddis – a work in progress) where the case has been mainly composed of N gauge model railway ballasting material in a mixture of different colours and glued to a fine tube over the body of the fly. It looks good and is a pretty exact copy of many caddis cases found in the river. I just have to perfect the gluing system now because the ravages of the current and the fly constantly banging into the gravel bottom or other objects can cause the ballast to wear off quickly. But that is part of the fun of trying new ideas isn't it? Once it is perfected it is boring and we need a new challenge!

Some years ago Oliver Edwards put his mind to the problem of creating a realistic imitation of an 'entombed' caddis and came up with the world famous Peeping Caddis. This fly uses a coarse fishing split shot weight squeezed onto a strip of nylon to get the fly down to the bottom of the river. I suspect, had beads been common tying materials at the time, that the split shot would have been binned and substituted

Prepared caddis heads

with a black bead set on the hook rather than above it.

I have used the Peeping Caddis for years and it is a great fly. However, I wanted something that looked more realistic and so set about creating such a fly. First of all I used a black tungsten bead instead of the split shot. Then, the only other change, I took a piece of extra fine chenille in fluorescent yellow and, instead of setting fire to the end to create a burnt black blob I reached for my UV resin. A small blob of this on the end of the chenille looked very realistic as the head of the caddis once it had been coloured with a dark brown or black marker pen. Thus was born the Peek-a-boo Caddis and it has been a very successful fly for me.

I can thoroughly recommend it to anyone who needs a realistic-looking cased caddis pattern.

## Peek-a-boo Caddis
*Fly tied by the author*

**Materials:**

| | |
|---|---|
| **Hook:** | Any wet-fly hook with a longish shank, size 10 to 14. |
| **Silk:** | Black. |
| **Bead:** | Black tungsten in a size to suit your needs and the hook. |
| **Rib:** | Gold or silver wire. |
| **Body:** | Hare's ear or squirrel. Mix the colours as you go up the shank using light grey, dark brown, black, etc., to create the impression of bits of material of different shades. |
| **Head:** | Extra fine chenille with a UV Resin 'blob' head. Colours that can be used include fluorescent yellow, chartreuse, cream. |
| **Legs:** | Partridge, waterhen or CdC hackle. |

**Tying Instructions:**

1. First prepare your head by taking a piece of chenille and adding a small blob of UV resin to the end. It may take two blobs dependent on the resin you use. After applying the resin cure with your UV torch and colour it with a dark brown or black marker pen.
2. Put the bead onto the hook and slide up to eye ensuring the rebated part is to the bend of the hook. Run the silk onto the hook and put several turns behind the bead to help lock it in place.
3. Run the silk down to the bend and here tie in your chenille leaving about 4 or 5 mm, dependent on hook size, hanging out over the bend. Remember we tie this fly back to front.
4. Tie in your chosen feather (partridge, waterhen or CdC) on top of the chenille, by the tip, part way up the hook from the bend and judge the point at which you tie it down so that, once wound on and the fibre butts have been trapped down as you move the tying silk towards the bend, the fibres will splay out beyond the end of the chenille and appear as legs coming out of the case. Take the silk right to the bend.
5. Tie in the rib.
6. Dub the silk with the hare's ear or squirrel and wind back to the back of the bead. The body can have a reasonable degree of 'fullness' to it.
7. Rib up to the bead in the opposite direction to that in which you wound the dubbing.
8. Tie off, remove waste, and whip finish. Varnish if you like.

**Fishing Method:** Just like the SBE Caddis, this one needs to be fished on the bottom of the river using any nymphing technique.

# 67 Chad Cad

Grayling anglers, especially those who frequent the chalkstreams, have all been conditioned into thinking the only Chadwick's darning wool of any use is shade 477. They are wrong! Chadwick made lots of shades and, although that company has long gone, there are other makes of mending wool mixtures still around. A furtive dive into a haberdasher's – make sure your drinking mates don't see you or you will be on the receiving end of some stick – and you can find lots of great colours of mending wool. You can also ferret about in your local charity shop where it is often relatively easy to find cards of Chadwick's, or similar, in shades that anglers haven't yet thought about using. The Chad Cad comes from just such an exercise, although my ferreting was done in my mum's sewing box some years ago!

Lots of sedge (caddis) flies make their homes from minute pieces of stone or sand which they find on the riverbed and then mould into a delicate and quite exquisite tube in which they can live until it is time to think of hatching into a fly. The Chad Cad tries to mimic these stone homes by having a body made of 4 different wools applied randomly to end up looking like bits of different coloured stone. The

Chad Cad Wools

# Chad Cad

*Fly tied by the author*

## Materials

**Hook:** Any wet-fly hook with a longish shank, size 10 to 14.

**Weight:** Flat lead 0.2 mm or 0.3 mm thick, or square lead or lead sheet.

**Silk:** Black.

**Body:** Mending wools – Chadwick's if you can get them – in 4 different colours – white, beige, grey, black, sand, etc., to match the colours of real caddis cases in your local river.

**Head:** Extra fine chenille with a UV resin 'blob' head. Colours that can be used include fluorescent yellow, chartreuse, cream.

See Peek-a-boo Caddis for instructions in creating the 'blob' head.

**Legs:** Partridge, waterhen or CdC hackle.

## Tying Instructions:

1. First prepare your head by taking a piece of chenille and adding a small blob of UV resin to the end. It may take two blobs, dependent on the resin you use. After applying the resin cure with your UV torch and colour it with a dark brown or black marker pen.
2. Add a layer of flat lead onto the hook. Run the silk over this a couple of times to help lock it in place.
3. Run the silk down to the bend and here tie in your chenille leaving about 4 or 5 mm, dependent on hook size, hanging out over the bend. Remember we tie this fly back to front.
4. Tie in your chosen feather (partridge, waterhen or CdC) on top of the chenille, by the tip, part way up the hook from the bend and judge the point at which you tie it down so that, once wound on and the fibre butts have been trapped down as you move the tying silk towards the bend, the fibres will splay out beyond the end of the chenille and appear as legs coming out of the case. Take the silk right to the bend.
5. Tie in the mending wool but tie each one a little apart from each other. This is so you can create a more random pattern as you wind them up the hook. For example, tie in a couple at the bend then one about 4 mm towards the eye and another a similar distance away.
6. Wind the first wool to the eye and tie off. Start with the one nearest the bend.
7. Now start taking each of the remaining wools to the eye but don't make the winding regular so there is a random look not a pattern.
8. Tie off each in turn then remove waste and finally whip finish.

**Fishing Method:** Just as with the previous SBE & Peek-a-boo Caddis, get this one down to the bottom of the river using any nymphing technique.

Chalkstream caddis cases constructed from stone

implementation must have some degree of realism because it has fooled many a grayling into unwisely eating a Chad Cad.

If you decide to design a fly using this material then make sure you thoroughly wet the prototype and check the colours out before committing to bulk production because wool can often change shade dramatically when wet. The Killer Bug is a supreme example of this, of course.

## 68  Caseless Caddis – *Hans van Klinken*

Hans van Klinken is not just a creator of superb dry flies. His Caseless Caddis is a great nymph, designed to represent the caseless varieties of caddis: it has immense potential for the grayling angler throughout the UK and Europe. The two most common forms of natural caseless caddis, *Rhyacophila* and *Hydropsyche*, are both very common in the UK and Hans' fly is a very good and successful pattern. Here is how Hans developed the fly:

*In 1986 I started to collect caseless caddis species from several rivers, which I tried to imitate as close as possible during the winter months. The first patterns I tied were not pretty looking creatures, but rougher bottom bouncers. They were a little too heavy and too bulky and did not look like the real insect I was trying to copy. However, the flies worked reasonably well. Despite this, I discovered that it was not easy to tie realistic nymphs! Improvements were made several times but still I was not satisfied. My large Scandinavia nymph was even better and I had more confidence in it because it had proved to* be very effective all over Europe.

It is no secret that the caseless caddis imitations which I use today were developed after some long discussions with England's Oliver Edwards, accepted as one of the finest fly tiers in Europe. I told him a lot about my large Scandinavian patterns, fishing techniques and thoughts. We are good friends and share each other secrets and techniques without hesitation. Oliver taught me not only how to study the anatomy of an insect, but he also showed me how to combine and handle natural and synthetics in a more effective way. He also convinced me that heavily leaded patterns are not always better catchers then sparsely weighted nymphs. Nowadays I even believe that under some circumstances unweighted patterns can be more effective than weighted ones.

The first prototypes of the Caseless Caddis in my series were developed in the winter of 1987. At that time I still tied my patterns in probably 15 different colours. The first successful attempts to use the Caseless Caddis occurred in a German river where my friend Jack and I caught plenty of fish with this very effective nymph pattern. Now I use mainly yellowish and greenish variations. Therefore I have large quantities and sizes of those colours in my fly-box today.

After my conversations with Oliver it was time to experiment. I improved several of my patterns in the first months of 1988 and tried to give them a more

## Caseless Caddis
*Flies tied by Hans van Klinken*

**Materials**

**Hook:** Daiichi Klinkhåmer hook, no 1160 or 1167.
**Thread:** Uni thread 8/0 Black.
**Underbody:** Lead wire – 1 layer on shank, 2 layers on thorax.
**Rib:** Monofilament 0.20 mm – at least 12 windings.
**Abdomen:** Furry Foam or other fine dubbing.
**Thorax:** Dark brown fitch (polecat) or mink, well picked out, or black Straggle String.
**Shellback:** Flexibody.
**Head:** Black marker pen.

## Tying Instructions

1. Put fine lead wire on the hook shank (two layers around the thorax). Optionally coat with varnish.
2. Tie in 0.20 mm/0.08" diameter clear monofilament for use as rib and to create the body segmentation.
3. Secure the underbody well with thread and lacquer to be sure the materials will not twist around the hook shank when the fly is finished.
4. Cut out a small piece of transparent Flexibody trimming the end you will tie it in with to a truncated cone.
5. Tie in the strip of Flexibody.
6. Tie in a narrow strip of furry foam. If Furry Foam is not available use Haretron or fine dubbing material.
7. Wrap the Furry Foam around the shank to form the abdomen.
8. Use some dark mink or fitch guardhairs/underfur spun in a dubbing loop for the thorax. Make a well defined thorax.
9. Pull over the Flexibody. Secure it with your tying thread.
10. Wind the monofilament in at least 12 turns to the eye of the hook and tie off. You now have a good and effective segmentation, which is of vital important for this pattern.
11. Pick out the mink hairs to define the legs, and the Caseless Caddis is complete.

**Note:** As an interesting, modern, alternative you can use Straggle String Micro Chenille for both abdomen and thorax, as below.

**Fishing Method:** Hans loves to sight-fish with the Caseless Caddis in clear water. However he fishes more often in deeper or more coloured water where he can't see the fish – here he uses an indicator and fishes upstream, dead-drift, in the classic style.

*realistic and better-looking appearance. One of them was my imitation of the caseless caddis nymph. I think I had learned a lot from Oliver's vision about realistic nymph patterns. About the same time Gertjan Doedens, another Dutchman, designed a similar caddis larva. His idea of using flexibody as back material finally led me to this excellent caddis larva imitation. The reason that I used a curved hook to present my caddis is because I find that disorientated larva will often drift in this way. This is why I mainly fish the pattern in a dead drift. Another important reason for curved hooks is because the hooking power is much better.*

So there we can see a good demonstration that the process of development can be a complex affair involving several ideas from different contributors. However it was devised, there is no doubting the effectiveness of this fly which can be used to represent both Rhyacophila and Hydropsyche larvae.

# 69  Der Wurm – *Christian Mohr*

Christian was for many years the Area Secretary of the Grayling Society in Germany. Here is what he has to say about the development of 'Der Wurm':

*Many years ago, a friend of mine and one time member of the Grayling Society, Michael Wenzel, told me that he was expecting to be invited to a fabulous private stretch of fishing below the dam of a reservoir, which allegedly held some very large grayling. These were deemed to be uncatchable, because they had been growing big on fish being chopped up by the hydro-power turbines, when electricity was being generated. We both thought that fishing bait would most likely bring success, but the stretch was fly and nymph only.*

*Shortly after our discussion I visited my local fishing tackle shop, which had a sale on of large stocks of handmade Partridge of Redditch hooks, many of them in odd sizes. That's where I came across the model K4A shrimp hooks in size 2, which I had never seen before that large. Packets of a blood-red, D-shaped plastic material nearby immediately gave me the idea for artificial worms. At home I experimented a bit with stretching the tie-in point of the plastic to avoid the worms to have fat bottoms and dressed a couple of dozen. Next time I met Michael, I gave him a few of the 'worms'; I also gave a few to my wife and then just forgot all about them. Incidentally, Michael never received that invitation, and he apparently also forgot all about the 'worms'.*

*A couple of years later, Michael, Stefanie and myself were out fishing for grayling in our local stream, the River Dhünn. Michael and I had fished all the likely holes but hadn't had any luck with the ladies of the stream. We had withdrawn from the river and sat on the bank to regain the circulation in our stone-cold feet, when Stefanie came strolling down from upstream fishing the stretch we earlier had vacated. Well, sitting on the bank we at least saw the first grayling of the day. And the second. And the third. After the fourth, we inquired about the fly which had done the trick that day and upon hearing about it, Michael speedily rummaged through his vest to look for the film canister holding the forgotten treasures. We resumed our efforts, which were rewarded with several nice grayling for each of us.*

*All during this winter we tested the 'worm' extensively and found it to be near unbeatable for catching grayling in cold conditions. If I remember right, the first time the 'worm' was christened in UK waters was in the Wylye at a stretch of the Wilton Fly Fishing Club. We had been invited to fish for grayling by Steve Skuce, Mike Tebbs and Roger Cullum Kenyon. Fishing was slow, when I was placed by (I think) Steve at a very nice bend which I thought had to yield a few grayling. If my memory serves me right, I caught some 7 fish in 8 casts, a fact that did not go unnoticed by Steve. He asked what was tied to the end of my line, I gave him some worms, and the rest as they say, is history.*

History indeed, and what Christian probably does not know is that a few days afterwards I was fishing close to that spot and caught eight grayling in ten casts on his magic fly. Mathematically not quite as good a performance as his was but jaw dropping nevertheless. Give it a go and show them the early worm!

## Der Wurm
*Flies tied by Christian Mohr*

**Materials**

**Hook:** Any big curved hook – but originally a Partridge K4A size 2! Currently the K4A only goes up to size 8 but the Partridge Patriot Czech Nymph CZ/SHR has large sizes and is a good substitute.

**Silk:** Red.

**Underbody:** Pearlescent tinsel. This is an optional variation which was not on the original fly. It works both with and without an underbody. Steve Rhodes feels that it adds some lustre which may attract grayling in slightly coloured water.

**Body:** Blood-red Bodyglass or Magic Glass with a 'D' profile.

**Tying Instructions**

1. Take red silk down around bend quite some way – see photograph.
2. If choosing to use an underbody then tie it in now.
3. Tie in Bodyglass or substitute, having cut a slight V to the point where it is tied in to make it less bulky.
4. Take the silk back to just behind the eye.
5. Wind the underbody material (if using) to the silk in touching turns and tie off and remove waste.
6. Stretch the Bodyglass as you wind it forwards to start off with a nice taper then release some tension so a segmented look is created.
7. At the eye tie off the ribbing very securely because it has memory and will spring back if not controlled.
8. Remove waste Bodyglass, form a small tapered head, tie off and whip finish.

**Fishing Method:** This is a big fly for a big hole and big grayling! Fish as an upstream nymph – although I caught my 8 out of 10 fishing downstream.

# 70 Squirmy Wormy – *John Zimmerman*

Mention the Squirmy Wormy amongst grayling anglers and you will get all variations of polarised responses, with many in favour of using it and many who would not touch the fly with a wading staff. Why? Well, because it is one of those flies, like the Alexandra, the Dog Nobbler and the Booby, that work brilliantly but are so 'non PC' that some people want them banned. In fact I believe this fly really has been banned in flyfishing competitions in the Czech Republic!

I was first introduced to the Squirmy Wormy by John Zimmerman, an American guide who was in the UK taking some of his pupils (he is a college lecturer in North Carolina) on a European tour. They came to fish on – let's just say a nameless chalkstream – with me, and at some point during the proceedings John pulled out of his box a Squirmy Wormy and asked if I had ever seen one. Remembering my first experience with Christian Mohr's Worm fly, I just had to give this monstrosity a go. It worked very well and has now gained some popularity, or notoriety, as other anglers have also had success with it.

This is what John subsequently told me:

*The Squirmy is the ultimate naughty fly. The only naughtier fly is a Squirmy with an egg tied at the head of the*

John Zimmerman with a tasty brown

## Squirmy Wormy

*Flies tied by John Zimmerman*

**Materials:**

- **Hook:** Any suitable wet-fly hook, size 14 upwards.
- **Silk:** Pink or red or whatever matches the colour of squirmy material you are using.
- **Bead:** Gold – heavy!
- **Body:** Squirmy Wormy material – red is most popular but purple and orange are also good.

**Tying Instructions:**

As John says; "the fly is stupid simple to tie."

1. Place a suitable bead on the hook and push up to the eye.
2. Tie in the material at the bend end of the shank, with it facing towards you. Use a loose wrap so that when you tighten it the material pulls away from you and onto the top of the hook. Tighten too much and you will cut the material. Don't tighten enough and the material will not roll up onto the top of the hook. It is very slippery stuff!
3. Run the silk up to behind the bead and, if you want the material at the front to lie backwards then put a few turns in front of it and behind the bead.
4. Tie off, remove waste and put on your best disguise to go fishing!

*I recently came across the definition of what constitutes a gentleman: it is someone who knows how to play the bagpipes but chooses not to! I wonder if we should have a broadly similar definition of a gentleman angler: someone who has a Squirmy Wormy in his box but chooses not to use it! I certainly have some in my box, and I choose to ... aha, that would be telling!*

*Happy fly-tying!*

Now that'll make a LOT of Squirmy Wormies!

**Tip:** There are companies selling the material – by that I mean respectable fly-tying supply companies – and you will pay a reasonably high price for a smallish amount. Do what I do myself, and what John recommends, and look for a Spaghetti Stress Ball on the internet. A friend and I both bought one, from a company selling special needs toys, full of hundreds of red and blue strands for only about twice the price of a miserably small packet from a respectable fly-tying material supplier.

*hook! I first became acquainted with the Squirmy Wormy when my fishing partner and I were gearing up for an upcoming flyfishing tournament in 2011—has it really been that long? Being very competitive chaps, Taylor and I were looking for a secret weapon—so I called Dave Hise. Dave is one of the best fly-tyers in the United States and has an incredible eye for fishy materials. The Squirmy is Dave's invention, and he let me in on the secret. I tied a few of the bugs up, and we showed them to some well-trained trout on the river closest to us and caught fish that had just a few days before remained safely unfooled. The competition came and we came within four centimeters of taking first place—the two fellows who won the comp own and guide daily on the water the comp was being held on. Since then, the Squirmy has gained new colors, but it's gone through a slight alteration. The original material came on Mondo Spaghetti Balls and was cut off in packs of ten and sold at retail for astronomical mark-ups. A Spaghetti Ball used to cost me about $1.50 ... but now they're upwards of $7-$19 and I can't choose my color! So I have started importing all manners of colors from a wholesaler. Steve has a few of my favorites!*

I have seen many variations of this fly but this is the original one as shown to me by John.

Flyfishing
The Richard Walker Angling Library
GRAYLING
THE GRAYLING ANGLER
JOHN ROBERTS

# Chapter Seven

# Gray Matter

WHEN I AM ASKED by Kirsty Young, on *Desert Island Discs*, to choose the book that I can take with me to the remote and mythical desert island I will be hard pressed to decide between one of those great books by John Roberts, *Fly Fishing for Grayling* or his earlier one, *The Grayling Angler*, and that superb book by Reg Righyni just entitled *Grayling*. I could add Francis Walbran's *How to Catch Grayling* or Carter Platt's *Grayling Fishing* or Pritt's *Book of the Grayling* to this list because they are great books also. Of course, my friends at the Grayling Society will beat me up if I don't mention the two books by the late President, Dr. Ron Broughton, *Grayling: the Fourth Game Fish* and *The Complete Book of the Grayling*, both of which are excellent.

Of course, there had better be a crystal clear stream full of grayling on that island where I can use my one luxury item which will be a flyfishing kit consisting of a top of the range fly rod (Winston probably), reel (Danielsson), line (Snowbee Thistledown) and box of flies – the ones in this book of course!

The following pages form a guide to some of the resources available to the questing grayling angler.

The first section features books that are specifically on grayling, listed by date of publication.

This is followed by a brief selection of video material found in media such as DVDs and the internet.

Finally, at the end of the chapter is an alphabetical list of other angling books and papers consulted during the research and writing of this book.

# Books

### The Practical Fly-Fisher: More Particularly for Grayling or Umber – John Jackson.

*Charles Farlow, London & J Swallow, Leeds, 1854.*

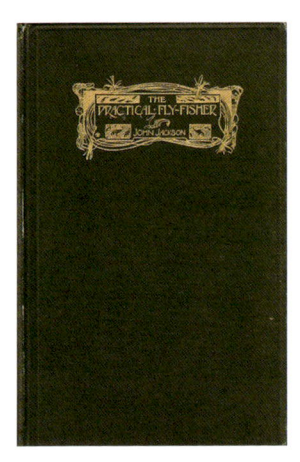

A gem that is unfortunately beyond the pocket of most of us. You can actually read the text of this (as with many other early angling books) on-line on the archive.org website. Jackson lived on the banks of the River Yore (Ure) in Yorkshire and was a great lover of grayling. This charming book explains how to tie flies (as practised in 1854) and lists no less than 64 patterns. It also gives information on the distribution of grayling in the Yorkshire rivers. Well worth a read.

### The Book of the Grayling – T E Pritt.

*Goodall & Suddick, Leeds, 1888.*

Pritt was a Lancastrian who just happened to emigrate across the Pennines and is best known for his book *North Country Flies* which is a great showcase for those super soft-hackled spiders so much liked in Yorkshire. He tells us about the fish and where and how it can be caught, and lists dressings for 15 wet flies which were to be found on the casts of notable grayling anglers. It includes a section on worm-fishing for grayling.

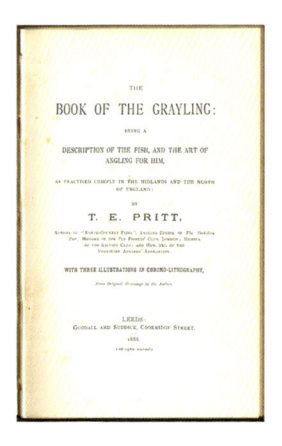

### Grayling and How to Catch Them – Francis M Walbran.

*The Angler, Scarborough, 1895.*

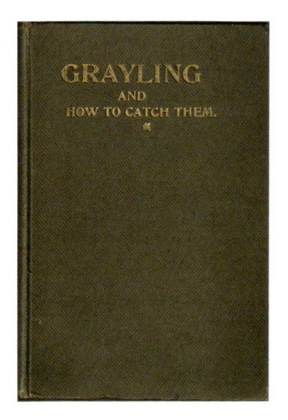

In February 1909, Francis 'Max' Walbran was drowned whilst fishing for grayling in the Ure in Yorkshire. He was a well-known angler and tackle-dealer, and his book takes us through the grayling story from its introduction and distribution to flyfishing and flies and, finally, bait fishing. The second section of the book is anecdotal with chapters on individual grayling fishing excursions. Many of the flies are the same as those in Pritt's earlier book, which just goes to show that there is a solid cadre of well-respected grayling flies that have existed for many, many years.

## Grayling Fishing in South Country Chalkstreams – H A Rolt.

*Sampson Low, Marston & Co., London, 1901.*

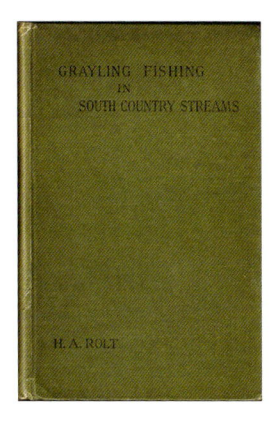

This is a delightful, if somewhat dated, little book, following a familiar pattern of discussing the fish and then how to catch it, and including a list of twelve flies, both dry and wet. Rolt also discusses the question of whether grayling should be introduced into trout streams, or even if they should be eradicated where they existed already, coming down decidedly on the side of the grayling. This was, until not that long ago, a real issue on the chalkstreams and it is only recently that wholesale culling was stopped on these rivers in the South.

## Grayling Fishing – William Carter Platts.

*A & C Black, London, 1939.*

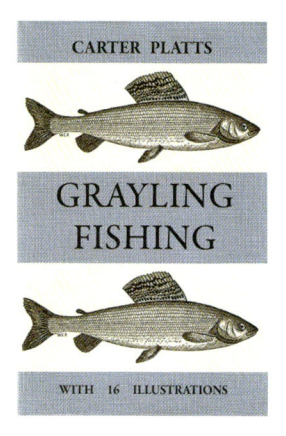

It is said that the stimulus for writing this book was that no-one had written a book on grayling for a long while! That seems to me to be a good enough reason and it is a magnificent book. Carter Platts really understood grayling and had a passion for them.

## L'Ombre Poisson de Sport – L de Boisset.

*Librairie des Champs-Elysées, Paris, 1941.*

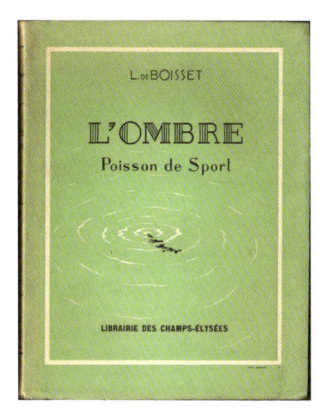

This is the one book here which I haven't yet read. I understand it is a comprehensive look at the fish and methods to catch it. One day when my French is better, I may give it a go!

The Grayling – Richard Lake.
*Wilding & Son, Shrewsbury, 1942.*

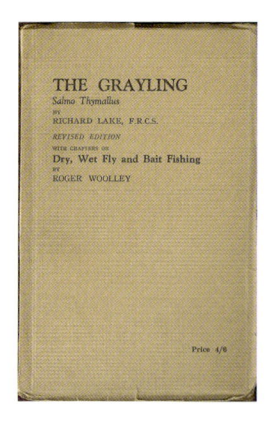

This is a small book and I would say that, by modern thinking, it has some misconceptions about grayling, in particular the supposed behavioural differences between those living in the North and those in the South. In my copy, which is the second edition of 1946, there are chapters on Grayling Flies and Bait Fishing written by Roger Woolley, and anything written by Woolley is worth reading. Buy this book if you feel you need to complete your collection.

Grayling Fishing – 'R A M.'
The Fishing Gazette, *Beckenham, 1944.*

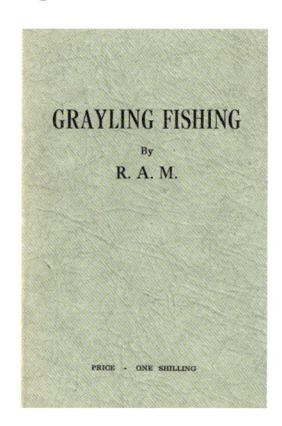

This diminutive book is just 17 pages long and is probably best described as 'quaint.' It covers both fly and bait fishing, although the float he recommends would make us laugh these days. It demonstrates the thinking of the day – which has not stood the test of time! Mainly for collectors, I think.

Grayling: How To Catch Them – H G C Claypoole.
*Herbert Jenkins, London, 1957.*

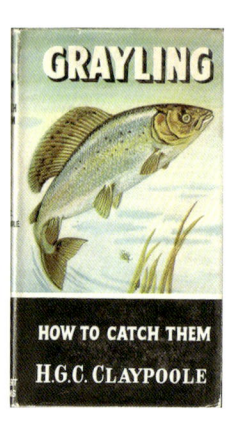

One of the famous and collectable *'How To Catch Them'* series, this covers almost everything you need to know. Chapters include those about the fish, its behaviour, flies, tackle, dry-fly fishing, wet-fly fishing and bait fishing. A good little book which I can recommend.

Grayling – R V Righyni.
*Macdonald, London, 1968.*

This famous Yorkshire angler was a co-founder of the Grayling Society. He was a mustard-keen grayling angler and his book is undoubtedly a classic. Looking on my bookshelf I see that I have two copies, one of which was spotted by my eldest daughter in the 'Withdrawn For Sale' rack at Farnborough Library in 1992 and she bought it for me – for 40 pence. When I looked inside I saw that I had been the only person that had borrowed it from the library in the previous five years so I felt that it was destined to be mine!

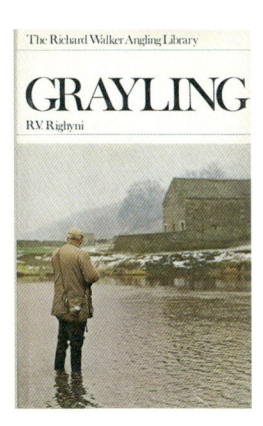

The Grayling Angler – John Roberts.
*H F & G Witherby, London, 1982.*

John Roberts's original book on grayling, which also covers bait-fishing, is where I started my own reading – my copy is well-battered from excessive use. This book lit the blue touch paper for me and grayling fishing.

Grayling: the Fourth Game Fish – Ronald Broughton.
*Crowood Press, Marlborough, 1989.*

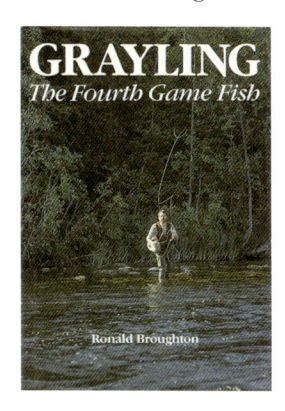

Ron was a founder member of the Grayling Society and served as Chairman and President. Fondly known as 'The Doc,' his knowledge of grayling fishing, especially in Northern waters, was immense. His book is essentially a compendium of great writing from a variety of authors. A second, revised and enlarged edition was published by Robert Hale in 2000 as *The Complete Book of the Grayling*.

Vlagzalm & Vliegvissen – Hugo Martel.
*Published by the author, Bruges, 1998.*

The title translates as *Grayling and Flyfishing*. I would like to tell you more about the contents but it is written in Flemish. Hugo is a long-term supporter of the Grayling Society and has been involved with its management in his native Belgium for many years. He is a well-travelled and highly experienced grayling angler and, should you happen to speak Flemish, this will be a great book. I just know that because he is a great man! I can, actually, work out a bit of it because, although it is written in Flemish, after a couple of stiff ones it seems to be written in Anglerish.

Fly Fishing for Grayling – John Roberts. *Excellent Press, Ludlow, 1999.*

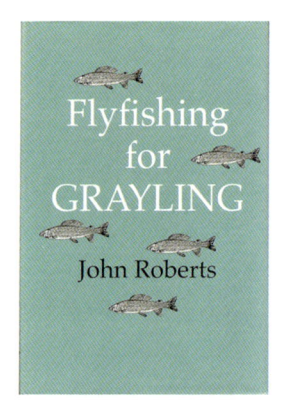

John Roberts is a very knowledgeable, experienced and thoughtful angler, and his passion for grayling, and trout, shines through whenever and whatever he writes. This is a book you *must* read if you want to be a successful grayling fly fisherman.

The Lady of the Stream – Compiled by Paul Morgan and Hugo Martel. *The Medlar Press, Ellesmere, 2003.*

An attractive anthology of writing on grayling with chapters from such notables as Reg Righyni, W Carter Platts, Oliver Kite and Charles Ritz. Nicely put together by two grayling enthusiasts and produced to a high quality.

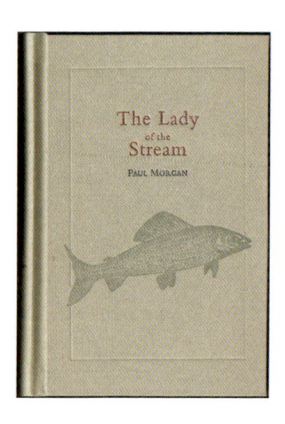

Flyfishing for Alaska's Grayling: Sailfish of the North – Cecilia Kleinkauf. *Frank Amato, Portland, Oregon, 2009.*

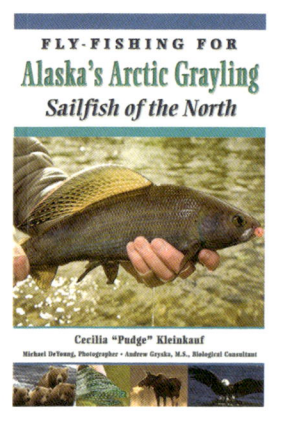

A very nice book from a very keen and experienced lady angler. 'Pudge' Kleinkauf is a retired professor and lawyer who only took up flyfishing at the age of 40: I am sure she wishes she had found it earlier. She is a gifted fly-tyer and is extremely well-known in Alaska where she has a guiding business. There are, of course, many similarities between the European and Arctic grayling.

**Fishing in Grayling Paradise** – Karel Krivanec.

*Published by the author, Czech Republic, 2014.*

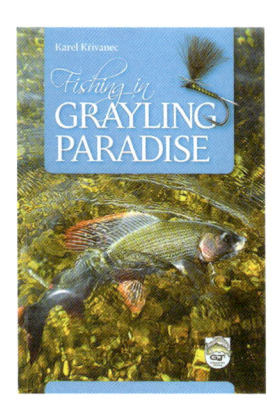

Karel is a well-known angling author, fly-tying innovator, and the author of *Czech Nymph*. This book is a collection of tales of his fishing on his local river, the Vltava, in the Sumava mountains area. A gentle anecdotal book which you can pick up and delve into at any time.

**The Complete Book about Grayling** – Bob Willis.

*Published by the author, 2015.*

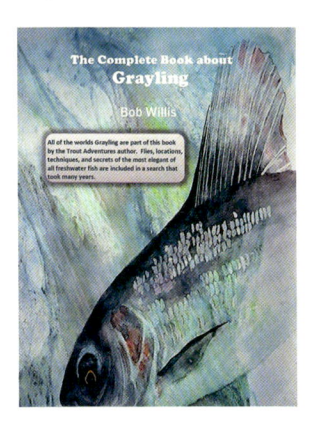

I met the author when I took him fishing on the Wylye whilst he was researching for this book. On that day he couldn't buy a grayling and got a bit fed up just catching wild trout! Bob is a retired American who has a mission to travel and catch, and write about, every species and sub-species of trout and grayling in the world, and has self-published a number of books on the subject. It is an interesting read and the sections on Mongolia and Russia are fascinating and original. An angler's book and not one for the scientists who may question some of his conclusions regarding genetics.

And now, for something completely different – an ebook!

**Inspiring Ties: Grayling Flies** – Richard Ellis.

*Self published via blurb.co.uk, 2015.*

Richard is a well-known member of the Fly Dresser's Guild and I once had the great pleasure of being invited by him to act as a co-instructor at an FDG Grayling Flies fly-tying day. This ebook is beautifully produced with 20 varied and outstanding flies and excellent step-by-step photographic sequences. Well worth the few bob it costs to download.

## Grayling Society Publications

The Grayling Society have produced two excellent booklets on flies which can be obtained from the society's website at: www.graylingsociety.net.

### Some Favourite Flies for Grayling: Volume One – Edited by Reg Fuller.
*The Grayling Society, 1990.*

Twenty flies from leading members of the Society, fully described and with some colour illustrations.

### Some Favourite Flies for Grayling: Volume Two – Edited by Brian L Clarke.
*The Grayling Society, 2012.*

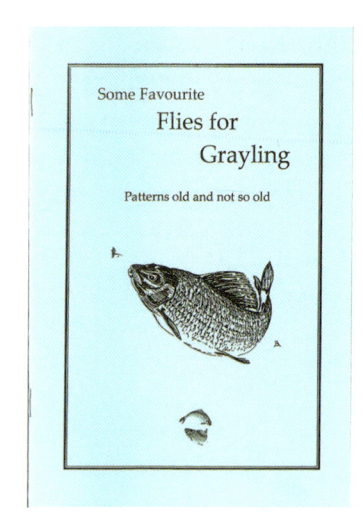

Twenty-one patterns from various officers of the club. The booklet contains descriptions, tying instructions and colour photographs of each fly.

## Other Media

### DVDs

Great DVD's which I think you should watch. There are some great discs around these days and these ones are particularly good in my opinion.

### Oliver Edwards 'Essential Skills'
*www.essential-skills.tv*

Oliver is such a well-known angler and fly-tyer that I won't say much except that all eight of these are excellent. I particularly recommend the following:

   Wet Fly Fishing on Rivers

   Czech Nymphing & Upstream Nymphing & North Country Spiders

   Search & Sight Fishing: The Deep Diving Shrimp & Chalk Stream Entomology

### River Academy Series
*Fish On Productions (www.fishonproductions.co.uk)*

Featuring John Tyzack and Dean Andrews, the well-known TV actor, these are all extremely well produced, very educational and highly entertaining. In particular the following are very good:

   Grayling Through The Year.

   French Nymphing and related long leader techniques.

   Urban Fly Fishing.

A River Runs Through It – A major movie directed by Robert Redford and starring Craig Sheffer, Brad Pitt and Tom Skeritt, based on Norman Maclean's novella of the same name. No grayling to be seen anywhere but what a movie and what fantastic flyfishing scenes.

## YouTube

Of course, there are thousands of clips on www.youtube.com with a fishing bias and you could spend your life getting screen-boggled, but these are my favourites:

Oliver Kite – Taken from his 1960s Southern TV series.

Grayling Festival with Friends.

Frank Sawyer – A silent movie!

Tying a Pheasant Tail Nymph.

Davie McPhail – Fly-tying Videos

Davie is such a highly skilled fly-tyer and his videos are just the best on YouTube. He has done many and there are several directly relevant to grayling.

And for something completely different look up:

Hank Patterson, Your Flyfishing Guide – on YouTube!

# Further References

## Books

In addition to those grayling books above, the following were consulted during the research and writing of this book, and may be found useful by readers. All of these, as well as the grayling books above, can be found on the website of my esteemed publishers – www.anglebooks.com.

Baeza, Luis Meana. *The Pardon de Meana and the Feather of Gallo de León.* Published by the author, Madrid, 2011.

Deane, Peter. *Peter Deane's Fly-Tying.* Batsford, London, 1993.

Edmonds, H H & Lee, N N. *Brook and River Trouting: a Manual of Modern North Country Methods.* Published by the authors, Bradford, 1912.

Graham-Ranger, Clive. *Fishing with Bill Sibbons.* Crowood Press, Marlborough, 1990.

Harding, Mike. *A Guide to North Country Flies and How to Tie Them.* Aurum Press, London, 2009.

Hayter, Tony. *F M Halford and the Dry Fly Revolution.* Robert Hale, London, 2002.

Hayter, Tony. *G E M. Skues: the Man of the Nymph.* Robert Hale, London, 2013.

Horsfall Turner, Eric. *Angler's Cavalcade.* A & C Black, London, 1966.

Kite, Oliver. *Nymph Fishing in Practice.* Herbert Jenkins, London, 1963.

Kite, Oliver. *A Fisherman's Diary.* André Deutsch, London, 1969.

Krivanec, Karel. *Czech Nymph.* Published by the author, Czech Republic, 2007.

Lawton, Terry. *Nymph Fishing: a History of the Art and Practice.* Swan Hill Press, Shrewsbury, 2005.

Maclean, Norman. *Trout & Grayling: an Angler's Natural History.* A & C Black, London, 1980.

Mold, Frederick E. *Presenting the Fly to the Trout.* Herbert Jenkins, London, 1967.

Moss, H W. *The Elements of Fly Fishing for Trout and Grayling.* Faber & Faber, London, 1951.

Moutter, Ian. *Tying Flies the Paraloop Way.* Swan Hill Press, Shrewsbury, 2001.

Overfield, T Donald. *Fifty Favourite Dry Flies.* Ernest Benn, London, 1980.

Overfield, T. Donald. *Famous Flies and their Originators.* A & C Black, London, 1972.

Pritt, T E. *Yorkshire Trout Flies.* Goodall & Suddick, Leeds, 1885. Reprinted as *North-Country Flies.* Sampson Low, London, 1886.

Roberts, John. *A Guide to River Trout Flies.* Crowood Press, Marlborough, 1989.

Sawyer, Frank. *Nymphs and the Trout.* Stanley Paul, London, 1958.

Skues, G E M. *Minor Tactics of the Chalk Stream.* A & C Black, London, 1910.

Skues, G E M. *The Way of a Trout with a Fly.* A & C Black, London, 1921.

Skues, G E M. *Nymph Fishing for Chalk Stream Trout.* A & C Black, London, 1939.

Skues, G E M. *Itchen Memories.* Herbert Jenkins, London, 1951.

Smith, Robert L. *The North Country Fly: Yorkshire's Soft hackle Tradition.* Coch-y-Bonddu Books, Machynlleth, 2015.

Smith, Roger. *Flyfishing the Welsh Borderlands.* Coch-y-Bonddu Books, Machynlleth, 2011.

Stewart, W C. *The Practical Angler.* A & C Black, London, 1857.

Vallack, Harry. *Fishing Flies for Upper Teesdale.* Published by the author, Middleton-in-Teesdale, 2008.

White, Philip. *Observation: A Flyfisher's Guide to Reading the Water.* Coch-y-Bonddu Books, Machynlleth, 2016.

Wiggin, Maurice. *Teach Yourself Fly Fishing.* English Universities Press, London, 1958.

Williams, A Courtney. *A Dictionary of Trout Flies.* A & C Black, London, 1949.

Woolley, Roger. *Modern Trout Fly Dressing.* The Fishing Gazette, London, 1932.

## Papers & Documents

Nick Dawnay, Louise Dawnay, Roger N Hughes, Richard Cove & Martin I Taylor. *Substantial genetic structure among stocked and native populations of the European grayling (Thymallus thymallus, Salmonidae) in the United Kingdom, Conservation Genetics 12, 731-744, 2010.* Available to view on the Grayling Research Trust website – www.graylingresearch.org.

*National Trout & Grayling Strategy.* The Environment Agency, 2003